ph
2.1.07

# SOCIA[...]OPLE WITH DEMENTIA

## Partnerships, practice and persistence

Mary Marshall and Margaret-Anne Tibbs

Consultant editor: Jo Campling

Revised Second Edition

P≈P

BASW
BRITISH ASSOCIATION
OF SOCIAL WORKERS

First published as 'I can't place this place at all': Working with people with dementia and their carers in 1996 by Venture Press, 16 Kent Street, Birmingham, B5 6RD

This revised second edition published in Great Britain in November 2006 by

The Policy Press
University of Bristol
Fourth Floor
Beacon House
Queen's Road
Bristol BS8 1QU
UK

Tel +44 (0)117 331 4054
Fax +44 (0)117 331 4093
e-mail tpp-info@bristol.ac.uk
www.policypress.org.uk

British Library Cataloguing in Publication Data
A catalogue record for this book is available from the British Library.

Library of Congress Cataloging-in-Publication Data
A catalog record for this book has been requested.

ISBN-10 1 86134 702 2 paperback
ISBN-13 978186134 702 2 paperback
ISBN-10 1 86134 703 0 hardcover
ISBN-13 978186134 703 9 hardcover

Cover design by Qube Design Associates, Bristol.
Front cover: photograph supplied by kind permission of Getty Images.
Printed and bound in Great Britain by Hobbs the Printers, Southampton.

This book is dedicated to social workers who will get dementia
and to those who will care for us,
and to Jo Campling, our editor, without whose insistence
this book would not have been written.

# Contents

# Introduction

First, some words about the title of this book. Clearly, we wanted to say that this is a book about social work and people with dementia. We would like to have said 'and their carers' because social work is substantially about working with families and relationships, but this would have been too long. Our subtitle consists of three words which we think further clarify what this book is about. *Partnerships* because we expect social workers to see the person with dementia, as well as carers and colleagues, as partners in a shared endeavour where possible; *practice* because this is primarily a book about practice and it is full of accounts of practice; and *persistence* because we believe that this is an essential quality of work in this field. It is not a quick fix type of social work. Ageism and stigma beset this field and social workers need to be really persistent to ensure that the best social work is provided.

This book is written by social workers for social workers. We have written it with four groups in mind although we hope it is useful to any social worker working with people with dementia:

- social work students;
- social workers doing post-registration training and learning;
- social workers transferring into dementia care from another field;
- social workers in the field of registration and inspection.

Although much of what we cover is appropriate for social workers in any country, we have had to include a lot of British policy and legal material because so much social work is specific to the context in which we work. We believe that British social trends are very similar to those of other industrialised countries.

We have assumed that readers will have a good basic grounding in social work and that this book provides additional material on attitudes, knowledge and skills specifically related to people with dementia and their carers.

The book is a very substantial update and extension of a book written for a wider range of professionals: *I Can't Place this Place at all: Working with People with Dementia and their Carers*, which was published by the Venture Press (the publishing arm of the British Association of Social Workers [BASW]) in 1996. Much has changed since then. Our understanding of dementia and how to improve the lives of people with dementia and their carers has increased at a formidable rate and there is now a very substantial literature on the subject.

Sadly, the same cannot be said of social work, specifically with people with dementia and their families where there has been very little published, except Tibbs (2001), and little research on social work per se. There is some research on assessment and care management but none specifically about social workers. However, this dearth of specialist research has never hindered social work in the past. We are used to drawing our expertise from a wide field and incorporating it into our practice. We have tried to do this in this book without drowning readers in references.

This book inevitably reflects the interests and background of the authors. Margaret-Anne Tibbs has worked in England all her life in a local authority and more recently as a freelance trainer. She has special links with South Africa. Mary Marshall has worked mainly in Scotland in the voluntary and academic sectors, most recently in service development. She worked for a brief spell in Australia and has maintained an interest in Australian models of care.

Devolution has had a major impact on policies and services, although this can be overstated given that Scotland and Northern Ireland have always had their own legislation and service structures. However, since devolution, Scotland in particular has some legislation which is different from the rest of the UK. In our view, with some exceptions, the preoccupations of legislation and social policy have been very similar so we have decided to focus mainly on England and Wales rather than attempt to provide a description of each country of the UK. We are aware that, in the near future, Wales will have some of its own legislation.

The book also reflects the expertise of our friends and colleagues, to whom we are most grateful. We have tried to reference them where possible but it is clearly impossible to identify everything we have learned from them. Many of them also provided the stories which illustrate the text although most of these derive from our own experience. Special mention needs to be made of Kate Allan, Carole Archibald, Juliet Cheetham, Sylvia Cox, Colm Cunningham, Mary Dixon, Michael Farrington, Ann Ferguson, Graham Jackson and John Killick. Eileen Richardson provided invaluable assistance with the references and Ron Smith with text editing.

This has not been an easy book to write because it is very hard to generalise about social work with people with dementia and their carers in 2006. It varies enormously from place to place and agency to agency. In some places it is limited to competent form-filling whereas in others it is a creative and responsive process. We are, on the whole, optimistic that the latter is on the ascendant, which we evidence from developments such as the 21st Century Social Work Review in Scotland (Scottish Executive, 2006). Certainly, whilst trying to be realistic about what social workers can reasonably achieve in some agencies, we hope we have set the bar high in terms of our aspirations.

We are also clear that writing a book like this is difficult because the whole field is developing so fast. We therefore hope that we have provided enough of an infrastructure to enable readers to build on it and continue to learn and develop their practice. We cannot claim to be all-round experts; indeed it would be impossible to be one.

We firmly believe that social work has a lot to offer, and that it is best offered alongside other professions with complementary approaches. In our view the International Association of Schools of Social Work (IASSW)/International federation of Social Work (IFSW) definition of social work is very helpful: 'The social work profession promotes social change, problem solving in human relationships and the empowerment and liberation of people to enhance well-being' (www.iassw-aiets.org). This also fits with the theoretical underpinnings we have used in this book: those of three approaches to dementia as well as person-centred care. These have been developed to inform dementia care more widely but we believe they have particular resonance with social work practice.

We need to say something here about terminology. We use the term 'person with dementia' rather than 'dementia sufferer' throughout because we know that people with dementia prefer it. We have not used the word 'carer' for paid staff, although we know they can have a lot in common with family and friends, as we believe it causes confusion and we know that many unpaid carers object to its use for paid staff. We have been very uncertain whether to use the word 'client' or 'user' for people with whom we work and have opted for both since 'user of social work' seems odd to us, whereas user of social services sounds perfectly right. This may reflect our belief that relationships are at the heart of social work. We have used the term 'behaviour that challenges' rather than 'challenging behaviour' throughout although we know that this has resulted in some rather clunky phrases. There are a lot of strong feelings about behaviour and simple, non-judgemental terms have yet to emerge. Finally, we have written in the first person since we see ourselves as social workers talking to social workers.

We have tried to write a book that is free of jargon and engaging to read. It is nevertheless based on sound experience and theoretical and research literature where this exists. We hope that it encourages social workers into this rewarding field.

# ONE

# The new culture of dementia care

## Introduction

In this chapter we look at two factors that underpin the 'old' culture of dementia care: the stigma of mental illness, with its deep historical roots, and the prevalence of task-centred care. We then describe the 'new' culture of dementia care. Kitwood was the first person to write about the changes between what he describes as the old and new cultures and we refer to his work in some detail. The second half of the chapter introduces the social and citizenship models of dementia care. In Chapter Two, we introduce the medical model. As you will see, we believe that although social work is primarily about the social model, social workers need to understand all three in order to provide the best dementia care.

## Factors underpinning the old culture of dementia care

### Stigma

In his useful chapter looking at sociological perspectives and dementia, Bond (2001, p 227) provides a good, clear definition of stigma: stigma 'refers to a relationship of devaluation in which one individual is disqualified from full social acceptance. Stigma is a social attribute, which is discrediting for an individual or group'. In our view, stigma needs to be understood as arising from long historical attitudes to mental illness.

Just as we need to understand the biography of a person with dementia in order to be able to understand the way they are now, we also need to know about our own professional biography. We therefore briefly examine the history of the way in which people with dementia have been cared for in our society.

## A short history of attitudes to mental illness

### From earliest times

Records of people suffering from memory loss in old age go back a long way. In the 16th century Shakespeare gave us a vivid description of dementia in old age in his play *King Lear* who describes himself as:

> ... a very foolish fond old man,
> Fourscore and upward, not an hour more nor less
> And, to deal plainly,
> I fear I am not in my perfect mind.
> Methinks I should know you, and know this man;
> Yet I am doubtful.... (*King Lear*, Act 4, Scene 7)

In Western Europe at that time, and still to some extent today, it was believed that memory loss and confusion were an inevitable part of old age. People like King Lear were cared for within their own families and communities, with varying degrees of kindness and sympathy and often with downright cruelty. In cultures all over the world today, where dementia and other mental illnesses are not yet recognised as such, there is a range of attitudes. In some these illnesses are seen as a blessing from the gods, in others a punishment and in some they are attributed to evil spirits. It might be useful to differentiate between people with dementia who are simply confused and others whose behaviour is challenging to other people. The latter are more likely to be seen as mentally ill.

### The age of confinement

If you had dementia and were to some extent troublesome you would have been regarded as 'mad'. From the middle of the 16th century onwards a person with dementia would probably have been incarcerated in one of the new public institutions. The workhouses, as they were called, were created under the Poor Law, which was passed in the reign of Queen Elizabeth I to provide for people – children and adults – who were unable to support themselves financially and whose families were unable to do so either. These institutions were also built to contain the misfits, the political dissidents, the social casualties and the 'mad'. No distinction was made between these unfortunate people. This movement – referred to by Foucault (1973) as 'The Great Confinement' – was to continue, in one form or another, until the end of the 20th century.

By the latter half of the 18th century the dominant Western European world view had changed from the religious to the scientific. The Age of Reason – the Enlightenment – had dawned. Scholars came to believe that the universe operated on logical and scientific principles. As part of this belief system it followed that the ability to be rational and order our thoughts was what defined 'personhood' and set human beings apart from animals. 'Madness' was understood to be the opposite of 'Reason' and therefore to be feared. Because of their impaired capacity to reason, those who were 'mad' were viewed as being nearer to beasts than human beings and this belief justified the cramped, squalid and brutal conditions in which they were kept.

In the early 19th century the 'mad', including people with dementia, particularly those with behaviour that challenges other people, were segregated in their own institutions. The most famous of these in England was Bethlehem Hospital in London, which was used as a mental institution from 1547 to 1815. It became a place whose name passed, in the abbreviated form of 'Bedlam', into popular culture as a word to describe uproar, chaos, anarchy and terror.

### Reform and the asylums

A Quaker, William Tuke, built the first 'asylum' or 'place of sanctuary' in 1796. He called it 'The Retreat'. The Quakers did not believe that 'personhood' resided in reason but believed in the 'Inner Light' burning within each person, regardless of age, gender, race or religious belief. It was this belief that set them apart from other religious movements of their time and had led to 150 years of persecution. Their experience made them particularly sympathetic to marginalised groups, including the 'mad'.

The reformers believed that a regime of kindness and humanity using exercise, hard work and moral teaching provided an alternative to 'Bedlam'. Instead of treating people as ravening beasts to be subdued, they treated them as confused children to be guided and protected. This was a completely radical idea and it is extraordinary that the model was so quickly adopted. By the last quarter of the 19th century every town in the UK, as well as many other countries, had its own 'lunatic asylum'. Many people will be familiar with these great buildings, which often had 1,000 or more beds. They had their own farms, provided work for the inmates and became major employers of local labour.

### From asylums to mental institutions

However, they quickly became overcrowded and, as so often happens when the model of a new idea is adopted by people who do not understand the underpinning philosophy, practice became distorted in the face of huge demand and insufficient resources. It was these institutions, which evolved into mental hospitals, which were a familiar part of life in the UK for so long. It was in these institutions that many people with dementia, with behaviour that challenges others, were kept.

This may all seem very remote but there are still some people alive today who have spent 50 years in such institutions.

> Agnes McKay baffled the staff in her care home by walking round and round in circles in the middle of the morning for no apparent reason. At a conference one of the staff described this behaviour and one of the other delegates was able to explain it. He had been a student in a large hospital where each morning every ward had an exercise hour where they walked round and round. Agnes had spent most of her life in this hospital.

In the institutions people were divided up strictly on the basis of gender and age. Changing their names through the 20th century from 'lunatic asylums' to 'mental hospitals' and then to 'psychiatric hospitals' was not enough to reform them. By the last quarter of the 20th century the physical fabric of the structures of the institutions, dating largely from the first half of the 19th century, was becoming increasingly expensive to maintain. At the same time, most people's acute symptoms and behaviour could be controlled by the use of psychotropic drugs, which were developed in the 1960s. There was therefore no longer a need to keep so many people locked away for years of their life in institutions.

### The closure of the mental institutions

In the mid–1980s a national programme of closing the psychiatric hospitals began. National Health Service (NHS) beds for people with dementia are now quite rare and exist mainly to assess and deal with crises. Much reduced, traditional back wards still remain, caring for people with the most challenging behaviour. They are an area of NHS provision frequently needing a great deal of attention. They are often in old buildings, using isolated and disaffected nursing staff caring for disabled and challenging people, many of whom have a history of violence and cannot be cared for in any other setting. On the other hand, some of these wards for people with dementia and behaviour that challenges are run as specialist units doing an important and difficult job and they are sources of much expertise for the field of dementia care.

After the Second World War the workhouses or poor houses for destitute elderly people were slowly replaced by old people's homes developed on a hotel model, mainly run by local authorities and some voluntary organisations. The huge expansion of the private sector followed a change in the law in 1983 when it became possible for the social security system to fund places in nursing and residential homes. The NHS also bought beds to facilitate the dramatic shrinking of the long-stay NHS sector. The responsibility for paying for long-term care was shifted to the individual and arguments have raged ever since about who should pay for long-term care for chronically ill people, especially those with dementia. In the 1980s many large Victorian and Edwardian houses were adapted to meet demand. The type of housing available, of course, dictated the location of care homes, so that we may find a concentration of care homes in one area of a county and very few in another. Large new buildings appeared too; in most cases they were an improvement on the physical environment of long-stay wards of hospitals. However, new buildings do not necessarily change the practice of staff and pessimistic attitudes to people with dementia still persist.

An online Mental Health Time Line produced by Roberts of the University of Middlessex (see www.mdx.ac.uk/www/study/mhhtim.htm) provides a helpful detailed history of the treatment of people with mental illness, including dementia, from earliest times to the present day.

## Task-centred care

Task-centred care is characterised by approaching the care of someone as a set of tasks – washing, dressing, taking them to the toilet, activities, meals and so on. These tasks are undertaken for everyone often in sequence and result in routines such as 'toilet drill' or getting everyone up and dressed by a certain time regardless of their individual preferences. Task-centred care is still widespread although generally recognised as undesirable.

Its origins are complex and lie mainly in acute hospital nursing.

Firm routines were seen as essential and, perhaps, they still are when life and death procedures have to be followed. Huge efforts have been made in nursing since the early 1980s to move to a more individual model of care. An example is the introduction of a named nurse for each patient. Task-centred care has never been a good model for psychiatric nursing although it has been widely practised in these settings.

> As students in a psycho-geriatric ward in the 1960s we had to have everyone out of bed and the beds made by 8.00 and bath times were twice a week when everyone was bathed whether or not this was their normal routine.

People trained in these settings are still around, managing wards and nursing homes, and some of them will struggle with the concept of working without fixed routines.

The tendency of staff to focus on routines and physical tasks when caring for people in institutions is pervasive and deep-seated in all care settings. This is not an issue that is specific to the care of people with dementia. It is like a powerful undertow, which we have to constantly resist as we struggle towards more person-centred care. Many staff find it easier to focus on practical tasks rather than to engage with the complexities of individual needs and behaviour.

It is important to understand why this happens. One reason must be that this is a way of avoiding the emotional pain (Samut, 2003a, 2003b) of much of the care of people with dementia. Empathising with what dementia must be like is simply too hard for some people and it is easier not to see them as ordinary people. Staff need to be well supported to move towards individual care and we will return to this in Chapter Nine. Social work in the community is not immune to routinised practice. Some assessment processes deny the complexity of human experience and biography, and they can be undertaken with very little attention paid to seeing the perspective of the person with dementia or the carer.

## The old culture

By 1995 the large asylums/mental hospitals/psychiatric hospitals had gone. Most people with dementia were living in small, homely and often attractive buildings. But, deep down, many people still believed that the ability to be rational and order our thoughts was what defined personhood and set human beings apart from animals. 'Madness' was still understood to be the opposite of 'Reason' and it was still something to fear.

In 1995 Kitwood wrote a chapter in a book that he co-edited called *The New Culture of Dementia Care* (Kitwood and Benson, 1995). He was concerned to observe that what he called 'the old culture of dementia care' was still alive and well – a 'culture of 'alienation and estrangement' was still dominant' (Kitwood and Benson, 1995, p 11). He made this assertion on the basis of his personal observation of staff and residents in care homes in the early 1990s.

Some of the characteristics he identified were:

- Dementia care was seen as a backwater. The work was seen as placing high demands on staff in exchange for few rewards. It was thought to suit staff with few qualifications and little ambition.
- The care task was about providing a safe environment and meeting basic human needs. The aim was to provide good physical care.
- The 'primary degenerative dementias' were seen as devastating diseases of the central nervous system in which personality and identity were progressively destroyed.
- It was important to have a clear and accurate understanding of a person's impairments, especially those of cognition.
- 'Challenging behaviour' was seen as an inevitable part of dementia to be 'managed' and 'controlled' as skilfully and effectively as possible.
- The personal feelings of staff must be set aside. The 'Us' and 'Them' feeling that went back centuries was still in place.

## The new culture

Kitwood was one of the earliest and most influential exponents of the new approach. It became a powerful movement for change, which amounts to a cultural revolution in the way we think about dementia.

Although we were all taught that dementia is a progressive and inexorable decline into helplessness, many of us had become aware through our own experience that the reality is far more complex. We knew that much more potential remains than we had been led to believe. Kitwood collected this anecdotal evidence and formed it into a coherent theory, which he referred to as 'the new culture of dementia care'. The new culture is in good part about knowing what we have yet to learn; in realising how little we know about the impact of the neurological damage of dementia on the experience of individuals.

The person-centred approach is a direct challenge to the way that the traditional model of dementia care functions. We used to believe that, because there was no medical treatment or cure for dementia medically, there was nothing we could offer except support to carers and sedation to people with dementia when they displayed behaviour that challenged other people. We refer at different points in this book to this 'pessimistic' view of dementia.

## A person becomes a person through other people

Kitwood said: 'Personhood is a status or standing which is bestowed upon one human being by others, in the context of relationship and social being. It implies recognition, respect and trust' (Kitwood, 1997a, p 8). The same idea is expressed as a proverb, which occurs in all the black South African languages. In Zulu the proverb says 'Umuntu ukumuntu ngibanye abantu', translated as 'A person becomes a person through other persons' or 'We can become human only together'. This proverb is closely linked to another black South African concept – 'Ubuntu'. 'We say each one of us matters and we need each other in the spirit of 'Ubuntu' [eating from a shared dish], that we can only be human in relationship, that a person is only a person through other persons' (Tutu, 2004).

The person-centred approach asserts that every person has their own unique personality and life history. These are integral to the person and make up their own unique identity. In order to provide person-centred care we must focus on the whole person. We try to learn as much about them as we can by discovering as much as possible about their biography. We also use very detailed observation of their actions and non-verbal communication. Communication is key and we look at it further in Chapter Five.

## Emotional needs

Kitwood identified four main emotional needs that are common to all human beings but that are particularly in danger of being undermined in people with dementia. He said that these needs are all interwoven and that a deficit in meeting one need will affect all the others.

The needs are:

## *Identity*

Our sense of who we are and what we stand for depends upon past memories of things that have happened to us in our lives. Remembering our family story and the way in which our personal story fits into that story reinforces our own identity. It has been known for many decades that children who are adopted very often experience a great sense of loss or confusion. Kitwood emphasised that people with dementia – whose sense of their own past is disappearing or has already disappeared because of impaired memory – can also feel a sense of loss and confusion.

## *Inclusion*

It has become fashionable to talk about 'social inclusion' as a desirable goal for public policy. Exclusion is seen to be caused by many factors, such as social deprivation, poverty and the marginalisation of various minority groups. It is not often applied to people with dementia. However, they are often marginalised by others in care homes and even in their own homes because their behaviour is misunderstood. A common response to this social exclusion by people with dementia is behaviour that challenges others. This creates a vicious circle, increasing their isolation still further.

## *Occupation*

Meaningful activity is another fundamental human need. The social care world has become fairly skilled in providing activities and entertainment for people with dementia in care homes but there is insufficient attention to making them meaningful to individuals. General activity does not always meet this need for occupation (Craig, 2003). Occupation carries an emotional meaning with it. If we are occupied we have a sense of purpose, we have a role, we are needed. We can see that a lack of occupation is felt by people with dementia when they talk about the job they used to do, when they mistake a care home for a workplace, when they say that they have to go to work. Women who feel that they need to go home to look after their children are expressing this unmet need for occupation and a role as well as a need to give and receive love.

## *Attachment*

In recent years psychologists have identified that the need to feel safe is experienced as strongly in many people with dementia as it is in very young children. The work of Miesen and Jones (1997) has built on the original work of Bowlby and Ainsworth in the 1950s and 1960s and shown that many people with dementia are spending a great deal of their time in what Ainsworth called a 'strange situation' (Ainsworth et al, 1978). This is because the person with dementia is unable to make sense of their world. This fact triggers feelings of danger and then evokes the person's attachment response to these feelings, which will have been developed when they were a small child.

The strangeness of the situation arises from the loss of memory and ability to recognise familiar people and places, as well as the fact that people with dementia are often cared for in very unfamiliar environments. These factors, combined with the loss of the coping strategies developed throughout life to handle feelings of danger, can make the world seem a very frightening place. Much 'attention-seeking' behaviour shown by people with dementia is in reality 'attachment' behaviour that is misinterpreted by other people.

We now know that dementia does not inevitably result in a loss of personality and identity, nor does it change the essence of the person. We now believe that we are dealing with people who, given good care, can be assisted in maintaining their skills, personalities and well-being to a remarkable degree.

Kitwood challenged the traditional way of thinking about dementia with the notion that a major force in the incapacity of many people is the way we relate to them; that it is our problem, not their problem. Starting with ourselves means that we need to strive for a degree of empathy. It will be helpful if we imagine ourselves with the disease and consider what will be most help to us. This allows us to see that many of the more painful aspects of the experience of dementia are caused by the way others relate to people with dementia. It may not be comfortable to take the view that part of the disability of dementia is caused by the way we relate to people with dementia. Many carers find the medical model, in which behaviour and other aspects of dementia are related primarily to brain damage, easier to understand and cope with. The answer is, of course, that we need both the social and the medical model to understand dementia fully and we need the expertise of both health and social care professionals.

## Stages of dementia

Stages of dementia have been identified and can be a useful starting point for understanding, but they must not be treated as gospel. It is like the concept of stages in the grieving process. It is useful to know about them, but each person's experience of grieving is different. Some people have the stages of dementia in different degrees, some miss stages out. For many people the stages go back and forth. Most people with dementia will tell you that they have good and bad days. If you consider the social approach to dementia, which suggests that numerous factors interact with the brain damage, this is not surprising.

> John Phillips is a very articulate man with vascular dementia. He teaches a lot of staff about his experience of dementia. Nevertheless, some days he is unable even to dress himself.

There are many versions of the stages of dementia. We decided not to outline any of them in this book because they can detract from a truly person-centred approach. As social workers we do, however, need to be familiar with the concept of stages so that we can hold our own in discussions with our nursing colleagues who are more likely to use the term.

Social workers have an important role in helping families to understand that people with dementia have a real struggle in relating to others in a way that reinforces their uniqueness. As social workers, we understand that, because this is so difficult for people with dementia, others need to support them in doing so. This is an area in which social work values are particularly important. The IFSW defines social work in the following way: 'The social work profession promotes social change, problem solving in human relationships and the empowerment and liberation of people to enhance well-being. Utilising theories of human behaviour and social systems, social work intervenes at the points where people interact with their environments. Principles of human rights and social justice are fundamental to social work' (www.iassw–aiets.org). You may well find that you have a role to play in educating your fellow professionals from other disciplines, as well as families, about the need to support the human rights of people with dementia.

# Ways of understanding dementia

There are three ways of understanding dementia and we need to understand all three. The first and longer-established is the medical model (called the 'organic' model in Cheston and Bender's (1999) thoughtful book), which focuses on the brain damage and its progressive nature. What we see in people with dementia and what they experience is attributed to the brain damage.

Because there is no cure for dementia, the medical model is a pessimistic one. It tends to see all manifestations of dementia as due to brain damage. The following quotation from a textbook for general practitioners (GPs) published in 2000 illustrates this point with some force: 'Throughout the book we will be emphasising how much damage dementia does to the lives of sufferers and those around them. No one can doubt the magnitude and importance of this damage. It poses an enormous challenge to health and social services and to the community as a whole' (Jacques and Jackson, 2000, p 4).

The social model (or disability model as it is sometimes called) suggests that what we see and what is experienced results from an interaction of the person with brain damage and a whole set of factors, which we present below. We also need a third model to understand that people with dementia are fellow citizens who make a contribution to society as well as receive services. You will notice that we use the terms 'model' and 'approach'. They are both used widely and mean the same thing.

## The social approach to dementia

It will be helpful if we start presenting the social approach by suggesting that we see dementia as an impairment, which becomes a disability because of the social and the built environment. This is the way social workers are trained to think of social models of any illness or impairment (Oliver, 1990; Bartlett, 2000; Barnes and Mercer, 2006).

The impairments of dementia are, generally speaking:

• failing memory;
• impaired learning;
• impaired ability to reason.

One of the most profound effects of diminishing cognitive competence is the high level of stress experienced by many people with dementia, which is very obvious when you meet them. We also need to bear in mind that people who are not fully in control of their social and built environments will depend on them being helpful. It seems likely that if you cannot remember and cannot work out what is going on, you are acutely dependent on buildings and the people around you to 'tell' you in some way.

Figure 4.1 in Chapter Four is the simplest way of describing the social model of care since the essence is that the experience of dementia results from the interaction of a person with a degree of brain damage with a host of factors within him/herself and many aspects of the social and the built environment.

One of the characteristics of the social model is that it has a positive message. All the factors that interact with the person can be optimised to make the experience of dementia a better one. We are all potential experts at this and our aim in this book is to help social workers to play their part, by describing how to do this for each of the factors in the figure.

If we accept that dementia is a disability, we can adopt a rehabilitation approach. This is not a word often used in dementia care but it fits well with a positive approach to dementia and enables us to explain some of what we mean to our medical colleagues who are very familiar with it. Marshall (2005) summarises the key concepts of rehabilitation as:

- teamwork;
- working with families and other support mechanisms;
- prostheses (in this case people as well as some aids, adaptations, tools and environmental modifications);
- removing causes of excess (or unnecessary) disability;
- learning and motivation (perhaps the most problematic concepts for dementia care);
- focus (we cannot sort out every aspect of people's lives so we need to be clear where we can help).

Preventing excess or unnecessary disability is a very useful concept in dementia care since much of the help given to people with dementia actually increases their disability. This can be about the manner in which people with dementia are treated as well as more tangible forms of help. Using the term 'rehabilitation' we can perhaps explain to commissioners and providers of care that if we do not provide the right kind of care, people with dementia will be more disabled than they need to be.

## The citizenship approach to dementia

One of the most exciting developments in our understanding of dementia over the last few years has been in communicating with people with dementia. We have learned that they want to communicate and that they have lots to say. We devote a chapter to this important topic (see Chapter Five). We mention it here because it is this change that has led to a third approach to dementia.

The citizenship approach turns the other two approaches on their heads by asking 'what can people with dementia give us?' rather than 'what can we do for people with dementia?'. It is, however, more than simply listening to people. Drake (1999) asserts that citizenship is more than consumerism, which is where the expression of power is limited to making choices or expressing preferences. It involves civil, political and social rights and participating in the sort of activities most of us take for granted such as work, leisure, political debate and religious observance. Drake further makes the point that it is about equality of opportunity and process although the outcome may be limited by the abilities of any individual.

Citizenship is based on reciprocity, which is why this approach is so new. In the past, nobody was thinking about people with dementia as being able to give as well as receive. We might need to pause for a minute and consider what they can give. Everyone who works with people with dementia will have their own list.

Ours is:

- creativity (which we cover in Chapter Nine);
- emotional veracity;
- courage;
- views and preferences (which we cover in Chapter Four);
- opinions – for example we believe that people with dementia should vote;
- humour.

In terms of expertise, for this model or approach, people with dementia are the experts in dementia.

In summary, we cannot stress often enough that this book is based on our conviction that social workers need to respect all three approaches even if our expertise and special contributions are in the social or disability approach. These approaches are not alternatives, but are three sides to a triangle without which it would not be whole.

## Hearing the voice of people with dementia

As we have said, this is a tremendously exciting new development in the field and is of vital importance in transforming the culture of care. We cover this in some detail in Chapter Five. The fact that for so long we did not hear what people with dementia were saying about their condition may have contributed significantly to the survival of the old culture with its roots in the long-distant past. Earlier diagnosis and, for some people, the drugs for the symptomatic treatment of Alzheimer's disease have meant that certain gifted people with dementia are now telling us what it really feels like. What they have to say can be very challenging. These talented and courageous people are telling their stories at conferences, on radio and television and in books.

Many people with dementia have written about their experiences (Davis, 1993; Bryden, 2005). Most people writing about dementia these days include material written by people with dementia or transcripts of the views of people with dementia (Wilkinson, 2002; Basing, 2004; Marshall, 2005; the Trebus project, see www.alzscotland.org). This material takes us into a completely different stage of our cultural revolution. Nobody any longer has the excuse of saying 'I didn't realise what it was like'. So far, contributions have been from articulate, white, educated people. We have yet to hear from other groups of people with dementia.

## Transferring learning

Social work has always been good at incorporating learning from other fields. We are really a hybrid profession although we have our own particular value base. The field of dementia care is no exception. We have borrowed from a wide range of different therapeutic fields and other groups. We make this point at the start of this book to emphasise that the best social work is a highly creative process where we are constantly on the alert for material that improves our ability to help people with dementia and their carers. We could have chosen palliative care or cancer care to illustrate how we can learn from other fields, however we have chosen learning disability, some aspects of which are:

- People working in the field of learning disability are much further ahead of us in thinking through concepts of 'normalisation'.
- They have a well-established tradition of developing care facilities for people with high levels of behaviour that challenges staff.

- They have learned much about stress reduction techniques without resorting to medication to pacify people.
- We can also learn from their more innovative models of day care and day opportunities.
- They have developed advocacy where there is a conflict between the person and their family to an advanced degree.
- There is a much clearer understanding of the human rights of the individual and the boundaries of what other people can do on their behalf in the field of learning disability.

The fact that many people with a learning disability (Jokinen, 2005) are now developing dementia because they are living longer means that there is a need for joint training (Kerr and Wilson, 2002). A collaborative model between these two fields could be very beneficial to both groups.

## Conclusion

If we think of the incarceration of 'mad' people as a huge and ancient tree, we can see that it was finally cut down in the 1990s. But its roots penetrate deep into the earth in which new trees have been planted. Values and beliefs, which spring from the old incarceration roots, are still managing to strangle the growth of the new young trees.

However, you cannot stop new growth forever. Every day new approaches are being tried, many transferred from other fields. Fundamentally what we need in the new culture of dementia care is care that recognises the uniqueness of each individual and their relationships but at the same time benefits from as wide a trawl of knowledge and practice as possible. It is very difficult, very demanding and very rewarding for all concerned when it works.

Our intention is to communicate a spirit of optimism and excitement that encourages readers to be constantly alert to new approaches and to share the process of learning.

### Further reading
Kitwood, T. (1997a) *Dementia Reconsidered: The Person Comes First*, Buckingham: Open University Press.

# TWO

# Demography, diagnosis and alcohol-related brain damage

## Introduction

This is a book about knowledge, ideas, skills and expertise for social workers. However, in order to understand our task we have to understand the context in which we work. Demography is a very important part of the context. All developed countries have rapidly ageing populations, which means that dementia, which is so closely linked to age, may be called the key health issue for the 21st century. We discuss demographics and then take a medical approach to dementia, which social workers need to understand. We include a special section on alcohol-related brain damage (ARBD) because social workers will be working increasingly with people with this condition.

## Demographics

Over 750,000 older people in the UK have a diagnosis of dementia. Using population figures for 1996, this can be broken down as shown in Table 2.1.

The primary risk factor for dementia is age. As social workers, we need to be aware, therefore, that demography is a key factor in our field because it affects both current services and future planning.

**Table 2.1:** The number of people with dementia in the UK

| Country | Number of people |
| --- | --- |
| England | 652,600 |
| Scotland | 63,700 |
| Wales | 41,800 |
| Northern Ireland | 17,100 |

*Source:* Alzheimer's Society (2004a; www.alzheimers.org.uk)

There is a great deal of research in progress looking at risk factors such as family history, diet, stress and head trauma (Gow and Gilhooly, 2003). So far it is inconclusive although it is clear that the risk factors for vascular dementia are related to those for other vascular problems, like smoking, poor diet and little exercise. There is increasing attention to the possibility that there is a vascular component to all dementias (Snowden, 2001).

## Prevalence

A large study published in 2004 compared prevalence rates in nine Organisation for Economic Co-operation and Development (OECD) countries – Australia, Canada, England and Wales, France, Germany, Japan, Spain, Sweden and the US. It found some differences but the results were broadly similar. The authors concluded that 'ageing OECD populations will increase the prevalence of age-related diseases, in particular dementia. Furthermore, improvements in health and social care will prolong survival, further increasing the pool of people suffering from dementia and Alzheimer's disease' (Moise et al, 2004, p 64).

By the year 2010 the authors predicted 'dramatic increases in the projected prevalence rates for dementia for the population aged 75 and over with even larger increases for people with moderate to severe dementia' (p 19). They also predicted 'a further dramatic increase when the post-war baby boom cohorts reach the age where susceptibility to dementia is significant' (p 19). They do not, of course, mean that a greater proportion of older people will have dementia but that the numbers will increase very dramatically as the number of older people increases.

## Younger people

The number of younger people with dementia is also increasing. Some groups of people with high risk of dementia are living into older age for the first time. People with Down's syndrome, for example, are now living longer and get dementia in their forties and fifties (McQuillan et al, 2003). There is a possibility that people with acquired brain injury are also at high risk. There are also small numbers of younger people with AIDS who get dementia.

## Carers

Many carers are themselves older people: 1.5 million are aged over 60 and 8,000 over 90 (Carers UK, 2005). Alongside the increase in the number of very old people we have a decrease in the number of people available to care for them, at least as far as paid staff are concerned. There are fewer people available in the working population, both because of lower birth rates over many years and because of other employment opportunities. Between 2005 and 2020 we will see the retirement of the baby boomers, many of whom will be available to be volunteers and informal carers. When they need care, there will be a problem because they had relatively few children and there will be many of them.

Caring for the old and sick has traditionally been seen as a female task – both within the family and as a job. However, there has been an increase in the number of male carers because men are living longer (Neno, 2004).

## Family composition

The shifts in patterns of family formation and dissolution that have happened since the 1970s have potentially adversely affected the ability of the family to care for its own. The experience of family life is now far more diverse than it once was – serial relationships and single-parent families are common. Increasing numbers of women are working outside the home. Couples who remain married to each other for many decades have become the exception rather than the rule, which may affect the extent to which spouses/partners look after each other in the future. People who are step-parents as well as parents, having created more than one family unit, and who are holding down a job, may be unable to care for their own parents – let alone their ex-partner's relatives, aunts or uncles. There is, as yet, little evidence one way or the other about the impact of changes in family structure and patterns on willingness to care for relatives with dementia.

Estimating future needs for the health and social care for older (and younger) people with dementia is extremely difficult. To do this we need to look at morbidity as well as demographic trends. We can estimate the likely number of older people, although projections were adjusted upwards in 2003 because the current cohort was living longer and future projections are based on current trends. The really difficult question is how healthy older people are going to be in the future (morbidity being the issue rather than mortality). The fact that many baby boomers drink more than the previous generation (NHS Scotland, 2006) and often have rather sedentary lifestyles (Wanless, 2006, annex 6, p 153) may bode ill for their health and may mean that they will need more care. On the other hand there may be better treatments for the chronic and progressive illnesses of old age including dementia. One trend is certain: there will be more people with disabilities in the younger old group and some of these people, such as those with Down's syndrome, are at high risk of dementia. The long-term impact of increasing use of recreational drugs is so far unknown, although worrying. At present, studies of future needs for care are based on the current older population.

## International trends

It is clear that in the industrialised world the demographic challenge is forcing governments to face up to the key health issue of dementia. It is a huge challenge and is likely to remain so for the foreseeable future. There is no such clear trend common to all of the less industrialised countries. In sub-Saharan Africa, for instance, the AIDS pandemic has had a devastating effect on people of working age. At present this means that there is a much-reduced adult generation available to care for older people and in the future there will be fewer older people to be cared for. But in other less industrialised countries, like much of the Indian subcontinent, South East Asia and South America, more people are now living longer because increasing numbers have survived infancy, which is a time of high mortality. Reduced rates of infant mortality started about 50 years ago and these people are now ageing in numbers never seen before. Dementia is thereby becoming a key social challenge in those countries as well.

Alzheimer's Disease International makes this point forcefully when it points out that 'For at least 15 years, the majority of people with dementia worldwide have been living in developing regions of the world. They account already for 60% of all cases; by 2040 this proportion will have risen to 71%' (www.alz.co.uk).

At present we have no very clear evidence of prevalence rates of dementia in different countries. 'To estimate the numbers of cases of dementia, we apply prevalence rates from previous studies to population figures. Very little is known about the prevalence of dementia outside the more developed countries (Europe, North America, Australasia and Japan), so it is difficult to estimate the number of cases of dementia worldwide. ADI [Alzheimer's Disease International] supports the 10/66 Dementia Research Group which aims to quantify prevalence and incidence rates in developing countries, so that we can make better estimates in those regions' (www. alz.co.uk)

'Pilot studies are now completed in 25 centres in Latin America, Africa, India, China and South East Asia. Lack of awareness of dementia as a health condition, coupled with unresponsive health services are two of the biggest problems facing those with dementia in the developing world' (www. alz.co.uk).

## What is dementia?

We have deliberately not started this chapter on context with the usual medical approach. This is because it is often seen as more important than other approaches, rather than as one of many. Nevertheless, knowledge of the illness, or, more accurately, illnesses, is essential for social workers.

There are many medical definitions of dementia. Some people use the term 'types' of dementia, others refer to 'causes' of dementia. Alzheimer's Australia says: 'Dementia is the term used to describe the symptoms of a large group of illnesses which cause a progressive decline in a person's mental functioning. It is a broad term which describes a loss of memory, intellect, rationality, social skills and normal emotional reactions' (www.alzheimers.org.au).

We take the view that it is useful to include ARBD because social workers will meet increasing numbers of people with this diagnosis and most of the practice issues are similar. However, unlike most other dementias it is not always progressive. Everyone's pathway through dementia is different but there are overriding similarities.

## The importance of differential diagnosis

The label 'dementia' is, by itself, not very useful as an indicator of the kind of help people need. It has led to very negative consequences, since people with this label may be thought to be mentally incompetent in every respect. It means little without more information about, for example, the person's remaining abilities, their present mental competence, behaviour, emotional needs and physical health. Assessments need to cover a wide range of factors, as we discuss in Chapter Five.

First we need to ensure that the person with dementia receives a differential diagnosis, partly to determine the kind of dementia but also to make sure that the person actually has dementia. Many people experience loss of memory, behaviour problems and disorientation

Table 2.2: Quick guide to the clinical features of dementia, depression and delirium

| | Dementia | Depression | Delirium |
|---|---|---|---|
| **History of duration of illness** | Gradual onset and unremitting course for at least 6 months prior to consultation | Gradual onset for weeks or months prior to consultation | Sudden acute onset where the carer can be precise about the time – generally hours or days prior to consultation |
| **Cognitive assessment** | **Memory**<br>Impairment noted possibly by others, usually short-term memory and recall most affected but in some individuals remote memory is also affected<br>**Orientation**<br>Can be impaired for place and time but in some individuals in the early stages of the illness orientation may be unaffected<br>**Level of consciousness**<br>Fully conscious and alert normally | **Memory**<br>Impairment generally reported in the short-term memory and recall<br>**Orientation**<br>Rarely impaired<br>**Level of consciousness**<br>Fully conscious and alert | **Memory**<br>Only recent memory impaired<br>**Orientation**<br>Almost always impaired for time, place and person again with sudden onset<br>**Level of consciousness**<br>Fluctuating levels of consciousness and not always fully alert |
| **Thoughts and perception** | Often reduced interest and poor levels of concentration slowing of thoughts, occasional feelings of worthlessness. Can present with visual or auditory hallucinations in some cases | Often preoccupied with sad thoughts and feelings of hopelessness, generally thought process is slowed and can be preoccupied | Often paranoid and bizarre, topics often do not relate to current situation and there are often vivid visual and auditory hallucinations present |

**Table 2.2:** contd.../

|  | Dementia | Depression | Delirium |
|---|---|---|---|
| **Emotions** | Can present as emotionally labile in some cases, may be apathetic or agitated or quite irritable | Sad, fearful and emotionally 'flat'; on occasions can be irritable | Usually quite irritable, frightened and often aggressive or agitated |
| **Sleep pattern** | Can often be disturbed and night-time waking and confusion is often present | Usually wakens early in the morning and/or has difficulty getting to sleep. In some cases daytime sleeping is common | More confused in the evening and at night leading to disturbed sleep and restlessness |
| **Other indicators** | Likely to confabulate to cover up the gaps in memory, may not be aware of the deficits in cognition | May have a past history of depression | Physical exam may indicate an illness or other physical cause for sudden deterioration |

*Source:* adapted by P. Bree (2005) from S. Colles, A. Kydd and A. Chapman (eds) (2001) *A Practice Guide for Community Nursing,* Stirling DSDC.

when they are acutely ill or very distressed. This is known as an acute confusional state (or delirium). When the underlying cause is treated they return to normal (Manning, 2003). Some medications can cause similar symptoms. It is particularly important to identify depression, which can appear to be very like dementia in some people (Manthorpe and Iliffe, 2005).

A thorough diagnosis will always include a detailed history that will, among other things, establish the speed of onset. Alzheimer's disease is usually characterised by a gradual onset. Both delirium and vascular dementia can start quickly. Words like 'confusion' should, in our opinion, be avoided because the term is not sufficiently precise to be valuable. People sometimes think it is synonymous with dementia, but there are many different causes of confusion.

There are two main common causes/types of dementia – Alzheimer's disease and vascular dementia and a large number of people have both. We quote some figures here, which must not be taken as absolute because there are slight differences in diagnostic categories in different studies. Bender (2003) provides a useful critique of the standard disease typology we provide here.

## Alzheimer's disease

The most common cause of dementia is Alzheimer's disease accounting for 50% to 60% of all cases. It destroys brain cells and nerves disrupting the transmitters which carry messages in the brain, particularly those responsible for storing memories. During the course of Alzheimer's disease, nerve cells die in particular regions of the brain. The brain shrinks as gaps develop in the temporal lobes and hippocampus, which are responsible for storing and retrieving new information. This in turn affects people's ability to remember, speak, think and make decisions' (www.alz.co.uk). Alzheimer's disease, generally speaking, starts imperceptibly and is characterised by a steady global deterioration.

When Mrs James was found walking along a main road in her nightdress in the middle of winter, a social worker was asked to make an assessment. Her daughter told the social worker that Mrs James had been diagnosed with Alzheimer's disease by the GP two years previously. Looking back, however, she felt that her mother had been behaving 'strangely' in small ways for some years before that; she remembered a time, three years previously, when Mrs James became confused and frightened at the local shops.

## Vascular dementia

'The next largest cause is vascular dementia which accounts for about 20% of all cases, another 20% of people having both Alzheimer's disease and vascular dementia. The most common type of vascular dementia is multi-infarct dementia (MID) where the brain has been damaged by repeated small strokes. However, vascular dementia can be caused by a number of other conditions including high blood pressure (hypertension), irregular heart rhythms (arrhythmias) and diseases which cause damage to the arteries in the brain. Their dementia proceeds in a less global way with stable periods and sudden deterioration as sections of the brain are affected' (Alzheimer Scotland, www.alzscot.org.uk).

> Miss Wills was an active woman of 80 who lived alone. Her friend visited her every Saturday. On one visit she found that Miss Wills had a large bruise on her face, was very confused and failed to recognise her. She concluded that Miss Wills had knocked herself out when she fell. Miss Wills' GP, knowing that she had high blood pressure, thought it likely that she had vascular dementia and had suffered a small stroke, causing her to lose consciousness and fall, banging her head.

## Dementia with Lewy bodies

'The third most common cause of dementia is dementia with Lewy bodies and may occur in 10% to 20% of cases which start after the age of 65. It is similar to Alzheimer's disease in that it is caused by the degeneration and death of nerve cells in the brain. It takes its name from the abnormal collection of protein, known as Lewy bodies, which occur in the nerve cells of the brain. Half or more of people with Lewy body disease also develop signs and symptoms of Parkinson disease. People with Lewy body disease often have hallucinations and are very sensitive to some tranquillisers known as antipsychotic or neuroleptic drugs and their use should be avoided if at all possible' (www.alz.co.uk).

## Rarer types/causes of dementia

These include fronto-temporal dementia, Creutzfeldt–Jakob Disease (CJD) and ARBD. There are a few even rarer kinds of dementia for which a medical briefing needs to be sought.

### Fronto-temporal dementia

Fronto-temporal dementia 'covers a range of conditions, including Pick's Disease, frontal lobe degeneration and dementia associated with motor neuron disease. All are caused by damage to the frontal lobe and/or temporal parts of the brain. These areas are responsible for our behaviour, emotional responses and language skills. In the early stages, memory is still intact but the personality and behaviour of the person changes. Younger people, specifically those under the age of 65, are more likely to be affected' (Alzheimer's Society, 2003a, www.alzheimers.org.uk).

### Creutzfeldt–Jakob Disease

Creutzfeldt–Jakob Disease (CJD) is a prion disease. Prions are abnormal forms of protein. There are several forms of CJD. Sporadic CJD is very rare, affects those over the age of 50 and progresses very rapidly. Familial CJD is an inherited form where some families seem to be predisposed to producing the abnormal prion proteins. Most people with CJD are younger people and the course of the illness is usually longer.

In 1996 a new type of variant CJD was reported. It appears to affect younger people more than the other forms of the disease. The average age of death is 29. There is now evidence that variant CJD is caused by Bovine Spongiform Encephalopathy (BSE) – a form of prion disease affecting cattle. The consumption of infected beef products appears to have led to the development of BSE in humans (Alzheimer's Society, 2003b, www.alzheimers.org.uk).

## Alcohol-related brain damage

The number of people with ARBD is increasing at the moment and social workers are likely to be involved because of the complex needs of this group of people. There is as yet very little awareness of causes and symptoms of this condition and very little information about the needs of people with ARBD. Unlike other dementias, there is potential for partial or full recovery. Most of this book is about the dementias that are progressive so this section is an extended one about ARBD to include more than simply medical information.

## Demographics

There are no figures about numbers of people affected, except perhaps locally of people known to service providers. We know that numbers are increasing as more and more alcohol is consumed but there are no actual numbers that might galvanise attention. There is a tendency to think of this as a problem of homeless men whereas the reality is that 'it affects all parts of society regardless of age, gender or social class' (Community Care Works, 2005, p 3). Although there are plenty of older people with ARBD, most of them will be younger than retirement age.

## What is ARBD?

Cox et al (2004, p 2) provide a useful framework: 'ARBD refers to the effects of changes to the structure and function of the brain resulting from long term consumption of alcohol. There is no single cause of ARBD, which usually results from a combination of factors. These include the toxic effects of alcohol on brain cells, vitamin and nutritional deficiencies, head injury and disturbances to the blood supply to the brain. ARBD encompasses a range of conditions characterised by impaired mental function such as Wernicke-Korsakoff's syndrome, alcohol-related dementia, alcoholic dementia and alcohol amnesic syndrome'.

'Alcohol causes damage through:

- Its toxic effect on the central nervous system
- Changes to metabolism, heart function and blood supply
- Dehydration – damage to brain cells
- Interfering with thiamine absorption
- Its association with poor nutrition
- Falls, accidents and possible head injury.' (Community Care Works, 2005, p 3)

## Recovery and rehabilitation

Professionals do not always take ARBD seriously enough and there is also a stigma in seeking help. Recovery is more likely if people abstain from alcohol and it will vary according to the extent of brain damage. It can take up to two years, which can complicate long-term care planning. Many people with alcohol problems also have other problems such as breakdown in relationships, debt and homelessness, so giving up alcohol is a real challenge. Many live with long-term impairments, such as poor learning ability and difficulties in dealing with abstract concepts.

Even if people are lucky enough to get the right diagnosis early enough there is a serious dearth of age-appropriate services and support to help with rehabilitation. There are few specialist services and this group of people does not usually do well in mainstream services for older people with dementia. Clearly, properly coordinated assessment and care planning from knowledgeable staff who can work with a wide range of people is needed.

## Care planning

People with ARBD can manage at home with support but 'this depends on the following factors:

- Abstinence from alcohol, or at least a carefully managed harm reduction programme
- Consistent support from staff with understanding and knowledge of ARBD
- Developing/redeveloping skills in daily living, developing/ maintaining routines
- A safe living environment (house may require some adaptations)
- Good diet/nutrition
- Meaningful daytime activity
- Support from family and friends
- Activity-based rehabilitation strategies to improve memory and other cognitive impairment' (Cox et al, 2004, p 24).

These are challenging to provide although there are more and more models of provision. Finding appropriate accommodation is often the big hurdle especially since many people with ARBD will have had a chaotic housing pattern.

Teamwork between professions and agencies is essential especially during the rehabilitation period, when a specialist unit may be required. In the longer term a range of options is needed depending on the extent of recovery. Individual, person–centred assessment and care planning is the only way forward given the diversity, complexity and fluctuation of individual need. As social workers we may well be involved in supporting families to support people with ARBD. We will certainly be involved in explaining the particular needs of this group to colleagues in many settings and providing support for them too. Whether we work within a dementia service, a mental health service or an alcohol service is less important than that we ourselves are knowledgeable and supported.

This brief introduction to ARBD is meant to do no more than alert readers to this emerging group of people with dementia from which they can wholly or partially recover if they are given the right help at the right time. There is not a great deal of literature about ARBD. A good starting point is Cox et al (2004).

## Conclusion

This chapter has covered three topics: demography, medical information about dementia and ARBD. As far as demography and dementia are concerned we have only provided an introduction to a vast literature. Medical and nursing colleagues are obviously the source of a great deal more medical information. There is not a great deal of research or literature available yet on ARBD but people with ARBD are undoubtedly going to be a major user group in the near future.

### Further reading
Alzheimer's Society associates' websites

Bender, M. (2003) *Explorations in Dementia*, London: Jessica Kingsley Publishers.

Shenk, D. (2001) *The Forgetting*, London: Harper Collins.

# THREE

# Policy context

## Introduction

We work in complex and ever-changing organisations, which themselves operate in a complex and ever-changing policy context. In this chapter we look at recent policies in England and Wales. Many policy trends in Scotland and Northern Ireland are similar. Since the majority of our readers will be in England and Wales we concluded that we had to limit ourselves or this chapter would be far too long. We clarify the policy trends by describing them under five headings:

• Raising standards
• Fairness and equality
• Empowerment
• Partnership
• Social inclusion

In the last of these we look at groups we consider to be generally excluded: younger people with dementia, black and minority ethnic groups, people in the early stages of dementia, people with complex needs, homeless people and older people in prison. We also look at staff from overseas.

## Raising standards

Older people with mental health problems whose needs cut across all health and social care boundaries have received, until recently, relatively little attention and insufficient new resources to address their specific difficulties. We approach policies aiming to raise standards by reviewing relevant legislation.

### Care management (1990 NHS and Community Care Act)

Care management is now well established as the working framework for staff in community care teams, including social workers. It is one of those ideas which is plainly sensible, and a reaction against years of inflexible provision of standardised services. In the UK, care management means organising and coordinating a multiplicity of providers, since we have generally assumed that it is undesirable to provide flexible, individually tailored care packages from the local authority alone. Many local authorities in the UK have severely cut back on their 'in-house' services, including day, home, respite and residential care. This is not universally the case and there remain some exceptions to this trend, especially in Scotland.

One of the problems is commissioning flexible services. Commissioning the right service, in the right amount, at the right time is really difficult. Failure, however, to do this can mean that some people are receiving too much, others too little and some inappropriate support. This is, in part, the result of multiple funding streams, each with its own criteria and monitoring system.

The UK systems of care management have generally not been seen as requiring an interdisciplinary approach. This means that opportunities to provide a seamless health and social work service have been limited. Dementia is especially challenging for care managers. Care plans and packages have to be constantly reviewed and updated. Staff also have to be aware of the constant shifting of available services and the ability of their client to meet the eligibility criteria. Needs can change from low to moderate to substantial to critical and back again to low within a short space of time.

There are abrupt changes, for example sudden deterioration with vascular and Lewy body dementias, which can throw the best care plan into disarray. Acute confusional episodes can also cause a sudden loss of cognitive function, which dramatically disables the person. When the physical condition causing the acute episode has been successfully treated, the person returns to their former level of ability, needing reassessment. Social circumstances can change equally rapidly.

There is also the issue of control. Who is in charge of a care plan? Some carers feel very diminished if another person is managing the help they receive. One essential skill needed when working with carers is the ability to give help in a way that makes them feel that they are in control, while bearing in mind that there may be a conflict of interest between them and the person with dementia.

## Modernising Social Services *(DH, 1998a)*

The intention to drive up standards gave rise to the publication of the White Paper *Modernising Social Services*. Principles for services for adults were outlined as:

- better coordination between health and social care providers;
- more clarity about what services are provided, for whom and how much people should pay for them;
- more consistency of provision across the country;
- services designed to promote independence;
- the raising of standards in service delivery.

### Regulation of the workforce

The creation of the General Social Care Council/Scottish Social Services Council led to a new central register of qualified social workers, putting social workers on the same footing as comparable professionals. Other staff in dementia care are also in the process of being placed on a register.

### The Forget Me Not *Reports (Audit Commission, 2000, 2002)*

The Audit Commission produced a landmark report in 2000 entitled *Forget Me Not*, which was the result of a thorough review of mental health services for older people. It asserted that 'services for older people with mental health problems are patchy and inconsistent across the country, and often fail to link together into a coherent service network' (p 97). Two years later there was a second *Forget Me Not* report (Audit Commission, 2002), which looked at how much progress had been made. This showed some evidence of improvement but not nearly enough. Specialist mental health teams for dementia were still only available in 50% of the areas studied. Although the Audit Commission only covers England and Wales, these reports have been very influential throughout the whole of the UK.

## The National Service Framework for Older People *(DH, 2001a)*

*The National Service Framework for Older People* (England and Wales) challenged all professionals working with older people to review their practice in the light of the standards that it laid down. Unfortunately only Standard 7 referred to older people with mental health needs, including dementia. No additional funds were allocated to its implementation as they had been to the National Service Framework for people of working age with mental health needs. This probably explains why progress in improving these services has been frustratingly slow.

## Fairness and equality

### Eligibility criteria (Fair Access to Care, DH, 2003a)

Social services departments in England and Wales were required to produce and publish their eligibility criteria for services by the 1990 NHS and Community Care Act. Further guidance entitled *Fair Access to Care* was produced in 2003 (DH, 2003a). The framework for eligibility was graded into bands: Critical, Substantial, Moderate and Low. The criteria were defined as factors 'which describe the seriousness of the risk to independence or other consequences if needs are not addressed' (DH, 2003a, p 4).

Although the original concept was an attempt to introduce fairness and equality into the system, the *Fair Access to Care* guidance contained the sentence: 'In setting their eligibility criteria, councils should take account of their resources, local expectations and local costs' (p 5). This has allowed social services commissioners, working in a chronically underfunded environment, to use the eligibility criteria as a means of rationing services, under the guise of 'targeting' those most in need. In some parts of the UK, people living in the community had their funding capped at the same level as that set for residential care. In recent years, most local authorities have adopted a more flexible approach.

There is an ongoing debate about the extent and implications of the lack of low-level support in the community. A recent report by the Institute for Public Policy Research (Rankin, 2005, p 19) asserts: 'Currently most resources are focused on older people with the highest levels of need. One of the results of the community care reforms in the 1990s was the shift of resources towards people with high levels of need, which it is widely acknowledged has had the consequence of removing low level support'. However, Supporting People funding has provided low-level support to people with dementia, as part of projects to help them remain at home, throughout the UK.

Some of the small group of people with early dementia, particularly younger people who are receiving Direct Payments, currently receive generous funding for care packages.

It remains true, however, that people who are assessed as having low or moderate needs may be deemed to fall outside the remit of social services. Others who are assessed as having critical or substantial needs may not qualify for social services help on financial grounds. It has become quite common for families to be told, after an initial referral, either that their needs are not serious enough, or that they have too much money to qualify for a social services care package. This can be stressful for social workers who make the initial contact, as they face the pain and distress of people's lives as they struggle with dementia.

## Devolution of budgets to local level (from 1990)

Social workers are now aware how much money their team has to spend each week. Team leaders will be making extremely difficult choices between families in extreme need at the funding panels, but someone else in the local authority decides how much money is available to be spent. Increasingly, if you are able to pay, there is an astonishing range of services to help you. There is a possibility that those who are well off will benefit enormously, as will those who have very limited financial resources. Those who are assessed as having less than critical or substantial needs and those who are above the poverty level, but not rich, are suffering. Many are likely to refuse help if they have to pay for it. This should have been evident in the planning stages. Instead it has come as something of a shock to many frontline workers who see people in extreme need refusing services.

> Mr Potter was 75 years old and cared for his wife who had dementia and his 40-year-old son who had Down's syndrome. He had been much helped over the years by home helps who did the shopping and helped him keep the house clean. When charges were introduced for the home help service he thought he could manage without them. Three weeks later he died from a heart attack while carrying heavy bags from the supermarket.

Charges can be a nightmare when the person has dementia. Their grasp of their finances may be unreliable, so asking them to sign financial agreements may sometimes be legally dubious. This will be discussed further in the section on mental capacity.

## The funding of long-term care

We feel this particular part of social policy deserves special mention as it is so central to the role of the social worker as care manager. It has been a dilemma since the closure of the long-term hospitals for older people. An early initiative of the New Labour government in 1997 was the setting up of a Royal Commission on Long Term Care, which reported in 1999. It divided the costs of long-term care into living costs, housing costs, nursing costs and personal care costs and took the view that the last two of these should be free. Scotland accepted all these recommendations but the rest of the UK did not and still charges for personal care. The Royal Commission was very much influenced by the fact that older people with acute conditions like cancer receive all their health and personal care free, whereas people with dementia, which is a long-term condition, have to pay for a lot of it.

In 2006 The King's Fund published a major review of social care spending for people over the age of 65 in England, chaired by Sir Derek Wanless (Wanless, 2006). The report confirms that the question of long-term care, its funding and quality, remains a very challenging area of public policy. 'In terms of service mix, the evidence suggests that most individuals would prefer to receive care at or close to home and that most would prefer 'prevention rather than cure' if they thought it would work. By contrast, the services which are available at present are focused on people with high end need and are still substantially provided in care homes' (Wanless, 2006, p 58).

## Empowerment

### The Carers Acts (1995 and 2000)

The role of carers has long been recognised as being crucial in the field of dementia care. The 1995 Carers (Recognition and Services) Act gave statutory recognition and the right to an assessment of their own needs as carers in England and Wales for the first time. However, it was not until 2000 that the provision of services for carers became mandatory, with the passing of the 2000 Carers and Disabled Children Act. This Act marked a significant milestone by giving funding directly to carers through the provision of Carers' Vouchers and Direct Payments in England and Wales to carers as well as to people in early-stage dementia. In practice, relatives make a lot of decisions on behalf of a person with dementia. Staff consult them all the time. Generally speaking, this is entirely appropriate since they have the best interests of the person at heart. However, we all need to be alert to occasions when there is a conflict of interest.

## Direct Payments (1996)

The system of Direct Payments where social services assess entitlement to care and give people the money to buy it for themselves was recently extended to older people in some parts of the UK. Clark et al (2004) found that cultural change is required to encourage care managers to take advantage of the undoubted benefits of Direct Payments for older people. It has huge potential for people with dementia who really need a few consistent familiar helpers, rather than a traffic of strangers. In England the government is designing and implementing pilots of 'individual budgets', which further extend the potential.

## Carers' Vouchers (2000)

These are paid directly to carers from the Carers' Fund in England and Wales. In some places the scheme is running successfully and has the advantage that, after an initial social work assessment, the carer can decide to use the vouchers how and when they need them.

## 'Supporting People' (2003)

'Supporting People' was introduced in 2003 as a new integrated policy and funding framework for housing support services. The aim is 'to enable vulnerable people to live independently in the community in all types of accommodation and tenure' (www.Scotland.gov.uk/Topics/Housing/Housing/supportpeople/intro). It replaced Housing Benefit and other funding streams. It is UK funding but its use has varied greatly. It is now allocated to local authorities who are the primary commissioners, at levels capped in April 2004.

This money has extended the availability of basic levels of support to a wider group of people in some areas, since, as we have seen, social services tend to target only those in the direst need, but it has made for complications. Some people will have help from a lot of different individuals, some providing support, others care and others health inputs. This can be confusing and distressing to people with dementia, one of whom commented that 'it is like living in a railway station'.

## Mental capacity legislation

The 2005 Mental Capacity Act (England and Wales), which followed a considerable time after the 2000 Adults with Incapacity (Scotland) Act, means that we are better able to offer protection in law to adults who lack mental capacity, including people with dementia.

A fundamental change resulting from this Act is that we now have a 'presumption against lack of capacity'. In other words, a person is now presumed to be capable of making informed decisions until proved otherwise. The fact that a person forgets that they have made a decision does not invalidate it. If a person is unable to communicate their wishes the decision as to whether they lack capacity must be based on a balance of probabilities. It is up to the professionals to show that a person lacks capacity to make a decision about a particular issue and they must take considerable care in reaching that conclusion.

The old Court of Protection has been reformed and the Enduring Power of Attorney is replaced with a Lasting Power of Attorney. A donor can confer a Lasting Power of Attorney on a donee/s, which gives them the authority to make decisions about all the person's welfare, property and finances. This power of attorney is subject to the 'best interests' test, taking into account the person's past and present wishes and feelings and the factors they would consider if able to do so (Section 4).

This Act addressed the problem that, under the old legislation, you are either wholly incompetent or wholly competent in law, whereas many people with dementia remain able to decide about some aspects of their lives but not about others.

Mr Sexton, for example, could tell his wife that he wanted his money left to his daughters but was nevertheless unable to stop walking out of the care home and getting lost.

### The Bournewood Judgment (2004)

One of the tasks in which we as social workers are very much involved, which we discuss in Chapter Six, is the moving of people from their own homes to hospitals or care homes. The Common Law doctrines of 'necessity' and 'best interests' have been used for many years to remove older people who lack mental capacity, including those with dementia, from their own homes and transfer them to care homes, without their consent or even knowledge of what is happening to them. The principle was successfully contested by a family in what has come to be known as the Bournewood Judgment.

In this case, a family contested the right of the Bournewood NHS Trust to remove an autistic man, unable to speak and with limited understanding, from a day centre to an in-patient unit without his consent. In 2004 the European Court of Human Rights upheld the family's view that detention, under the Common Law, of an incapable patient, using the 'best interests' argument was unlawful because it is 'too arbitrary'. In 2005 the Mental Capacity Act (England and Wales) was passed. We quote the useful principles from the 2000 Adults with Incapacity (Scotland) Act in Chapter Six.

## Other key policy changes (1997-2000)

Several generic policy and legislative initiatives have also had an impact on our field:

- the Social Exclusion Unit was set up in 1997, including regular reporting mechanisms;
- the 1998 Human Rights Act;
- legislation for the Protection of Vulnerable Adults (POVA) (2000);
- the 2000 Race Relations Amendment Act.

# Partnerships

We decided to make this part of our book title because we feel that it is and will in the future be of increasing importance in our field. We focus in this section on partnerships between professionals. However, partnerships with friends and family and above all with the person with dementia are equally important for social workers.

Miss Harris illustrates a common problem of receiving the uncoordinated attention of two organisations. She had mild dementia and lived on her own in a Scottish town. Neighbours alerted the social work department on one occasion when Miss Harris was very distressed. The GP was called out separately by a visiting nephew. The social worker visited several times to make an assessment. Miss Harris refused all offers of help. At the same time, the consultant psychiatrist visited, prescribed medication and asked the community psychiatric nurse (CPN) to visit. Miss Harris quite enjoyed the visits although she had no idea who was who. Each service gave up on her although they were called in at a later date. Had they known the other service was visiting, they might have got together to discuss Miss Harris and they might have realised that she would have preferred female rather than male visitors (the GP, psychiatrist, social worker and CPN were all men). They could have usefully shared information about the neighbours, who were the main carers.

## Developments towards joint working in the field

It can be helpful to see different professional groups as tribes with their own language, culture, traditions and history. Their relationships can be characterised by competition, mistrust and power-seeking. We discuss this in some detail in Chapter Five. Even today the tensions of joint working between health and social work/social care staff remain problematic. It is to be hoped that new joint arrangements may finally have an impact. Northern Ireland has had joint health and social service trusts for many years (Birrell and Williamson, 1983) and this trend is now happening throughout the UK. Social workers are increasingly likely to be working in mixed teams and we talk about this further in Chapter Six.

## The 1999 Health and Social Care Act

This was an enabling piece of legislation, which indicated how health trusts and social services departments in England and Wales could work more effectively together by removing some of the legal and administrative barriers that had previously existed. Specifically these were:

- lead commissioning – partners could agree to delegate commissioning of services to one lead organisation;
- pooled budgets – partners could contribute agreed funding to a single pot to be spent on jointly agreed projects;
- integrated provision – partners could integrate their staff (at all levels), resources and management structures to deliver a 'seamless' service. By 2000 the concept of 'care trusts' was emerging. These were to be integrated, single health and social care organisations delivering a range of specialist services to vulnerable people.

We continue to see great organisational and structural change in the NHS. The clear demarcation of budgets between Primary Care Trusts (led by GPs) and Hospital Trusts is also well established but the reconfiguration of Trusts and Strategic Health Authorities and definitions of their roles is an evolving process.

Community Mental Health Teams (CMHTs) for adults of working age are well established. CMHTs for Older People are now being established by Partnership Trusts in many parts of the UK. Real change for older people with mental health problems began to be seen in the middle of the first decade of the 21st century when the creation of Partnership Mental Health Trusts gave the move towards the creation of specialist multidisciplinary teams a kick-start. The results of this are becoming evident. The emphasis in the Partnership Trusts is strongly towards integrated working with shared paperwork and one referral point for GPs to access.

## The Single Assessment Process (2001)

The point was made in *The National Service Framework for Older People* that 'assessments are often duplicated with no coherent approach across health and social care services' (DH, 2001a, p 24). The final implementation date for the Single Assessment Process (SAP) was April 2004 by which time all NHS Community Trusts and social services departments in England and Wales had to have suitable structures and shared assessment paperwork in place (DH, 2004).

Shared forms are now required everywhere in the UK. This has both advantages and disadvantages in our view. The advantages are that assessment covers the whole ground, whereas, in the past, it was often partial, depending to some extent on the interests and background of the person doing the assessment. It is also easier to share a standard process with users of services, so transparency is an advantage. Another advantage, in theory at least, is that service users and their carers are not subjected to a series of assessments from different professionals.

The extent to which this has happened in reality is uncertain, since in more complex situations professionals will do their own assessment over and above the shared forms. Indeed, in some places, social workers are not involved in situations where only the basic assessment is required; they are involved only when situations are more complex.

The SAP dictates that the basic forms are used by all relevant professionals. In many local authorities, for example, they come as packs of self-carbonated copies, one of which can be placed in the different professional files. They contain brief information, often in the form of tick boxes, about a wide selection of areas of need. Because the assessor is expected to cover all these possible categories of need, there is also a summary assessment, which can include recommendations, instructions and objectives.

## The Care Programme Approach (for older people from 2000)

The Care Programme Approach (CPA) with its emphasis on joint working and a named worker who is responsible for the patient was introduced into community NHS mental health care for adults of working age in 1991. It was seen as the cornerstone of the policy to support people with complex mental health needs outside hospital and further developed the guidance on Section 117 of the 1983 Mental Health Act. It entitled people with complex needs to community care services.

However, for many years CPA was not applied to older people with mental health problems, who came instead under Care Management. This was a glaring example of the way in which services for older people were not even on the radar for mental health planners and was picked up in the first *Forget Me Not* report (Audit Commission, 2000). CPA was then extended to older people with functional mental illness and to people with dementia with complex needs.

## Everybody's Business (2005)

A new phase of attention on older people with mental health problems began with the publication in July 2005 of *Securing Better Mental Health for Older Adults* (Philp and Appleby, 2005). This was followed by *Everybody's Business* (CSIP, 2005) the new service development guide for integrated mental health services for older adults. It seemed to indicate a clear and welcome decision to adopt a 'whole systems approach' to the mental health needs of older people. The guide states that 'the complex nature of older people's mental health requires a whole systems response that cuts across health and social care, physical and mental health, mainstream and specialist services' (CSIP, 2005, p 8).

The service guide identified the urgent need to address the confusion existing between the SAP and the CPA. Although CPA is a specialist assessment and SAP is more generic, 'they aim to improve standards of assessment and care planning with a common method across agencies and care settings' (CSIP, 2005, p 15). Services are at different positions in integrating the specialist CPA and the more generic SAP methodologies. 'The two services should aim to have seamless care planning. During the transfer of care there should be a seamless transition between the two systems' (CSIP, 2005, p 15).

## Our Health, Our Care, Our Say *(2006)*

In this White Paper the government set out clear intentions to underline the duty of health and social care to work together and to indicate its intention to shift health resources to the community. *Everybody's Business* is to be read in conjunction with this White Paper. Pilot schemes are being set up to develop innovative approaches to sustain prevention work involving health and social care systems jointly to improve outcomes for older people.

### Partnerships with users of services

The Wanless review (2006, p 77) identifies that 'the government ... has two flagship policy strategies: social care and health integration and choice/personalisation of social care'. Partnerships with users of services is a strong current policy trend, as is prevention. 'People are increasingly seen as active participants in shaping, creating and delivering their care, in conjunction with their paid carers, so that it meets their distinctive needs and their hopes for themselves' (Leadbetter and Lownsbrough, 2005, p 6). Rankin (2005) draws attention to two ways of thinking about prevention: preventing illness and admissions to institutional care and preventing isolation, social exclusion and promoting quality of life. How these are achieved alongside 'choice and voice' will become clearer over the next few years.

### Continuing health care

Some money is allocated by the NHS in England and Wales for people with continuing health care needs. They receive free care. Wanless states: 'The operation of two parallel systems (of health and social care), and the difficulty of distinguishing between needs at the boundary of these systems, is at its most acute with NHS continuing care.... [It] has become a flashpoint for arguments about inequities in the system' (Wanless, 2006, p 65).

## New partnerships

It is a fact that policies may have unexpected results. An example of this is the way in which the commissioner–provider split, which was central to the 1990 NHS and Community Care Act, has affected social workers. Most of the expertise in dementia care has been built up, sometimes to a very high level, in care homes and day centres by care providers. This has left some social workers who are commissioners/care managers feeling deskilled. We play a crucial role in the assessment process and the initial decisions we make with people with dementia and their carers are vital in shaping the quantity and quality of support they receive. A new relationship between commissioners and providers that is more like a partnership is going to be the only way to bridge this gap, a point made by the *Changing Lives* report: 'We will need ... new approaches to strategic partnerships between public, private and voluntary sectors that make effective use of the knowledge and skills of all parties' (Scottish Executive, 2006, p 20).

## Housing

We have put a section on housing under partnerships because we feel that housing is often neglected as part of community care and a closer partnership between social services, health and housing is necessary. The right kind of housing can empower and support people with dementia. People with dementia and their carers will be living in every kind of housing and each one has advantages and disadvantages. The home owner in a detached house has the advantage of being able to take more risks than the person in a flat who can cause consternation among neighbours who imagine the flat burning down. Sheltered housing has the advantage of having a warden. However, this can also feel like a disadvantage to the person with dementia because behaviour that is unacceptable in these quasi-communal settings can mean that action, such as removal, is taken faster.

From the point of view of those with dementia, a familiar dwelling is a huge advantage. Their ability to learn new places is very impaired and they often fail to adjust to a new place. It is often a mistake for people with dementia to move closer to relatives because they have to learn not only a new house, but new faces and a new community. Having said this, some new housing options are very attractive, combining a small, domestic setting and care available on site. Indeed, in many places in the UK, housing with care has been given a real policy push to replace residential care.

'Very sheltered housing' and 'extra care housing' are terms for this model of housing plus care. Cox (2000, 2006) has written up examples of good practice of this model for people with dementia. She comments in the second book that a successful move hinges on the preparatory stages. 'People with dementia were reported to be fully involved in the preparatory stage ... including the decisions to take on the tenancy, plans to move, giving up their house and moving to a new one. These decisions were facilitated by involvement in furnishing their own room, use of familiar possessions, family members being involved and care being taken with introductions to other tenants' (Cox, 2006, p 80). These lessons would seem to be equally applicable to moves into care homes, which we address in Chapter Six. The status of being a 'tenant' is usually preferable to being a 'resident' in a care home in terms of attitudes of care staff. It is also financially advantageous because the person retains their place within the benefits system.

The policy thrust from residential care towards housing with support and care has led to a lot of new building, some of it dementia-friendly. We explain what this means in Chapter Seven.

## Social inclusion

The imperative for social inclusion arises, in good part, out of the European Convention on Human Rights, incorporated into domestic law in 2000.

The 1998 Human Rights Act initially identified only three areas where discrimination becomes illegal – race, sex and disability. Further legislation made discrimination on grounds of religion and sexual orientation illegal in 2003 and discrimination on grounds of age in 2006 (Department of Trade and Industry, www.dti.gov.uk). However, although discrimination is now illegal in the UK on six different grounds, we live and work in countries where discrimination is still a fact of life. Cantley and Bowes (2004) remind us that we need to be clear, conceptually, about the nature of inclusion advocated. We need to promote genuine recognition of diversity and equal rights.

In terms of diversity the concept of 'intersectionality' is useful (Hulko, 2004). It relates to the metaphor of a traffic intersection and suggests that many aspects of people's lives intersect, such as race, gender, class, age and disability. We have to be able to understand this complexity and the way that each person will have a different experience and perspective because of the intersection of these factors. With the social inclusion agenda in mind, we now look at six specific groups of people with dementia whose needs are not yet fully recognised or met.

## Younger people with dementia

'Early onset dementia refers to a progressive degeneration of the brain occurring before the age of 65' (www.thecliveproject.org.uk) but it is better to use the term 'younger' since older people with an early diagnosis are sometimes referred to as 'early onset'.

In recent years we have become much more aware of the existence of this group of people. It is very difficult to obtain an accurate figure since they are such a disparate group. The Alzheimer's Society estimates that there are about 18,000 younger people with Alzheimer's disease or vascular dementia in the UK (www.alzheimer.org.uk). This does not include people with complex combinations of conditions such as Down's syndrome and ARBD and dementia. Whatever the numbers, it is clear that they are a significant group whose needs have historically been neglected. One of the many problems that are specific to this group of people is that the support services that have been developed are largely designed to meet the needs of people over the age of 75.

### Problems with diagnosis

Because dementia in younger people is relatively rare, many doctors working at primary care level are unfamiliar with it and for this reason it often takes a long time for accurate diagnosis. Social workers need to be aware of this when working with families where a parent is experiencing memory problems. It is very important that the GP makes a referral for a mental health assessment as soon as possible, in order to treat other conditions that might be causing the symptoms. However, we need to bear in mind that diagnosis is much more difficult in the early stages and sometimes there are 'false positives'; that is, diagnoses of dementia that turn out to be incorrect over time.

The patterns of diagnosis in younger people are being clarified by recent research looking at all the dementias. We know that younger people are less likely than older people to have Alzheimer's disease (34% of those surveyed) and are more likely to have a rare form of dementia (19% of those surveyed). These include dementia as a result of multiple sclerosis, Parkinson's, Huntington's, motor neuron disease and Down's syndrome (www.alzheimers.org.uk).

*Different needs*

The needs of younger people with dementia may be different from those of older people:

- They are likely to be working and involved in raising a family.
- They will have financial responsibilities for other people.
- They are likely to be physically strong and healthy. As a result they will probably be more active.

Carers of younger people with dementia have a great deal to cope with. The sense of loss for all concerned may be enormous and there may also be serious financial implications for the family. It seems to be very difficult for other people to be able to accept that a younger person has dementia, when there are no obvious physical changes to be seen and so affected families can feel very isolated. If there are children at home, they are likely to experience powerful emotions, which they may be unwilling to talk about with their parents because they do not want to worry them. These families need a great deal of support.

*Financial pressures*

If the person with dementia has been working this cannot usually continue. If the carer has been working, this also cannot usually continue. Most services do not cover a working day nor can they be guaranteed to be absolutely reliable in terms of time. Many services are not able to cope with the person with dementia's illnesses and bad days. For a working carer this means that promotion prospects are lost, as are pension entitlements. The Invalid Care Allowance is supposed to fill the gap, but in practice fails to do so. The minority with plenty of money can sometimes buy in assistance; those with little or no money will have to go through financial assessments and claim benefits. The picture is further complicated by the difference between benefits, charges by the local authority and Supporting People monies.

*Services for younger people*

There has been considerable development in some areas of the UK in supportive projects, which usually include counselling and group work. Most Alzheimer's Societies have set up development projects including younger people's networks. There are other national services such as

CANDID (www.candid.org) and various regional initiatives such as the Clive Project in Oxfordshire, which have high levels of specialist expertise.

All these projects recognise that younger people are likely to go to the internet for health information and they have produced excellent material online for people to download and read about their own condition and its implications, and provide advice about getting a diagnosis and sources of support. They have also set up virtual support groups where people living with dementia can talk to each other online.

The 'Living with Memory Loss' groups set up by Alzheimer's Australia provide an excellent model for support. People are invited to attend with a friend, initially for a six- or eight-week session, one day a week and then for monthly support groups. In each case, two groups are conducted, one for people living with memory loss and the other for a family member or friend. The groups are free of charge and are held in various locations.

We can conclude that we have reached a stage where we are now aware of the specialist needs of younger people with dementia (Hodges, 2001) but have a long way to go in meeting those needs in a fair and just way throughout the UK.

## Black and minority ethnic groups

As in the case of younger people with dementia, we have become much more aware in recent years of the special needs of people who belong to these groups.

### Demography

'The 2001 Census revealed that the UK today is more culturally diverse than ever before. The 4.6 million people from a variety of non–white backgrounds are not evenly distributed across the country, tending to live in large urban areas' (ONS, 2005). In England, people from black and minority ethnic groups made up 9% of the total population in 2001/02 compared to only 2% in both Scotland and Wales and less than 1% in Northern Ireland. Nearly half (48%) of the total black and minority ethnic population lived in the London region, where they comprised 29% of all residents. Indians were the largest ethnic minority group, followed by Pakistanis, Black Caribbeans, Black Africans and those of mixed ethnic backgrounds (www.statistics.gov.uk).

These groups have a younger age structure than the white majority population because of the patterns and dates of immigration. The major immigration took place in the 1950s/1960s from the former British colonies. People came from various Caribbean islands and some South Asian countries (India, Pakistan and Bangladesh) as young adults of working age who came to the UK to fill gaps in the labour force caused by the Second World War. This means that the black and minority ethnic population as a whole has a younger age structure than the majority white ethnic population although – as so often in our field – it is not helpful to make sweeping generalisations. For instance, doctors were recruited from the Punjab to join the newly formed NHS in 1948. In the 1970s there was further immigration of people of South Asian origin, already British citizens, who were expelled from Kenya and Uganda.

### Cultural understanding of dementia

Throughout our history the UK has always exported emigrants and attracted immigrants. Rarely have we imported more than we have exported. At the start of the 21st century there is an even balance. We have, unlike some other countries, consciously adopted a pluralist and multicultural approach towards our diverse population. This means, at best, that diversity of dress, food, worship, family structures, methods of childrearing and care of elders is celebrated. At worst, it means communities of people from different cultures growing up alongside each other, living parallel lives and continuing to be remarkably ignorant of the cultures of their neighbours.

The field of dementia care is not exempt from the need for us all to educate ourselves about people of a culture that differs from our own. There are many different social constructions of dementia. It is important that professionals trained in the western medical construct do not undervalue the constructs of other cultures. We need to learn from each other. It is common in some black and minority ethnic groups to think of dementia as a normal part of ageing. There is often little awareness that it is an illness, still less that anything can be done to help people.

Mackenzie et al (2003, p 33) in their research project on South Asian carers of people with dementia found different beliefs at work: 'For South Asian carers the stigma around dementia had its roots in religious ideology. Ongoing tension between good and evil meant carers of relatives with dementia were accused of 'not praying enough' and therefore bringing about the cognitive decline in their relative. In addition, a belief in reincarnation introduced the notion that the person with dementia had been a bad person in a previous life and was now being punished. South Asian carers believed the family reputation would be irrevocably damaged if members of the community found out about their relatives' condition and that this would impact on subsequent generations' marriage prospects. Consequently, concealment was a coping strategy used by all carers'. There is much work to be done in raising awareness of dementia as a disability in all communities.

## English as an additional language

Most people born in the Caribbean islands speak English from birth, of course, but for South Asian elders English is an additional language. It should also be remembered that many of the first generation of South Asian immigrants do not read or write in their own first language, and we should be aware of this possibility when handing out printed information. As well as the large minority ethnic groups, there are many other smaller but significant minority groups such as Italians, Irish, Polish and Chinese. Sometimes these groups of elders are referred to as the 'First Generation' and in some places, where the community is large, there are good services for them, provided by the community.

Since the beginning of the 21st century new groups of immigrants have started to arrive from different European countries and the countries of the former Soviet Union. As social workers in our field, we hardly need to be reminded that the deterioration of short-term memory as a result of dementia means that people will forget the English that they have learned as an additional language as adults and revert to their first language. We should also not forget that in some parts of the UK, such as in Wales and the Western Isles of Scotland, English is an additional language for some white indigenous people.

> Mrs McLeod was a silent woman with dementia in a care home who startled the staff by having a perfectly normal conversation with a visiting clergyman who thought she might be a Gaelic speaker.

This raises the issue of the use of interpreters. It is tempting, because it is quick and easy, for social workers to use family members as interpreters for people with dementia who do not speak English, but we should avoid this if at all possible. The relationship between the professional interpreter and the social worker is relatively straightforward. If a family member is acting as the interpreter the situation can become very complex. The interpreter may put words into the mouth of the person, or they may feel reluctant to translate what the person is saying to the social worker, because it seems to be rude or critical. They may be so overwhelmed by their own stressful emotions that they simply do not hear what the person is saying and will unconsciously, or consciously, put their own 'spin' on it. Turton et al (2003, p 8), in a study commissioned by the Home Office of five local authorities across England and Wales, found that 'Despite all the good practice identified, the telephone survey found that 70% of respondents use family and friends as interpreters on some occasions.... There are definite problems concerning confidentiality, language skills and lack of familiarity with the professional field concerned which can lead to distorted or inadequate information reaching the client'.

As social workers we need to know what common languages, other than English, are spoken in our locality and be aware of the list of interpreters authorised by the Trust/Department who can be called upon as needed. The problem for us, of course, is that although the interpreters will have the necessary language skills, they may not have the dementia communication skills that are needed.

For social workers, to ask colleagues from a particular minority ethnic group to act as an interpreter for a service user from the same group is also problematic. In the case of people of South Asian backgrounds, for example, it is not reasonable to expect that, because the social worker comes from the same ethnic background, they will speak the same language as the service user. The chances are that they will not. In any case, they are employed as social workers, not interpreters.

## People of different faiths

The different countries of the UK contain people of many different faiths and people of no faith. It is important that as social workers we have at least a basic understanding of the belief and value systems of the different faith groups that are represented in our own local communities. Many cultural beliefs and customs have their roots in faith, which means that they have a deep and powerful meaning for the person. It is easy for people from any group to misunderstand people from another; to use language that is unwittingly offensive; to define our own way as normal and everyone else's way as not normal.

Social workers, working with people from many different groups, often come into contact with people whose ways are different from our own. We have a lot to contribute to this whole area of living in a multicultural society, provided that we are proactive in learning about other cultures. Nobody can become expert in the wide variety of ethnic groups in the UK. However, we can try to encourage a dialogue with people from other countries, other faiths and other languages from our own, about the nature of dementia and dementia services. We all have a lot to learn from each other.

### Family carers

Being able and willing to provide care at home is an issue in all the many minority ethnic communities that make up modern Britain. Assumptions about extended family caring networks are now plainly ill–informed as they probably always were. All minority ethnic groups – Southern Mediterranean, Irish, black and South Asian families – are finding that the task of caring for their elders within the home is increasingly difficult. We need to be aware as well that we are expecting an increase in the number of elders in these communities.

### Services for people from black and minority ethnic groups

The issue of the low uptake of services by people from black and minority ethnic groups has been the subject of much research in recent years (Patel, 1999). We have been very slow in developing culturally appropriate services that families really want to use. This clearly explains the low uptake of such services as are available. Moreover, research by Daker–White et al (2002, p 7) stated that 'Racism is fundamental to any understanding of the position of black and minority ethnic groups in dementia services. Black service users may also experience racism from white service users and their relatives'.

They also found that 'the fundamental issues in access [to services] relate to the small numbers of people involved, and their geographical dispersal ... it is mostly limited by virtue of the perceived cultural inappropriateness of services used almost exclusively by white people, a lack of awareness of mainstream provision and the possible reluctance of some to engage in services perceived to have authoritarian and racist functions within a "white officialdom"' (Daker–White et al, 2002, p 5).

Some clear indicators of what constitutes best practice have come from the work of the Policy Research Institute on Ageing and Ethnicity (PRIAE). PRIAE have found that black and minority ethnic (BME) day centres have a critical role in that they provide culturally appropriate care and information, advocacy and familiarity (Patel, 2004).

## Workers from overseas

As we pointed out in Chapter Two, there are increasingly few people available at present to provide care. The problem of recruitment and retention is being confronted at every level with much attention paid by all governments. The scale of the problem varies in different parts of the UK, but there is currently significant in-migration from other countries to fill the gaps in the health and care sector. The ethical issues surrounding the employment of health care professionals who have been trained in a developing country coming to work in a place like the UK are complex, however this is the situation in which we find ourselves. 'Since the social care sector has recruitment and retention difficulties, Britain has been looking to economic migrants to fill social care jobs. This is an important and viable interim measure. In the long term, however, there needs to be continued attention to the development of a coherent workforce strategy for social care' (CSIP, 2005, p 69, www.csci.org.uk).

At the start of the 21st century, the UK services would not be able to function without these workers from overseas. NHS Trusts and some of the large private care providers are currently recruiting in various overseas countries. Some of the countries in which they have recruited, of which we are aware, are Africa, the Philippines, India and Romania.

The immigrant workforce in the social care industry is different in various ways to the British-born workforce. Many people are better educated than their indigenous colleagues. Many have educational aspirations. Some are nurses who have qualified in their countries of origin but are unable to practise as nurses in the UK until they have completed an 'Adaptation' course and are working as care workers pro tem. These nurses are often used to working within a dominant western medical model, which has not been subject to the influences of the new culture of dementia care at all.

Because of the crisis in recruitment in the UK, the care sector is an easy field in which people can obtain work visas, at a time when this is becoming more and more difficult throughout Europe. Although the low wages paid in many care homes act as a deterrent to many people born and raised in the UK, they compare favourably with those earned in the countries from which overseas workers come. Also, a lot of these workers are regularly sending money home to support their families and the exchange rate between sterling and their home currencies is very favourable. This means that not everyone coming into the care sector is necessarily motivated by a strong desire to work in this field, although some people clearly are. Many are being paid very low wages and living in poor housing conditions.

There are some significant factors about this section of the workforce of which we should be aware. Immigrant workers from India and African countries, for example, may not have encountered dementia before, for the demographic reasons already outlined above. Their anxiety about working with people with dementia is often high. The social construction of dementia in different cultures, already referred to, will be a significant factor in the attitude of these workers. The situation is complex. Unless they are nurses, it is unlikely that they will be familiar with the western medical or social models. They will probably be more familiar with strong taboos surrounding mental illness, including dementia, which involves beliefs in spirit possession, being ill-wished by other people and the feeling of shame that dementia brings to the extended family.

On the other hand there are many positives. These workers are likely to arrive in the UK with a deeply ingrained respect for their elders and will naturally use surnames and titles when they approach people in care homes, as opposed to the sometimes inappropriate 'mateyness' of their indigenous counterparts. Many people from outside Western Europe who have not had medical training seem to behave in a naturally person-centred way towards people who need their help.

There is one important factor that we highlight here briefly and that is the question of the cultural meaning of body language, which varies so widely around the world. We take eye contact, which is so important to people with impaired language skills, as an illustration.

> The care worker from Essex remembers her mother saying to her: 'Look at me when I'm talking to you!'
>
> The care worker from Harare remembers her mother saying to her: 'How dare you look at me directly like that? Have you no respect for your elders!'

Clearly all workers need training in dementia care but care workers from overseas need additional training delivered by people who respect their own diverse cultures. Staff groups do not seem to discuss these issues among themselves unless they are helped to do so by someone from outside their group. This is a great pity because there is clearly a tremendous need for cultural as well as language interpretation at every level.

## *Travellers*

A minority group that has lived within the UK for many centuries, preserving its own culture and traditions is the Travellers. Gypsies and Irish Travellers are both recognised as distinct ethnic minorities and are granted protection under the 2000 Race Relations Act. However, they were not included as a separate ethnic category in the 2001 Census so there is no accurate figure for the number of people in this group as a whole. In their case, it is their lifestyle and customs that set them apart from the majority population. As in the case of all the minority ethnic groups they are spread unevenly across the UK. There are parts of the UK where they form a significant sub-group within a local area and in other areas there are none at all. If there is a numerically significant Traveller community there may be designated Traveller sites, which are often in rural areas around market towns.

In such areas the local authority should provide designated educational, community and social workers to serve their specific needs, but services are patchy. As in the case of the population as a whole, there are more people with dementia in these communities than ever before and they have very specific needs. As with all minority ethnic groups, it is often the small and comparatively isolated communities who experience the greatest difficulty in accessing culturally appropriate services. A good source of advice and support is the Shelter website at http://england.shelter.org.uk/policy and the Friends, Families and Travellers Service at www.gypsy-traveller.org.

Mr Cordona had lived in a local authority Traveller site for many years and he was the pitch holder. He developed dementia three years ago. His family would try to cope when he frequently left the site and got lost. When he was found several hours later he would be cold and hungry and very confused. They would then take him to the Accident & Emergency (A&E) Department of the local hospital. After a few days in an acute ward, the hospital social worker would arrange for him to transfer to a care home. He was unable to settle in this completely alien environment and after a few days his family would move him back home and try to look after him on their own. A few months later the same revolving door pattern would be repeated with another admission to A&E. The lack of culturally appropriate solutions to support the family meant that, despite the best efforts of his family and the social worker, this was inevitable.

## People in the early stages of dementia

Members of this group may very well be in the older age group (over 75) but their needs are very different from people whose dementia is at a more advanced stage. It is generally recognised now that less disabled people with dementia do not usually benefit from mixing with people who are much more severely disabled and vice versa, although in some situations there are affinities that override this general principle such as shared language, culture or micro-culture such as rural areas where people tend to know each other very well.

Unfortunately the way services are set up does not always reflect this knowledge and they can find themselves in day centres and care homes with people with more advanced dementia. They may well find this frightening. People in the early stages can have a great deal to contribute to society, as we explain in Chapter Nine.

People with dementia who are still relatively unimpaired can be very challenging for social workers who may be uncertain whether to be direct about the diagnosis or not. It can be very easy to underestimate their skills and they may sense very quickly if they are being patronised and react accordingly. They may want to be included in decision making about their lives. Working with this group requires additional skills and there is an urgent need for training for professional care staff who are making assessments.

Group work has been found to be very helpful for many people in the early part of the journey through dementia. We address this in our section on group work in Chapter Nine.

## People with complex needs

In a sense we have already mentioned people with dementia who have other conditions but we felt it important to have a section on this because people with complex needs inevitably need social work help. These are people who have a complex combination of conditions and often have very problematic personal circumstances as well. They might have a learning disability, and dementia, and have no relatives and a very low income. They might be people who have dementia, an alcohol problem, liver failure and difficult family problems. They might have epilepsy (Cochrane, 2004), be failing to take medication, have dementia and a housing problem. They might have dementia and a psychotic illness and be constantly in trouble with the police for aggressive behaviour. The neighbourhoods in which people live can also be fraught with problems that exacerbate these personal ones.

It is very hard to generalise about the social work role both because it will be so different in different situations and because it will always exist alongside other professionals. Person–centred planning and care is the only way forward because every care package will be so different and will change so often as health and other needs change. We all need a lot of training and support to provide our best in these challenging situations. Teams can be the best way to provide this, not just for ourselves at the care planning level but also for the people providing the day-to-day support and care.

We are much more confident than we used to be about how to work with people with dementia and our skills in this are a crucial contribution, but all professionals are learning how to work with people with really complex needs. They challenge all our expertise and all our systems. As we have said, numbers are increasing, as people with learning and other disabilities are surviving longer. Work with these groups is the cutting edge of social and health care in the first decade of the 21st century.

## Marginalised groups of people with dementia

In this section we consider the needs of homeless people and people in the prison service. We simply have no idea how many of these people have dementia. The statistic of 18,000 people under the age of 65 with dementia, quoted above, seems likely – if we include people in these marginalised groups – to be a serious underestimation of the numbers of people involved.

### Homeless people

The prevalence of dementia is probably higher in homeless people than in the population at large, which means that there must be many homeless people with dementia living on our streets. This does not only apply to older people as the increase in the incidence of ARBD obviously has special relevance for younger homeless people. Many of these people may well be drug users as well and it is likely that many long-term users of hard drugs, if they survive long enough, will form part of this group. It is an area that has not yet been researched and its implications for services are not even on the social policy radar yet. This group of people will inevitably be among those with complex needs.

Services for homeless people of all ages are virtually non-existent and, by default, many will find their way into the criminal justice system. Clearly this is not the right place for them. Advice on working with homeless people can be obtained from Shelter (see http:// england.shelter.org).

Creative social work can, however, provide solutions.

> Mr Wilder had lived for years on the streets of a large city, often using the day centres and night shelters in the area. The stress and confusion caused by his dementia became worse and he became increasingly frail, as his lifestyle took its toll. Through the day centre, Mr Wilder was persuaded by a local authority social worker to agree to try life in a local care home. They were able to meet his need to spend his days in much the same way as he had always done and most of his days were spent in the city centre. Fortunately he was able to find his way back to the care home, in time for tea. No questions were asked about how he spent his days, providing he was sober on his return. His physical and mental health improved dramatically with regular meals and a warm room in which to sleep. This was a very positive move for Mr Wilder in the last years of his life.

### People in prison

Although the needs of older people in prison were included in *The National Service Framework for Older People* (DH, 2001a), none of the standards related directly to their needs. The responsibility for the health care of prisoners in England and Wales was transferred to the NHS in 2006, which should make a difference. There seem to be two groups of older prisoners: one is people well known to the prison system, who have either been in prison for long periods or who are repeat offenders. Another is older people going into prison for the first time, many of whom are men who have been imprisoned for the first time for sexual abuse, often carried out many years ago. They are not well known to the system and staff in prisons may not be aware of changes in their cognitive abilities. The question of the care and management of older prisoners needs urgent attention.

Wahidin and Aday (2005) provide useful data about the numbers of older people in prisons and stress the need for attention to their particular health needs. There is little information about prisoners with dementia. However, Murray (2004, p 32) asserts: 'At present the numbers of both older prisoners and those with a diagnosable mental illness is increasing rapidly. However, within the current prison service there is a lack of recognition of this issue and the difficulties it raises'.

## Conclusion

This has been a long chapter because social policy relating to older people is complex and challenging and has become more so with devolution. We have focused on England as the largest of the UK countries. We have looked at these policies under the headings of raising standards, fairness and equality, empowerment, partnerships and social inclusion. We have paid particular attention to groups of people who can be excluded from services: younger people with dementia, people from black and minority ethnic groups with dementia, Travellers, people in the early stages of dementia, people with complex needs, homeless people with dementia, and people in prison with dementia. We also mention paid staff from overseas.

### Further reading

Innes, A., Archibald, C. and Murphy, C. (2004) *Dementia and Social Inclusion: Marginalised Groups and Marginalised Areas of Dementia Research, Care and Practice*, London: Jessica Kingsley Publishers.

Phillips, J., Ray, M. and Marshall, M. (2006) *Social Work with Older People*, Basingstoke: Palgrave Macmillan.

Wanless, E. (2005) *Securing Good Care for Older People: Taking a Long Term View*, London: King's Fund.

# FOUR

# The experience of dementia

## Introduction

Every person experiences dementia in a unique way. In this chapter we look at some universal emotional needs, the meeting of which is often compromised by dementia. We consider the person relating to different factors, which determine what the experience will mean to them, an approach known as the social or disability model of care. The various factors interact with each other and we explore two of them in some detail – general physical health and the way in which people with dementia are treated by others. We also look briefly at four areas of life that are still considered taboos where people with dementia are concerned: sex and sexuality, spirituality, death and dying and social class. Finally we explore some of the difficult dilemmas faced by social workers in the field, suggesting that a conflict resolution approach can be useful.

## Every person is unique

The foundation of the person–centred approach to care is the belief that all human beings are of equal value and therefore people with dementia are no less valuable than anyone else. A person is much more than their disability. We have already referred at some length to the writings of Kitwood because we believe that he was able to express coherently a lot of really crucial thinking about dementia. His work drew upon his background in the church, social psychology, psychotherapy and his work with people with dementia. We can all think of situations in which people with dementia have their personhood denied by those around them. It is alarmingly easy to do this. Working to safeguard the personhood – the uniqueness – of the person with dementia, is the responsibility of all of us who work with them.

## The social or disability approach to dementia

Figure 4.1 summarises the social or disability model to dementia. It lists a range of factors that interrelate with the brain damage experienced by those with dementia.

Here we begin to examine these different factors that make up the whole person and describe some ways in which we can understand the person with dementia in order to make life as good as possible for them and their carers. As social workers we are well able to understand the ways that different 'systems' impinge on each other and the person. We know that improving any one factor will impact on the whole. We are applying this thinking to dementia care.

**Figure 4.1:** The social or disability model

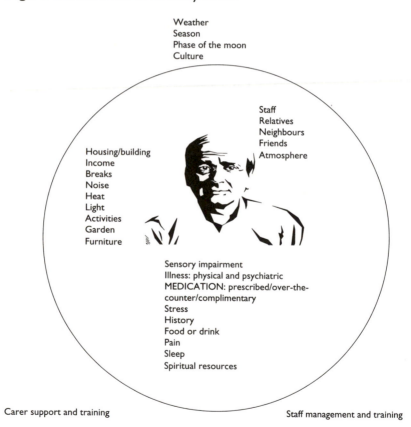

Weather
Season
Phase of the moon
Culture

Staff
Relatives
Neighbours
Friends
Atmosphere

Housing/building
Income
Breaks
Noise
Heat
Light
Activities
Garden
Furniture

Sensory impairment
Illness: physical and psychiatric
MEDICATION: prescribed/over-the-counter/complimentary
Stress
History
Food or drink
Pain
Sleep
Spiritual resources

Carer support and training

Staff management and training

## Personality

Everyone's personality is unique and is, on the whole, fixed by the time of adolescence. In the old, pessimistic culture of dementia care we used to believe that dementia actually changes personality. We now believe that it is more likely that most people with dementia – faced with a world that no longer makes sense – keep trying to understand and interact with the world using the coping strategies that were developed earlier in life. Sometimes these coping strategies work well. Many of the people with dementia who are willing to share their experience to benefit others have probably always been courageous and determined people.

For many people, however, there is a mismatch between these lifetime strategies and the environment in which they now find themselves. This causes much of the behaviour that challenges others. We need to put ourselves in their place. If our brain cells, damaged by dementia, are feeding us incorrect information about the world, we will try to deal with this strange world in tried and trusted ways that have always worked for us in the past. We will use humour or aggression or deceit or denial to extricate ourselves from awkward situations. The strategies we use will depend upon our personality.

## Life history

It is our life history or biography that interacts with our personality to give each one of us our unique identity. All the things that have happened to us throughout our lives influence the way in which we respond to situations. The life we lived as children with our parents at home, our school, our work, our relationships as adults, as lovers, as friends, as parents, all shape our personality. We know who we are because we know our own story – the story of our family, our community and our place in it as well as our belief system. This essential knowledge is absolutely dependent on memory.

Again – if we put ourselves in the place of a person with dementia who has impaired memory – we can begin to realise how dependent we are on other people to remind us of our own personal story. We need other people to help us to build the fragments that we can still recall into a coherent whole. Collecting as much information as we can about the life stories of people with dementia is not an optional extra. We discuss this in more detail in Chapter Nine because it is so important.

## Current physical health

The importance of maintaining as good physical health as is possible cannot be overestimated. People with dementia are struggling to cope with the world and anything that lowers their potential functioning should be minimised. Given that dementia is most common in people aged over 80, there are likely to be multiple disabilities and illnesses that occur in this age group.

Arthritis is common, as is heart malfunction. Chest conditions are relatively common too. Equally disabling are foot problems. Cutting long toenails, for example, can make an astonishing difference to morale and mobility. Treating constipation can make a huge difference to intellectual functioning and well-being. Eyesight and hearing impairments (see Allan, 2005; Allan et al, 2005, for useful information on hearing impairment and dementia) are often missed or attributed to the failing brain. There is often a degree of malnutrition for various reasons. We discuss this further in Chapter Seven. One of the difficulties is that the person with dementia is not able to explain where it hurts, how it hurts and whether they have a history of a certain condition.

## Acute confusional episodes, depression and dementia

It is important to distinguish between acute confusional episodes (delirium), depression and dementia, as we said in Chapter Two. The first two are treatable and we need to be sure we refer anyone we suspect with either for urgent treatment.

## Medication

Medication is a special issue when working with people who cannot always be relied upon to take it correctly and when the side effects can sometimes exacerbate disorientation. Mixing over-the-counter tablets with prescribed medication is a frequent hazard. In addition there are three dimensions of medication that are particularly relevant to dementia care.

### Polypharmacy

It is common for people aged over 75 to be taking several medications that have been prescribed by their doctor for different chronic and/or acute medical conditions. Some doctors are not always as vigilant as they should be and so may prescribe drugs that have side effects that are toxic in combination with other drugs. People in this age group may not always remember the names of the drugs and the conditions for which they are prescribed. If people have poor memories and confusion as a result of dementia, the problem can become very serious. Pharmacists can be very helpful with advice if you suspect polypharmacy.

### Neuroleptic drugs

These drugs, also referred to as sedatives, tranquillisers or anti-psychotics, have been much overused in the past and indeed are still overused in some places. Steps have been taken to attempt to control the use of some of them. They can be effective in reducing the intensity of psychotic experiences such as delusions and hallucinations and they do have a calming effect. However, they are less and less effective over time and have many undesirable side effects. They are powerful drugs that were developed for the relief of psychotic symptoms in adults of working age. They have traditionally been much used for the treatment of behavioural symptoms in dementia, including restlessness, aggression, emotional instability and loss of inhibition.

For many years Thioradizine (Melleril) was the drug of choice until the Committee on Safety of Medicines changed the license so that it could only be prescribed as second-line treatment for schizophrenia. Other so-called 'atypical' anti-psychotics such as Risperidone took its place and they were commonly prescribed, particularly for people living in long-term care homes. However, there is a growing consensus in the UK and other countries that these drugs are dangerous as well as being unnecessary, except in the case of a small number of people:

> In 2004 the Committee on Safety of Medicines (CSM) ruled that the risk of stroke when using Risperidone and Olanzepine is unacceptable. Research suggests that in 66% to 88% of cases these drugs are used inappropriately, as a form of restraint, to sedate people with dementia whose behaviour staff find too disturbing or difficult to manage. None of these drugs has a specific license for treating behavioural symptoms in people with dementia and the situation reflects the lack of training in dementia care of GPs, care home managers and care staff. (www.alzscot.org.uk)

There are real ethical problems in giving a powerful drug to one person in order to benefit other people. Now that we have the skills to understand much of the behaviour that challenges, it is seen as desirable to avoid giving them as far as possible. As the Alzheimer's Society succinctly puts it:

> The use of a person-centred approach will reduce the need to use neuroleptics, as will having an adequate number of staff who are well-trained in supporting people with dementia ... the use of neuroleptics will mask any underlying problem. (www.alzheimers.org.uk)

## Cholinesterase inhibitor drugs

These drugs are discussed in Chapter Six in relation to diagnosis.

## Sleep

Sleep disturbance is quite common for people with dementia, (Howcroft, 2003). Some people may become persistently wakeful and restless at night. There are lots of reasons for this, which the person with dementia will usually be unable to consider, explain or remedy. Social workers may need to use their detective skills (James et al, 2006). Some, for example, may be anxious about the time and may no longer be able to see a luminous clock. The solution may be a low light by a big clock. Digital night clocks are not usually understandable (Cunningham, 2005).

> Miss Green had been moving about at night in her care home for months before a care assistant tried a large clock on her bedside table. Miss Green was then able to get up at a suitable time.

> Others like Mrs O'Shea were responding to a change in their bedroom. Mrs O'Shea suddenly became very restless at night. Again an astute care assistant noticed that there was a new street light outside her room that could have been interpreted as daylight. Thicker curtains solved the problem.

'Detective work' is a concept we will come back to because it is an easy way for social workers to explain to care staff and relatives what is required in understanding behaviour. As usual, a first step is really knowing the person and their history. The answer may be simply that the person always worked a night shift.

People who do not sleep well at night can be really impaired by sleep deficit. At a minimum they tend to sleep a lot during the following day because they are tired and a pattern quickly becomes established. Eventually their body clock can become completely reversed. When people are living at home this can be very distressing and exhausting for their carers. Assuming there is no clear reason, medication can be helpful although the use of hypnotic medication does not guarantee that the person will sleep through the night, even if it does mean that they go off to sleep quickly. Increased daytime stimulation and physical activity may help the person to feel tired at the end of the day in a natural way. Knowing familiar night-time routines can also help so that people are cued into bedtime. Some people have always had a milky drink, others have always had the window open and so on.

Many people in care homes have trouble sleeping at night. The lack of physical exercise and meaningful occupation encourages sleeping in the daytime. Another possible cause is the routine of a home that may be unfamiliar to the person with dementia who might, for example, be used to sleeping until the late morning and going to bed in the small hours. A person–centred care plan should include information about familiar sleeping routines, which are best maintained as far as possible.

The review meeting may be a good opportunity for you to suggest that sleeping problems often have a practical solution. There is a danger of sleep disturbance being attributed to the dementia without consideration of other possible causes.

## Pain

Given that up to 84% of older people experience painful conditions, we should not be surprised that people with dementia are likely, as already discussed, to be suffering pain (Tsai and Chang, 2004). Osteoarthritis, osteoporosis, past hip fractures and cancer all cause chronic pain:

> Research suggests that when a person has dementia and pain is present they are at risk of not being treated, because of two misinformed beliefs – firstly that when a person has dementia they do not experience pain and secondly that nothing can be done for people with dementia. (www.alzheimers.org.au)

The problem is that a person with dementia may not be able to communicate their pain clearly, or they may not be able to interpret pain signals and convey their discomfort (Cook et al, 1999). Pain also goes unrecognised and untreated because of poor assessment and communication by staff (Cunningham, 2006). The people caring for the person need to recognise, through close observation, when the person with dementia may be in pain. Behaviour may be the clue. The person may lash out when moved or when getting up. They might cry, be reluctant to move or be restless. They may sleep more than usual or appear withdrawn. Their facial expressions may tell you that they are in pain.

When asking a person with dementia about their health try to use a range of words that might help the person describe their feelings. Words like 'discomfort', 'uncomfortable', 'hurting', 'aching' or 'sore' might be helpful. Ask at regular intervals, not just once (Cunningham, 2006). When people are living in long-term care homes it is important that staff regularly assess for pain, especially during movement (Abbey et al, 2004; Closs, 2005) and to make sure that they are doing everything possible to relieve pain through analgesia, heat and rest. Everyone has their part to play in making pain management successful. For example, on admission to the care home the social worker can provide information about how the person has previously managed pain, such as listening to particular music, or using a hot water bottle as well as taking painkillers.

There is a great deal of knowledge and experience about pain control held in palliative care teams and useful partnerships can be formed between them and long-term care homes. There is no justification for denying this knowledge to someone simply because they have dementia.

## The way a person is treated by others

You may have noticed that the factors on the right-hand side of our man in Figure 4.1 are mainly people. The way a person with dementia is treated by others has a profound impact, which can be both positive and negative. We start by considering some of the negatives.

### *Malignant social psychology*

If we recall the definition of personhood – 'A person becomes a person through other persons' – we will realise that the way people with dementia are treated by others is vitally important. Kitwood, having observed the depersonalising tendencies in dementia care in long-term care settings, decided to research the subject. He used a simple form of critical incident technique to observe and classify the examples he saw. The term he used to describe the phenomenon was 'malignant social psychology'. 'The strong word – malignant – signifies something very harmful, symptomatic of a care environment that is deeply damaging to personhood, possibly even undermining physical well-being....The term does not, however, imply evil intent on the part of caregivers; most of their work is done with kindness and good intent. The malignancy is part of our cultural inheritance' (Kitwood, 1997a, p 46). We explored this subject in some detail in Chapter One.

Kitwood finally identified 17 examples, which he had routinely observed at that time. He deliberately used words that would shock his readers – treachery, mockery, intimidation etc – in order to make them think about their practice. We recommend reading this book and looking at the examples, which sadly can still be seen in some places.

### The spectrum of mistreatment

A spectrum of mistreatment has been identified by Stokes (2001) in which malignant social psychology, which is largely seen and/or ignored by others, is at one end. Abuse/neglect, which is generally condemned, is at the other end. In the middle is what he calls maltreatment, which is known to others but condoned by them. This spectrum of mistreatment can be found in all care settings, from the person's own home through to acute hospitals and long-term care homes.

### Abuse

Abuse is more than violence against people with dementia. It is defined by Action on Elder Abuse as 'A single or repeated act or lack of appropriate action occurring within any relationship where there is an expectation of trust, which causes harm or distress to an older person' (www.elderabuse.org.uk, 2005). There are similar definitions in the government report for England entitled *No Secrets* (DH, 2000) and for Wales entitled *In Safe Hands* (National Assembly for Wales, 2000). There are no equivalent reports in Scotland or Northern Ireland although in Scotland the impending Vulnerable Adults Bill will undoubtedly have a definition. *No Secrets* identifies six different categories of abuse:

- physical abuse;
- sexual abuse;
- psychological or emotional abuse;
- financial or material abuse;
- neglect and acts of omission;
- discriminatory abuse.

It could also probably have added verbal abuse, which can be very frightening.

Abuse may be *active* (physical, sexual or financial) or *passive* (failure to give prescribed medication, neglect, failure to give help that is needed to perform the activities of daily living). Actions do not have to be deliberate to count as abuse. Ignorance – that is, not being aware that an action is abusive – does not mean that we have not acted in an abusive manner towards another person.

*Abuse within the family*

It is important to recognise at the outset that it may not be the carer who is doing the abusing; it can be another member of the family. It is often very hard to judge when a situation is abusive, and we are required to make some very difficult professional judgements. It can be the person with dementia who is abusing. Physical abuse from a family member can be symptomatic of a person at the end of their tether. Neither the person nor the relative is likely to use the term abuse and will tell a story and leave you to hear behind the words. Sometimes you are dealing with abusive relationships that have gone on for a long time. Sometimes sexual abuse in particular has been consensual and there are difficult decisions to be made about whether it still is now that one of the pair has dementia. In terms of sexual abuse one of the problems is finding words and terms to talk about it. Neglect can be hard to define because domestic standards are so different and abuse involving medication is almost invisible.

Sometimes the person with dementia clearly does not want you to act on the story they tell. They would prefer to remain with their relative in a troubled but familiar place than risk the unknown. Sometimes there is a cluster of abusive factors such as psychological and emotional abuse alongside financial abuse. Financial abuse is often very hard to determine. Is it abuse when a daughter asks her mother for her heating allowance to buy Christmas presents for the children? People with dementia may want to give their relatives money especially if that is the price for regular contact.

Abuse of vulnerable adults is a very difficult area of work requiring very careful judgement and tolerating knowledge of situations where intervention is not possible. Good, knowledgeable support from colleagues is essential.

*Abuse in long-term care settings*

Abuse is not merely a family issue, as some of the care home scandals have demonstrated. In these homes, physical abuse is as common as psychological abuse. Some of the poor standards that have existed in some long-stay care settings amount to abuse; standards that would never be condoned with more articulate residents and patients. Sexual abuse is probably rare and is certainly rarely recorded, perhaps in part because of the difficulty of finding the words to describe what is happening. Complaining about care is difficult. The correct route is through the levels of management. All organisations should have their own internal policy and procedures for dealing with allegations of abuse. These policies should be clear and straightforward. Sadly, neither of these is true of all homes.

The untrained care staff in The Noname Nursing Home were appalled to see their new unit manager apparently fondling the breasts of the women residents when they were in bed. He claimed he was checking for breast cancer but this plainly did not need to be done as often as he was doing it. The staff reported the matter to the manager of the home who was having difficulty recruiting staff to run his dementia unit and was unwilling to take action. The staff were not convinced he thought it was very important anyway. However, after the manager had discussed the situation with a colleague from another home run by the same company, he decided to contact the local Adult Protection Committee in order to obtain advice. Following this he conducted his own investigation and then relocated the unit manager to the mainstream residential unit. He also arranged for all staff in his home to attend training on the abuse of vulnerable adults to raise awareness of the issue and offer support to his staff

*Social work intervention in the spectrum of mistreatment*

It is clearly recognised that social workers who witness abuse or have abuse disclosed to them have a responsibility to, at least, report this. However, social workers can also have a preventative role, particularly in relation to abusive practice within care homes. Many care home staff have had limited training and may not understand that their behaviour could be abusive. In some establishments, practice has changed very little over the years and even new staff can find it hard to challenge such a culture.

A social worker visiting a care home and observing what they know to be abusive practice can, through their own behaviour, demonstrate an alternative model and sensitively challenge practice. It is important that discussion around bad practice is non-judgemental and supportive, offering advice or information where appropriate. It may be that rough handling is the result of poor training or lack of equipment and the social worker, by being supportive, may give the care assistant the confidence to raise this with management. If you make a point of including the person with dementia in your conversation with staff, deferring to them and allowing enough time to talk, the care assistant can follow your example.

You can build on this by having some positive dialogue with the care assistant afterwards about what has just taken place, reinforcing this as good practice. Much will depend on the relationship between the social worker and the care home staff, particularly if staff are to have the confidence to raise concerns or ask for advice or information. The skills that social workers possess are well suited to this sort of tactful support and informal education of care staff. In addition, because social workers are somewhat removed from the daily life of residents they can sometimes see things on review visits that care staff may have missed.

Mr Briggs lived in a specialist dementia unit within a mainstream residential home. He had never married and nobody ever visited him. His mental condition appeared to have declined since his admission, which was put down to the fact that the dementia had progressed. At the time of the review Mr Briggs, always softly spoken, had become almost monosyllabic. The social worker thought that he might be bored. As a result of the review Mr Briggs was taken upstairs every morning to join the residents in the other wing. He was soon playing cards and scrabble again – with assistance – and his cognitive abilities were found to be higher than staff had believed. More importantly he was much more cheerful.

Local authorities throughout the UK have been given the duty of developing inter-agency policies, procedures and joint protocols for the protection of vulnerable adults. The Department of Health report *No Secrets* (DH, 2000, p 1) stated that 'the aims should be to create a framework for action within which all responsible agencies work together to ensure a coherent policy for the protection of vulnerable adults at risk of abuse and a consistent and effective response to any circumstances giving ground for concern and formal complaints or expressions of anxiety'. People with dementia are clearly classed as 'vulnerable adults'.

All concerns about possible abuse in residential and nursing home placements and home care agencies should be reported to the Commission for Social Care Inspection (CSCI)/Scottish Commission for the Regulation of Care (SCRC)/Northern Ireland Regulation and Improvement Authority. There is a more general awareness of the issue of adult abuse than there was but we still have a long way to go in breaking the taboo surrounding the subject and preventing it from happening.

### Whistle-blowing

There are big problems associated with whistle-blowing, by which we mean formally complaining about standards and if necessary going to the press. Sometimes collecting evidence means taking the word of one staff member over another, which creates bad feeling – as in the case of The Noname Home.

There are policies now in place to protect whistle-blowers but they do still seem to suffer greatly from victimisation by their colleagues and often by their employers. The 1998 Public Interest Disclosure Act is designed to protect whistle-blowers. 'In general, workers should be able to make disclosures about wrongdoing to their employers so that problems can be dealt with internally within the organisation' (www.pcaw.co.uk/legislation). Public Concern at Work (see www.pcaw.co.uk) is an organisation that supports whistle-blowers.

## Some of the taboos in dementia care

Delivering person-centred care means that we have to know the person. This sounds obvious and straightforward but there are some topics that are often avoided. We have identified four of these. A fifth would be faecal incontinence, which we do not cover. Useful reading includes Jenkins (1999) and Muller-Hergl (2004).

## Sex and sexuality

One fundamental human aspect of our personhood is sex. Imagining that people with dementia are sexual beings is sometimes difficult. Sex and dementia are generally assumed to be about the sexually disinhibited behaviour of people with dementia. This is not an easy issue in itself, but it is immeasurably more difficult if we have not come to terms with the possibility of people with dementia having sexual needs.

First we need to be able to talk about sex. This requires a shared language to diminish the embarrassment and it may require practice. Archibald (2006) provides helpful training suggestions in her practice guide. Then we need to be able to see sexually disinhibited behaviour as an effort to communicate something; we need to understand the reasons for it. But this is only one dimension. Another is that people with dementia may want a physical sexual relationship, homosexual or heterosexual, or they may be scarred by sexual abuse at some time in their lives. The pain may come to the surface as their defences become less successful. Because relatives of people with dementia and staff in care homes alike may find this whole area of sex and sexuality hard to talk about, social workers may well be asked for advice in situations where it has become difficult. It will help you, therefore, if you have thought through your own attitudes beforehand and tried to widen your horizons, if necessary, through reading about this very tricky field. The following references cover the main issues social workers will need to have considered: Lichtenberg and Strzpek (1990), Sloan (1993), Duffy (1995), Teitalman and Copilillo (2002).

### Sexual orientation

The question of sexual orientation needs a special mention here. As with all these taboos, the issue is complex. The end of the 20th century saw a great improvement in the civil rights of the gay, lesbian, bisexual and transgendered community in the UK. The passing of the Civil Partnership legislation at the end of 2005, providing legal recognition of same-sex relationships, was a very significant step towards equality. However, public attitudes to homosexuality still remain very negative in certain sections of the population.

We must also remember that homosexuality was illegal until 1967. Many gay and lesbian older people with dementia will have lived all their adult lives in secrecy. 'Coming out' was not an option for them. This is not always easy for younger people, gay or straight, to appreciate.

Great sensitivity is called for and situations need to be approached on a case-by-case basis. Metz (1997) is a good resource for learning about gay issues.

Gay and lesbian carers of people with dementia are becoming increasingly well organised within the various Alzheimer's associations as they work together to address their special needs. As social workers, we need to be aware that initiatives to make services more 'gay friendly' than they have been do exist. Special packs and fact and information sheets are available from the Alzheimer's Society and some can be downloaded at www.alzheimers.org.uk.

In recognition of the special needs of this group some of the Supporting People funding has been used in Manchester to develop a citywide housing support service for older people from the lesbian, gay, bisexual and transgender community. The scheme employs a dedicated housing support worker who has specific knowledge and understanding of the issues faced by people in this community. The service aims to address issues such as homophobic harassment and to assist them with accessing appropriate services and with income maximisation (Alzheimer's Society, 2005).

## Spirituality

Another aspect of thinking in terms of personhood is to recognise the *spiritual* needs of people. This is not the same as thinking about their *religious* needs, which may or may not be important to people. We all know people who are 'high spirited' or 'lacking in spirit', by which we are meaning something about their inner liveliness, about what makes them 'tick', about what is that essential 'something' that feeds their inner being and helps them to triumph over adversity or to remain calm in the midst of turmoil. It has been well described in the following way:

> It is common for the words 'religion' and 'spirituality' to be used interchangeably. This tendency both narrows the scope of the latter and also fails to acknowledge the non-material aspects of life enjoyed by those without particular faith. Religion can be seen as the framework that some people use to make sense of the world and their place within it.... Spirituality is the experience of raw feelings – the

moments of joy, bewilderment, hope, understanding and awe – that we all experience at various points of our lives. These can be interpreted within or without a religious framework. Spirituality is the energy of the lived life. Religion is a community-shared story. (Airey et al, 2002, p 3)

Increasingly it is being recognised that we all have spiritual needs – including social workers and people with dementia. It does not mean that we are all religious, but that we all have a need to nurture whatever it is that gives us the strength and the courage to go on. For further reading see Everett (2000), Swinton (2001), Kimble (2002), Clarke (2003), Lee (2003), Shamy (2003) and Goldsmith (2004).

## Death and dying

### *Talking about death*

Most of us find talking about death extremely difficult (Cox and Watchman, 2004), yet settings where death and bereavement are part of normal conversation report that they are popular topics and that people with dementia derive great comfort in being allowed and enabled to talk about death. However, they are sensitive to the taboos that make it difficult to raise these subjects with family and friends themselves. We can provide these opportunities, if we ourselves are able to cope. Death is often a constant, if unspoken, preoccupation for very old people. They may want to share fears of pain or being alone for example, they may want to plan their own death, they may want to reflect on the deaths of others. Planning your own death is an important part of care planning in care homes.

### *Life review*

The theory that different life tasks need to be completed at different stages of life was developed by Erikson (1963), who identifies eight different life stages – each with its own task. The task of the final stage is to look back and sort out who we are so as to make sense of the lives we have lived. This helps us to die with self-respect. Feil (2002) has developed his work to apply to people with dementia. Most of us need to be able to communicate with at least one other person in order to complete this life task. Yet many people with dementia are not given this opportunity – even when they are living in a community with many other people.

### Our own attitudes to death

The fact that death and dying is such a taboo in the white majority ethnic populations of the UK has serious implications for care practice. In order to discuss death with someone else you have to feel comfortable with the idea of death – of your own dying. We must be careful not to oversimplify through generalisation but it seems likely that the taboo does not operate in the same way in people who belong to one of the many faith groups. Many of us are not comfortable with the idea of talking about death and so we deflect the conversation that the person is longing to hold with a sympathetic listener.

If we had lived at any time up to the Second World War, we would have been familiar with death as part of life because most people died at home, in their own beds. Now we live in a culture that seems to expect that everybody will remain healthy, as long as they eat the right food and take enough exercise, and probably live for a very long time. Death is seen somehow as a failure and we look for someone to blame and preferably to sue. This all adds to the sense that death is a pathological event that needs to be tidied away, instead of a normal part of living.

### Where should people die?

When someone is clearly deteriorating towards death, they are usually moved to hospital. Sometimes the family exerts considerable pressure for this to happen, in the vain hope that something can be done. However, for many people with dementia, when they have reached a stage of physical illness where nothing more can be done for them except 'tender loving care', it is clearly most undesirable to move them to a strange environment with unknown people, noises, smells and sounds around them. This really is a 'strange situation' for anyone and must be terrifying for a person who has problems making sense of their own world. Acute hospitals are not usually hospitable places in which to die.

The Alzheimer's Society's (2004b) position paper on palliative care (www.alzheimers.org) deplores the fact that the palliative care needs of people with dementia have received little attention to date. The Society believes that:

One to one nursing is needed. The use of a tube for artificial hydration and feeding should not be considered best practice but family members, carers and nursing staff who sit by the bed, offering sips of water or moistening a person's mouth provide a more appropriate and less invasive alternative ... early and ongoing involvement and consultation with family members is crucial – genuine shared decision-making. (Alzheimer's Society, 2004b)

### Bereavement

People with dementia vary greatly in the extent to which they understand that someone has died and the extent of bereavement. It is our view that it is often not recognised as an explanation of depression or behaviour. We may find ourselves having to insist that the person with dementia is fully included in wakes or funerals. They may have a particular need to be there to understand fully what has happened and to share in important rituals.

### Social class

Strangely enough, social class may be the most taboo subject of all in social work in the UK in the 21st century. The social inclusion agenda clearly covers social class but although we observe class differences we rarely talk about it nor record it. It is true, but often hard for us to accept, that there is a social stigma attached to social services/social work departments. Most adults who need the support of social workers are poor and inarticulate. When middle-class families of people with dementia who are confident and feel able to stand up for themselves, even to question our decisions, come along, it is easy for us to label them as troublemakers. They often want to know in great detail about the care package, the reasons for the decisions we have made and to challenge them. Some of us become wary, defensive and may feel hostile towards such families.

It is not surprising that when middle-class families have to turn to social workers for help when their friend or relative develops dementia, they find it hard because they are in uncharted territory. The doctor's surgery is familiar. Everyone has a GP and so everyone knows roughly what to expect. They may feel frustrated if they do not get the help they want, but they know how the system works.

The discovery that social workers are the gatekeepers to the help that they need so badly can be very hard for some middle-class families to accept. The distinction between health services, which are free, and social care services, which are means-tested, is something which is still not universally understood and learning this fact in the middle of a family crisis can be very hard. Having to disclose financial information to a social worker is often as unexpected as it is unwelcome.

Dementia is no respecter of persons. It can strike anybody in any walk of life. Because there are so many people with dementia, social workers in this field will probably work with far more middle-class families, in terms of numbers, than their counterparts in other client groups. We have to engage with this issue of social class because people are defined by it as much as they are by gender, age, race or sexual orientation.

Mr and Mrs Franks had two daughters, one a nurse and one a solicitor. When Mr Franks was diagnosed with vascular dementia the daughters came down to the town where their parents lived to discuss their care and support with a social worker. Mr Franks felt very uncomfortable, particularly with the nurse, because she commented on local services, comparing them unfavourably with services available in her own town. The family was about to make a complaint about the rudeness of the social worker when the senior practitioner in the team took over the case and was able, because she was more confident, to rescue the relationship.

In addressing all these taboos we need to be aware of our own underlying assumptions, stereotypes and prejudices about people who are different from ourselves.

## Dilemmas for social workers

It is no use pretending that there are always right answers. Judgement is required all the time. Here we outline some of the common situations with which we are all familiar.

### Risk

Risk is fraught with dilemmas. How much risk should we allow the person with dementia to take, given that they are often unable to work out the consequences. The line between allowing someone to be independent and to try to do things and simply allowing them to fail is not a clear one. Failure is every bit as bad an outcome as hurting themselves. Having dementia can feel as if it is all about failure in every aspect of life and leads to loss of confidence, low morale and great anxiety. We have to do everything we can to reduce the sense of failure. Activities should be failure-free as far as possible. Fine judgements are therefore required to allow enough calculated risk for the person with dementia to be able to succeed at something with enough protection to ensure there is neither failure nor injury of some sort. Perhaps occasional injury is a fair price to pay for some independence and success, but this should not be seen as an abdication of responsibility, rather a careful judgement.

> Mr di Rollo illustrates a considered approach to risk taking. He had had dementia for many years and was no longer able to speak properly. He was constantly near to tears, plucking at his clothes and the clothes of people near him. He was very shaky. He seemed unable to relate to anybody. His day centre used the preparation of the lunch as his main activity. The staff knew that Mr di Rollo had been an experienced chef and that some of his skills remained. His hands were washed, a chopping board was placed in front of him, upon which was placed a large potato that had been peeled by one of the other members and into his hands was placed a razor-sharp chopping knife. Mr di Rollo sliced the potato for the soup with no hesitation, placing the knife on the board when he had finished. Effusive thanks and approval were his reward.

## The needs of the individual or the needs of the group?

This is another recurring dilemma. Inevitably we are often involved in group care. This book takes as a starting point that the needs of the individual are paramount, but we have to recognise that this cannot always be so. How do we weigh up the welfare of a group of residents unable to go outside when they want to because one resident makes off if allowed through the door? How do we weigh up the rights of a group of residents who want to go out for an outing but cannot because there are not enough staff available to look after the two in the group whose road safety sense is impaired? A lot of this again is about understanding behaviour and this book should give extensive ideas on this if nothing else. But it would be foolish to pretend that there are not continuous and constant difficult decisions to be made, even when each individual has a care plan and these are being consistently implemented by all the staff.

## Should carers speak on behalf of people with dementia?

Most people with dementia need an advocate because they are unable to speak on their own behalf. Who better than someone who knows them really well? But it is not always in the interests of the person with dementia. Indeed there are sometimes quite sharp conflicts of interest and those are one of the reasons why work in this field is so very difficult. It used to be much easier when we believed that people with dementia had no meaningful preferences. Now we know that they have, we have to face the fact that it is often excruciatingly difficult to see a fair solution.

The fact that the law has now changed to reflect the fact that a person with dementia is assumed to possess mental capacity unless proved otherwise should make some of these choices easier to make. The rights of both people with dementia and their carers are now much more clearly defined and in time will help to make decision making in this difficult area somewhat easier.

## The needs of the individual versus the needs of the carer

Although dementia is primarily a disease of old age, younger people do get it and these families often illustrate the most difficult conflicts of interest.

Mr Shaw and his wife were both lawyers who married late and had a young family even though they were in their late forties. They both worked and were very successful until Mr Shaw got dementia. He gave up work, although not willingly. Mrs Shaw was very unwilling to give up her successful career; she was not only the main breadwinner but the only person who could keep her husband calm and relaxed. The children were very distressed by their father's behaviour. The conflict of interest was very painful. Mr Shaw needed to be with his wife all the time but Mrs Shaw needed and wanted to work. The children might well have been less stressed had their father been in hospital or a care home.

## Conflict resolution approach

Social workers are often seen as the profession to work in these situations where there is a painful conflict of interest and we sometimes need to consider some of the tried and tested conflict resolution approaches from other fields.

One way of working towards a solution which is fair even if it does not fully meet the needs of either party is the one used by trade unions and diplomats – negotiation. This is a process whereby each party specifies what they want and then works towards an agreed compromise where it is felt that concessions on both sides have been fair. In family situations, both sides need to be represented; certainly the person with dementia will need this. It will not be a process to be used very often but for some of the really difficult dilemmas it may be the way forward.

Mediation is another related technique used by the family conciliation service, which works with divorcing couples. With mediation, both parties are helped to put their case fully to the other. The tension between carers and people with dementia can have all the emotional components of any marriage, even when they are not married to each other. In many situations there are several staff involved who might undertake the role of negotiators or mediators. The social worker might assist the person with dementia, the occupational therapist might assist the children and the CPN might assist the carer in the case, for example, of Mr and Mrs Shaw. The solution is invariably a compromise for all parties. As social workers our role is to ensure that these compromises are as fair as possible.

## Conclusion

This chapter has mainly been about the social approach to dementia with a strong underpinning of the concept of personhood and the person–centred approach. Social workers make their major contribution in the social approach. This approach is a positive one on the whole because there is so much that can be done to improve the lives of people with dementia and their carers. Yes, dementia is a progressive condition, but it need not be a totally negative experience for all concerned.

### Further reading
Bryden, C. (2005) *Dancing with Dementia*, London: Jessica Kingsley Publishers.

Grant, L. (1999) *Remind Me Who I Am Again*, London: Granta.

Marriot, H. (2003) *The Selfish Pig's Guide to Caring*, Polperro: Polperro Heritage Press.

# FIVE

# Communication

## Introduction

Communication is central to the development of a truly person-centred approach to dementia care. In this chapter we consider four main aspects of communication – communication with:

- people with dementia;
- carers;
- colleagues;
- the public.

Written communication and advocacy are important issues that we also examine in this chapter. Communication is one of the most exciting areas of dementia care in which new developments are happening at a rapid pace.

## Communicating with people with dementia

Even as late as the 1980s it was generally thought that most people with dementia talked nonsense as a result of their brain damage. We have come a long way since then. We are now confident that it is possible to communicate with most people with dementia (Goldsmith, 1996) although we are still learning the necessary skills. Enabling people to share their wishes and preferences with us is perhaps the most urgent need, but, increasingly, the possibility of therapeutic communication is being recognised.

We have, in this book, tended to avoid talking about the stages of dementia because it can condition expectations, but we need to address the communication needs of people with different degrees of impairment. We have always to bear in mind that people with dementia have good days and bad days or even good mornings and bad mornings. As we have emphasised, there are a whole set of factors affecting their competence, some of which could be suboptimal at any time. Given that the same person with dementia can be impaired to different degrees at different times, we will look at three different degrees of impairment.

## People with unimpaired or mildly impaired verbal communication skills

Most people who have just had a diagnosis still have intact communication skills so we will refer explicitly to their needs and contribution to society here.

The development of the cholinesterase inhibitors for the symptomatic treatment of people in the early stages of Alzheimer's disease has led to an important change in the service that many GPs now offer to their patients. Because the drugs were initially developed to treat people in the early stages of Alzheimer's disease, there has been mounting pressure on GPs to refer people to psychiatrists for an early diagnosis which identifies those with Alzheimer's disease. This in turn has led to many people with dementia being diagnosed at an earlier stage, especially if they are under 65.

For people with less impaired communication skills it is important not to change your language style. The changes that are necessary for more impaired people will be picked up and interpreted by the person as being patronising. However, we all have to learn a different style of conversation. We need to change from a conversational style that is based on asking questions and therefore immediately places a person with short-term memory loss at a disadvantage. This does not come easily because our habitual style of social conversation is based on questions. However, starting a conversation with a statement rather than a question will avoid a lot of frustration for everyone. Thus you might say: 'Hello Mrs Dawson. My name is Mary Marshall. When I came to see you last time we talked in the sitting room. You told me about your memory problems'.

### Sharing the diagnosis

What is needed is skill in listening, which allows people to ask and to share whatever they will be grappling with in making sense of life with a progressive illness. If you are really attentive to the tone and hesitations as well as the content of the conversation you should be able to gauge better what it is that the person fears and what it is they want to know. The crucial skill is not offering false reassurance and comfort. Staying silent is better than doing this. Most people with dementia know there is something dreadfully wrong and they may need someone outside the family to talk to about their fears for themselves and their relationships.

People with dementia often advise that 'one step at a time' or 'one day at a time' is the best way forward since this is a condition with such an unpredictable prognosis in every sense. You may have to point out that everyone has their own pathway to follow and offer reassurance (when you honestly can) about the support and help that will be available. It is impossible to generalise about what information people in this position will want to know. It may be reviewing their life, it may be planning their future. Different people will want different amounts of information and will have different worries.

It is all much easier if the person and their carer know the diagnosis, even if they call it 'memory problems' rather than using a clinical term. There is a growing trend towards offering people the choice to be told their own diagnosis. Figures from the Alzheimer's Society National Helpline provide evidence of this growing trend. In 2000 they received 69 callers from people saying, in effect, 'I have been told I have dementia. What do I do?'. In 2003 that figure had risen to 168 and has continued to rise. When carers are told about the diagnosis, and the person with dementia is not told, it can put a great strain on relationships and can isolate the person with dementia yet further.

> Mr Fields would, from time to time, ask his daughter if there was something wrong with his head. She found this acutely stressful because she felt neither competent nor comfortable about being the person to tell her father about the diagnosis. As a consequence a barrier was erected between them and he was left alone with his fears.

It is not easy for the doctors to decide how, when and with whom to share the diagnosis and they often fall back on their own preferences. It would seem to be good practice, at least in the early stages, to assume that the person with dementia wants some information and to take it in tiny steps, providing only what they want to know. The person may need the social worker to provide more information and the same approach is needed. Alternatively, the social worker may need to support another trusted person in the process of telling the person with dementia.

> Mr Crerar lived in sheltered housing with his wife. The warden seemed to be the one person in Mr Crerar's life who did not shy away from

discussing his diminishing mental capacity with him. He was able to share his knowledge that he had dementia and the fact that he was very fearful of the future. It was a great comfort to him. The warden never used the word 'dementia', neither did she confront him with explanations. She simply listened, gave no false reassurance and told no lies. The social worker saw her role as supporting and informing the warden.

We have much to learn from the field of cancer care. In dementia care, as in cancer care, it is the non-medical staff who often find themselves sharing the diagnosis either because the person and their carer did not hear the doctor or because they did not feel comfortable asking for the information to be repeated and explained. Providing the right amount of information is not easy. Some people will want euphemisms, others will want all the factual information they can find. Leaving written information behind after your assessment visit can be useful so that the carer and the person with dementia can read as much or as little as they can deal with. This can be done at their own pace.

As in cancer care, some doctors prefer to tell the whole family with the person with dementia present. They claim that this sets a standard of treating the person with dementia as a responsible adult, which then makes relationships more straightforward as the disease progresses. Others tell the carer and the person with dementia, but tell them separately. Some simply tell the carer. Sometimes this decision is made on the basis of a judgement about what the person with dementia wants and the sense that this is obviously the right thing to do. The giving of the diagnosis is clearly a time when all the people concerned are greatly in need of support. A referral made by the doctor at this point to one of the Alzheimer's Societies should be standard practice.

### *Communication and assessment*

The continued emphasis on hearing the voice of consumers of services has implications for assessment and reviews as well as diagnosis, not least because the assessment and review forms often require the diagnosis. Social workers will often find themselves having to address the issue of whether or not someone knows that there is something wrong with their memory, whatever label they use. Communicating honestly about the assessment process has been a positive aspect of the current more standardised processes and forms. Certainly the best way to get around the interrogatory nature of form-filling is to do it alongside the respondent so that they choose what is written. Sitting side by side and going through it together can diminish a lot of paranoia about the forms. In a sense the information is then jointly owned.

All forms now require that the respondent signs the form and this is a great deal more appropriate if they have helped to fill it in. There are difficulties when there is a joint form for both the carer and the person with dementia, especially if they do not agree, which is very likely. Some local authorities use two forms and try to have them filled in separately. Completing a form with the person with dementia does, of course, assume that the person with dementia and the assessor can achieve some form of agreement. This can be very problematic since the person with dementia will often fear that recording their incompetence will threaten their lifestyle. There is a need for a great deal more research, written material and training on this issue of the sharing of the diagnosis. Staff support is vital too.

## People with impaired verbal communication skills

We now know that as dementia advances and if the person is having a bad day, verbal communication becomes more difficult although not impossible. Many research projects such as Mozely et al (1999) found that people are able to express their views even when they are severely cognitively impaired as measured by conventional tools such as the Mini-Mental State Examination (MMSE) (see www.minimental.com). In that project, residents with an MMSE score as low as 10 out of 30 were involved in the research. Similar results were found in the Bradford Dementia Group study into well-being in homes run by Methodist Homes for the Aged (MHA) Care (Bruce et al, 2002).

An example from the medical model that is helpful to social workers is the distinction that is made between receptive and expressive dysphasia. In receptive dysphasia the person with dementia has no problems in expressing themselves but cannot understand what the other person is saying to them. In expressive dysphasia the person with dementia knows what they want to say, but is unable to find the words. We should, however, assume that the person with dementia can express themselves in a straightforward verbal fashion until we are quite sure that the problem is dysphasia rather than our lack of skill in communication.

It may be necessary to choose the right moment and spend time engaging with the person initially. It is important to remember that English may not be the person's first language, as we pointed out in

Chapter Four. It can be helpful if we alter our conversational style more. Body language, particularly eye contact, becomes increasingly important; bearing in mind that eye contact has different meanings in different cultures. As the person with dementia finds it increasingly difficult to make sense of the words you are using, they will rely more and more on non-verbal signs to understand your meaning. For example, speak in short sentences – six words has been found to be ideal – match your voice tone to your facial expression, speak more slowly than you would normally do and be aware of your own voice tone. Choosing a good time of day, finding a quiet place and sitting in the light are helpful, as is awareness of hearing impairment, which often goes unrecognised. Allan (2002) has written some helpful guidance for communicating with people with hearing impairment and dementia. We too need to be able to concentrate fully in what is described as intense or exquisite listening, so a quiet place may be just as important for us.

It is often helpful to start with the assumption that people who are moderately impaired by their dementia communicate most powerfully through their emotions. They are seldom able to explain in plain, straightforward language what it is they want to tell you. This does not mean that they never can, but often they cannot tell you at the time you want to hear (Barnett, 2000).

> Mrs Turner's key worker thought Mrs Turner lived in about four different time zones, one of which was the present. When she was in the present it was quite possible to have a straightforward conversation with her.

Time is often the key. Everyone is short of time, but taking time to communicate is often time well spent if it means that you really find out what is bothering the person with dementia. As social workers we may need to encourage other people who spend more time with the person, such as the home carer or the care assistant, to do this. They may need our help in interpreting the stories and pictures they hear (Barnett, 2000).

In hospitals and long-term care homes staff often say that many of the best conversations take place in the bathroom with the warm water and scented bath essence encouraging easy communication. Seeing bathing as an activity rather than a task which has therapeutic as well as hygienic benefits can give staff great job satisfaction as well as enhancing the well-being of the person who is having the bath.

Most people who work with people with dementia, including social workers, will meet people who seem to be stuck in a groove about something. This is often because they cannot explain their feelings in a straightforward way.

> Why is it that Mrs Casson endlessly tells us about her brother's death? Could she perhaps be wanting to talk about death? A day centre in Geelong, which actively encourages the expression of feelings, finds that the people who attend the centre talk a lot about death. Mrs Casson needs a listener who will let her talk. She may simply be saying that she is miserable. We can encourage Mrs Casson to express her emotions by saying: 'Tell me about your brother. Was his death especially painful to you?'.

### Communicating with people with severely impaired verbal communication skills

Some people with dementia lose almost all the ability to communicate verbally. It is too easy to think that they have nothing to say and they can be deprived of any interaction with someone else at all. As we said right at the start of the book, we only have a sense of personhood in relationship to other people. Carers, staff and all the other people who come into contact with people with no apparent communication ability can be easily discouraged. They too need to have some response from the person with dementia to affirm them in their efforts.

Killick and Allan (2006) describe their efforts to communicate with people in the end stages of dementia based on work with people in comas. One of the essential skills they emphasise is that of mimicking the person with dementia. This sounds vaguely offensive, in reality it is the basis of a lot of communication with very disabled people with dementia because it puts them in control of it. Mullen, in the moving video about using music, *Responding to Music* (Mullen and Killick, 2001), shows how she mimics the efforts of people with dementia on musical instruments or singing and how this leads to very real and meaningful exchanges. It requires great concentration and focus but can have surprising consequences. More skill development work is clearly required.

Most communication with people with this degree of disability is through the senses: sound is one and we have mentioned Mullen's work as an example (we return to the subject of music in Chapter Nine since it has particular importance for people with dementia). Touch is another means of relating to people with dementia and many respond to touch when it appears that they are unable to respond to anything else. We need to be able to interpret their response to touch when this is possible. Visual stimuli can be important. Craig (2002) shows how she provided pleasurable touch and visual stimulation to people who were confined to their beds in very suboptimal environments. As social workers we may find ourselves having to insist on these kinds of improvements to the environment of people who are bedbound and can be deprived of any pleasurable sensory stimulation.

Care planning should continue to the end of life and should be more than keeping people clean and comfortable. Related to touch is kinetics or movement as a sensory stimulation; people can move their limbs sometimes to communicate. Smell is obviously important both for pleasure and memories. So many places for people who are very disabled smell unpleasant, either of urine or of disinfectant. We may need to point this out and suggest scented flowers, or pot pourri of a familiar smell.

The literature on communication with people without speech is very limited. Most social workers will not be expected to try to communicate but we do have a role in care planning and we can be consulted by visiting relatives who need advice and support.

## Advocacy

As we have seen – we cannot always assume that the best person to protect the person with dementia's best interests is a friend or family member. There is clearly a need for advocacy. Advocates are basically people with no vested interest (Burton, 1997). They are solely needed to represent the views of people with dementia in the countless decisions that are made about and for them.

Since the 1990s we have begun to see the development of advocacy for dementia services, although successful schemes are still relatively scarce. Scotland and Wales, using funding allocated by the Scottish Parliament and the Welsh Assembly, have led the way in this field.

Skills developed by people such as Powell (2000), Feil (2002) and Allan (2002a) in communicating with people with dementia can be taught to people who are working as advocates for people with dementia. We need to be realistic about how much time is involved. Even if advocates are volunteers, which they may be, this service cannot be done on the cheap.

The life-story book approach, which we discuss in more detail in Chapter Nine, can be useful in helping to work out what it is the person would have wanted to say had they been able to say it. Advocates need to know a lot about communication. They need to know that many people with dementia have fluctuating competence and that they need to persevere or wait until a better time. They need to be skilled at using non-verbal communication. Anyone, for example, who cannot bear to touch someone else is unlikely to be suitable for this work because so much communication is through touch.

It is puzzling that there are so few advocacy schemes given the dire need for advocacy for people with dementia who tend to be treated as of very low status. Many of them have outlived their relatives, if they ever had them, and have nobody to represent their interests. In long-stay care settings, for example, advocates could help in making good considered decisions about locked doors and other restraints, about activity programmes, outings and so on. In any long-stay establishment, there are many occasions where decisions are made that would be better if the person with dementia was given a stronger voice. Most provider agencies such as NHS Trusts, social services/work departments and independent and voluntary care providers will have policies on user involvement in making decisions. These policies will often mention advocacy.

The need has now been recognised in law with the passing of the 2000 Adults with Incapacity (Scotland) Act and the 2005 Mental Capacity Act (England and Wales). The latter Act provides for an 'Independent Mental Capacity Advocate' (IMCA) who is someone appointed to support a person who lacks capacity but has no one to speak for them.

The IMCA makes representations about the person's wishes, feelings, beliefs and values where decisions have to be made about accommodation or of a serious medical nature, at the same time bringing to the attention of the decision maker all factors that are relevant to the decision. The IMCA can challenge the decision maker on behalf of the person lacking capacity if necessary.

The Department for Constitutional Affairs has produced a booklet of guidelines and advice for social care professionals including social workers called *Making Decisions* (DCA, 1999) designed to help them carry out their own advocacy role more effectively. Advocacy within social work should not be seen as combative, as taking on the world on behalf of a person who cannot speak for themselves. Rather, it should be seen as giving people with dementia a voice in a world where they are generally silent. By asking questions and seeking clarification the advocate can assist everyone to pause and think again about decisions from the point of view of the person with dementia.

This should make for better decisions and more peace of mind all round, since justice is seen to be done.

## Behaviour as a way of communicating feelings

In this section we begin to talk about a recurring theme of this book, which is the importance of seeing behaviour as something we have to understand. Here we see it as a way of communicating. We use walking/wandering to make our point.

We are increasingly realising that people with dementia are trying to communicate in whatever way they can. Sometimes they tell us apparently unconnected stories, often about their past. Sometimes, they have only behaviour as a means of communicating. If we start with this premise we may begin to be able to 'listen'. In other words, we have to assume that there is a rationality about their conversation and behaviour rather than the irrationality that was the default position in the old culture of care. If we look at the behaviour of people with dementia with knowledge and experience, we can sometimes act as interpreters.

Why is it that Mr Allan, for example, will sometimes only pick at his food and leave most of it, causing his wife considerable distress and anxiety, whereas at other times he eats it all? If you watch Mr Allan it is clear that when he is agitated for some reason he is unable to eat. He also uses it as a way of expressing anger with his wife, which he cannot express verbally because he is only too well aware that he is totally dependent on her. If you talk to her you realise that she expresses a lot of love and care through food and she feels his behaviour is very rejecting of her. Mealtimes can easily become a battleground.

Mrs Baxter spits her food out in her residential care home, causing immense mess and consternation. Is she expressing her rage and impotence at her predicament?

Mrs Hughes stopped eating completely in her nursing home. It seemed that this started after she had realised that her husband was dead. This realisation had taken some weeks – she seemed surprisingly unconcerned at the time. Now she will only eat if she is hugged like a baby and fed soft foods with a spoon. She often weeps when she is fed. She is very fortunate to be in a nursing home where they are willing to give her this kind of care, because it can take an hour to spoon the bowl of mashed food into her mouth.

Perhaps we can interpret some behaviour of people with dementia as attempts to make sense of the bewildering situations in which they find themselves.

Mr Leith was in an acute hospital ward. He was sitting in a chair with a wheeled bedside table across his knees to stop him getting up because he had a drip in his arm. He seemed convinced that the table was a potato machine that needed fixing. To the dismay of the nurses he kept trying to get under it to see what was wrong. The nurses did not have the skills to get him to talk about the machine. He might have been able to express his fears about the fact that something was very wrong with his life through talking about the faulty machine.

### Walking

The behaviour that is described in the old culture as 'wandering' is an example of the kind of behaviour by which people are trying to communicate. 'Wandering' is not a very accurate term to describe this activity because it implies that it is without purpose. We now know that there are many possible reasons for it, many of which have a strong sense of purpose (Allan and Marshall, 2006). Here are some of them:

- There is no reason why a person who has always had lifelong patterns of walking and/or physical activity should not want to continue to walk when they are living in a care home.
- They may be distressed by strong feelings of anxiety, sadness or anger, which are reduced, as they are in anybody, by using up physical energy.
- This may be the way they have always responded to stress.

One of the reasons why the term 'wandering' persists is because there is no clear one-word alternative. This, in itself, should not be a problem – 'walking' might be a more accurate description of the activity. If we are person-centred we should be aiming to describe things more accurately for each person; for example, for some it will be agitated pacing, for others it will be strolling around the garden.

Mrs Wells lived in a village on her own and had always loved going for long walks in the countryside. After her husband died she used to visit his grave several times a week. When her dementia became more advanced she would get lost on the way back from the churchyard. Unfortunately for Mrs Wells she lived near the A1. It was not possible to make a plan with her to reduce the risk because her receptive dysphasia, combined with lack of insight because of damage to her frontal lobe, meant that she could not understand the words in which her social worker and family tried to explain the situation. She could not comprehend how dangerous it would be if she strayed onto the trunk road, putting herself and probably many other people in great danger. She just wanted to visit her husband's grave and took the shortest route to the churchyard. There was no alternative but to move her into a care home.

Mrs Knightly also lived in a village on her own. She was a devout Catholic and was in the habit of attending daily Mass in the nearby town. She would order a taxi to take her there. The taxi drivers knew her and made sure that, as her memory was quite impaired, she was always delivered safely back to her own home. When she got lost in and around the village, she was always set back on the right road home by other villagers who knew her well. Although her memory was impaired, her language was not and this clearly helped her to remain independent because she could talk to the taxi drivers and the other people in the village. Her social worker was able to use the supportive community to help Mrs Knightly to stay in her own home.

### 'Hearing' behaviour to underpin planning

It is worth assuming at the outset that behaviour is an attempt to communicate, although of course this will not always be the case. 'Hearing' what people with dementia are trying to say to us does not always make life easier for us because if we do understand what the person is communicating we often have to do something about it.

Working out why the person behaves in a particular way is a major step towards doing something about it. It may not be possible to allow a person to leave a building if there is some danger from a busy road or bad weather. A thorough risk assessment should always be carried out, paying particular attention to the person's remaining ability to judge road safety. In terms of the two people who communicated through food:

- we can teach Mr Allan's wife some relaxation techniques so that she stays calmer around mealtimes;
- we can allow Mrs Baxter and Mrs Hughes to express their rage or unhappiness more appropriately.

Learning to observe the behaviour of people with dementia closely as a means of helping us to understand the emotional need that they are expressing will help us to cope better ourselves and not become overwrought at their behaviour.

## Communicating with carers

Carers always tell us, if we give them the chance, that they need more information. If there is an early diagnosis, like for the person with dementia, they need as much information about the dementia as they can understand and cope with, but not more. It is not easy to know what to share because the individual pathway through the different stages and different types of dementia is so unpredictable.

Sharing the diagnosis of dementia has already been mentioned but here we want to address the needs of carers in this regard. In some ways it is little different from any diagnosis of a terminal illness. Some people want to know all the details of their relative's cancer, others prefer to ignore it. The point for us here is that we must be ready to provide the information in as small or large quantities as required by the carer. Although medical staff make the diagnosis, it is often the non-medical staff who have to explain it. Many carers simply cannot face the facts at all.

Mr Crichton's wife was diagnosed when she was still well able to talk about it. Her husband found this intolerable and refused to acknowledge that she had dementia or to talk to anyone about it.

Mrs Roise could not face the implications of her husband's dementia when he was first diagnosed. Her daughter, who was a nurse, sent off for fact sheets from the Alzheimer's Society. When the social worker visited Mr and Mrs Roise a year later it was only after a connection between them had been made that Mrs Roise went to the sideboard and withdrew the envelope from the Alzheimer's Society. It was still unopened. The social worker and Mrs Roise went through them together on a subsequent visit.

There are some very helpful books and leaflets now available. The Alzheimer's Societies are finely tuned to the needs of carers and have a range of materials in various formats. The websites of the national voluntary organisations are increasingly used as a source of information, by both people with dementia and carers and information can easily be downloaded on a great many topics related to dementia. Carers can often tell you what information they need but they may be so stressed and so exhausted by the time you make contact with them that they simply do not know where to start.

As the dementia progresses, carers need to know what help is available. Being able to ask for help is a real skill and one which carers seldom manage effectively without either feeling diminished or angry. They will ask for help when they are ready and will accept services when they are ready too. Managing your response to this apparent refusal of services that are offered requires particular skill, which often comes with experience on the part of the social worker.

It helps – when they have reached that particular point in their lives – if they know where to go and who to speak to in the first instance so that they are not pushed from pillar to post, losing their nerve and their energy as they go. Social workers need to know what is available locally. Being alongside a carer through this process is a vital job for social workers.

We appreciate that the advent of care management has made this increasingly difficult to do. If you are really not allowed to spend the time required yourself you should make sure that you provide a 'signposting' service to agencies which can do this. The Alzheimer's Societies, Age Concern and Help the Aged should be able to point people in the right direction. Although professionals sometimes have to speak on carers' behalf, we can be more helpful if we help them to ask themselves. It is very easy to make distressed carers dependent on professionals.

Carers do not need false reassurance about dementia and services. It is up to us to be as straight and honest as we can be. Many are anxious at the beginning about whether they will be able to cope and it can be helpful to emphasise that it is impossible to predict what they will have to cope with. One of the greatest strains is not being able to talk to the person with dementia in an honest way. Some people find that having to pretend there is nothing wrong is a great strain. Obviously this varies from one relationship to another, which is why really careful listening is so important. In some relationships coping without talking about their feelings has been their custom, in others they share everything. There can be no rules except the fundamental one of listening very carefully and responding, which of course requires skill and good support for staff. Several carers have written books about their experience, Grant (1999) and Marriot (2003) for example.

Carers often say that they want to be more involved in the services their relative is receiving, like Mrs Cross.

Mr Cross had been attending a day hospital for a year. Mrs Cross had no idea what went on there. When she asked Mr Cross he said that they took all his clothes off and that he had lunch. He could remember little else. Mrs Cross suggested to the charge nurse that she might attend with him one day but she was energetically discouraged on the basis that this was meant to be a day off for her. She was anxious because she felt that she knew what was best for her husband but nobody was asking her. She also wanted to be able to continue any treatment he received on the days he was not at the day hospital.

Miss Blair is another carer who should have had more information. Miss Blair's mother was in a residential care home, which she had believed was her mother's home for life. She was very distressed when her mother was suddenly moved to a psychiatric hospital because the home could no longer cope. She said she felt betrayed. If the staff had been honest with her they would have told her that the home would only keep residents as long as they did not disrupt the unit. Her mother had in fact become very aggressive.

Of course it is not always straightforward. Carers may want inappropriate degrees of control.

Mr Wheeler's mother had become attracted to Mr Green, one of the male residents, and the staff had not shared this information with Mr Wheeler because they felt he would not have coped with his mother's close relationship with Mr Green and would have asked the staff to intervene to prevent it. The manager of the home had known the social worker who had been involved in Mrs Wheeler's placement in the home for some years and she asked for his help. The social worker met with Mrs Wheeler and, using his communication skills, was able to discover that it was not a situation where she mistook Mr Green for her late husband, as the staff had believed. She had always enjoyed male company and she really wanted a special relationship. But neither she, nor Mr Green, wanted a physical sexual relationship. Having found out what was really going on the social worker was able to talk the situation through with Mr Wheeler so that he was able to accept his mother's right to make such a choice.

## Different attitudes to risk

The difference of opinion between staff and relatives is most common on the issue of risk. Relatives have often accepted the option of long-term care because they feel that their relative will be safer. They can be dismayed to find unlocked doors, kitchenettes and energetic activities. Social workers need to be open about the approach of the home, and this may even mean talking about risk, sex and death, before the admission in the context of the well-being and quality of life of their relative.

A good brochure about the philosophy of care is a useful starting point. Most relatives are not unreasonable people and appreciate a good discussion so that they can feel that their relative is going to receive planned care set within a well-considered philosophy.

Clear continuing information is the best basis for a real understanding. Social workers will be involved when there is a review or when there is a disagreement between staff and relatives. The care plan should be consistent with the philosophy and policies in the brochure although this may need to be talked through. If there is a difference of opinion about what is best for the person with dementia then it should be out in the open, discussed and some negotiated agreement arrived at.

Social workers may have to point out that implicit in all this is the approach of staff to carers, which should always be respectful. Carers can be very sensitive to any slight because they frequently feel that receiving help is an implicit criticism. Non-verbal communication is as important as verbal and the rule of thumb is that if people hear something and see something else, they will believe what they see. We may need to point out to the manager that when he or she says: 'We always have time to tell carers what is going on', and the relative sees that when the manager is talking to them they are constantly answering the phone and speaking to people who come through the door, carers will get the message!

We need to be aware that most carers feel guilty that they were not able to carry on caring for the person at home. These feelings can be very strong and can last for a long time after the person has gone to live in the care home. Many people also need to believe, understandably, that nobody can look after their relative as well as they could. These feelings need to be addressed and discussed with the carer. In one sense it is absolutely true that no care home can offer the same level of care as within the family because it cannot be on a one-to-one basis. However, the fact remains that the carer is no longer able to continue to offer care in that way any longer – and you may need to help them accept this.

Bryden gives a different view:

> Co-dependency is unhealthy for both the person with dementia and their family. We [people with dementia] can become more incapable than we really are and you [the carer] can become more exhausted than you need to be. And neither of us is being honest, each of us is journeying alone with dementia, struggling without any insight as to what to do. We need to move away from labeling ourselves as care-giver and sufferer towards becoming a care-partnership in which we accept, collaborate and adapt to new roles within the journey of dementia. (Bryden, 2005, p 150)

Insights like this from people with dementia are helping to push the debate about how to practise person-centred dementia care into new territory. For the first time we have the possibility of engaging in a dialogue with people with dementia about what they really want.

This highlights the issue, known for some time to social workers in this field, that we often have at least two clients – whose needs may vary greatly. One of the skills we need if we are working in this field is to learn how to balance two opposing sets of needs, empowering each person without disempowering the other.

# Communicating with colleagues

## *Tribal culture*

There are many types of colleagues. As we said in Chapter Three, it can be helpful to see people from a different profession as from a different tribe. Colleagues may be of the same tribe or even team as yourself. They may be from another tribe or team, and above or below you in the professional structure. Like yours, their tribe has its own language, its own set of traditions, which are different from yours. Each tribe spends a lot of time defending its own position. Tribes tend to be competitive and defensive and often look down on other tribes in order to reinforce their own sense of identity. It may be helpful to look at different levels in our own organisation in the same way.

So how do you set about communicating with another tribe? The first thing is to learn some of their language and traditions. This helps if they want to communicate with you so that there is a meeting halfway. It is useful to understand where they might compromise in decision making and where they might not. It helps to know what it is about your behaviour that makes them clam up and become defensive. There is a lot to be learned from watching international disputes and the way these are worked out because it is the same thing on a different scale.

Personal relationships that overcome mutual suspicion are always helpful because then candid conversations can take place. It is striking how in international conflict situations the two opposing sides often begin to talk to each other in secret. In South Africa Nelson Mandela met with Prime Minister F.W. de Klerk while he was still imprisoned, which meant that the vision of the dismantling of apartheid had already begun before it became public. Presumably they began to see each other as people with reasons for behaving as they did.

Mixed professional teams go through the same process. People come to see each other as people with the same aims but different languages and priorities: no one is right or wrong and each brings a perspective that sheds some light on the situation. In the past, organisations have been anxious about staff working in mixed professional teams because it dilutes their loyalty to the 'tribe', whereas now the advantages are clearly seen to outweigh the disadvantages.

George Bernard Shaw said that 'England and America are two countries divided by a common language' (www.askoxford.com/quotations). In other words, we are both using the same words but we attach different meanings to them. This causes problems because we think we are talking about the same thing when we are not. The tribal world of health and social care is littered with examples of this. 'Case conference' is one example. This has a formal and legal meaning for social workers but for health workers it is used to describe an informal meeting of concerned professionals, usually called by the consultant in a hospital setting.

Another is 'assessment'. All the professionals concerned carry out 'assessments' and yet they mean different things by them.

## The importance of recording and sharing qualitative information

Records are a way of collecting and storing information and making it available appropriately. Most agencies keep some sort of record of essential information such as addresses of next of kin, essential medical information and so on.

We address issues of shared forms and protocols in Chapter Six. However, there are situations in which social workers still need detailed recording, as they have always done. In these situations the computerised pro forma will never be sufficient. They will often be the situations in which there is a difference of opinion between the concerned parties, where it is extremely important to record detailed information that otherwise would be held in the social workers' head but not on the computer. The old adage that 'if it is not written down it never happened' is always worth bearing in mind. Examples of these situations are:

- Protection of Vulnerable Adults (POVA);
- Care Programme Approach (CPA);
- complaints;
- Care Standards Commission Inspections (CSCI) complaints procedures;
- risk monitoring;
- reviews.

Social workers who are working in the electronic world of the 21st century still need to be skilled in the clear, concise and detailed recording of information that enables another person to gain an accurate picture of the situation. Sometimes the pro forma is not up to the task and social workers need to use their initiative to ensure that the fullest possible record is made.

## Communicating detailed information across different care settings

As social workers we may have known the person with dementia before, during and after their move to residential care. We are in a strong position to make sure that information about routines and preferences, which is so important to the person's well-being, goes with them when they move. If the care home is not aware of how important this information can be, we may have an educational job to do.

Without a good record of the past and the present life of the person, communicating with people with dementia and organising their care and support cannot be achieved. This is particularly important in residential settings. Here we look at the present life of the person. We cover the subject of the person's past life in Chapter Nine.

When Mr O'Reilly was dying of cancer, his key worker had the foresight to seek his wife's help in preparing a life-story book about Mr O'Reilly, who also had dementia. This book also referred to his preferences and included the fact that he loathed striped shirts. The staff caring for him might have been bewildered by his difficult behaviour without this information if Mrs O'Reilly was not there to explain.

Mrs Jenkins was a lady who never felt properly dressed unless she was wearing her petticoat. Fortunately her daughter was able to explain this to staff when she moved into a residential care home. Even so the information was not always passed on. More than once when her daughter visited she found her mother in a distressed and angry state. The first thing she would check was whether she was wearing her petticoat. Usually it was this omission that was causing her distress.

The culture in care homes and day centres is basically an oral culture. Far more information is stored in the heads of the care staff than is written down. While it is good that individual care staff know so much detailed information about a person in their care, the danger is that the information is not passed on to the rest of the staff. If we could help staff to understand the disability approach to dementia and that they are, in fact, acting as the memory of the person, they might feel differently. The question of where this information should be kept in care homes is very important.

There is no point in having information in the office about the fact that Mrs Jenkins always likes to wear a petticoat. It needs to be in her bedroom. A better place to keep it might be on a summary sheet inside the wardrobe door.

A comfort food list for each resident can be pinned up inside a cupboard in the kitchenette as well as the more usual list of dietary requirements. We all use foods for comfort and there is no reason why people in care homes with dementia should be any different, just because they cannot tell us their preferences.

When Mrs Perreira became distressed, the care staff knew that she could sometimes be comforted by eating a couple of chocolate digestive biscuits, a supply of which were provided by her son and kept in the kitchenette on the unit. They also knew that she only drank black coffee with sugar and became upset if it was offered without sugar or with milk.

The small details of life are very important to all of us, and may seem to be extraordinarily trivial to other people. But we need to think of how intense some of our own likes and dislikes are and realise that people with dementia are no different. Gibson (1991) describes the positive impact of knowing preferences in residential care.

## Joint working

The creation of Community Mental Health Teams should go some way towards addressing the tribal culture of health and social care. Sharing the same workspace and meeting on a daily basis ought to improve communication between staff from different agencies.

What is needed is for us to bring the same thought we bring to the rest of our practice to this business of communicating with colleagues. Skills of diplomacy, negotiation, clarity and empathy are just as relevant. Written skills can be especially important when the opportunities of face-to-face communication are unavailable. GPs are a good illustration of this. They are seldom available for meetings and it is very important to communicate with them briefly and clearly in writing.

The same applies to colleagues in other parts of your own organisation, who can become very defensive if they are wrong-footed by not being in receipt of the necessary information. The intention to place the emphasis in the community care procedures on written forms is an attempt to improve communication so that everyone is collecting the same information and the sharing mechanisms are clear.

## Communication with the public

There is no doubt that there is much greater awareness of dementia now than there was in the 1990s. The Alzheimer's Societies have done remarkable work in raising awareness through their campaigns. They have been very successful indeed at using the media. However, an undesirable effect of this success with the media is that, in the past, they have tended to stress the negative aspects of dementia. It is clearly difficult to raise money for dementia by telling a positive story about the advantages of person-centred dementia care. The change in the message that is needed for today's world requires considerable skill on the part of the public relations and marketing departments of these organisations.

Of course there can be few people today whose lives have not been touched by dementia, either within their family or in neighbours and friends. Most people can talk about dementia, although they are often more comfortable using the term 'Alzheimer's disease', which seems to carry less stigma. This increased public awareness has also had the result that many older people are very frightened about the possibility that they might have dementia. After some experiences, we have learned not to give false reassurance. People know only too well that something is wrong even if they seem to be functioning adequately. It is better to suggest that they talk to their GP who can do some tests or refer them for a full diagnosis. With the emergence of Memory Clinics and Assessment Centres, more GPs will be able to refer these worried people once they have checked that their memory problems are not caused by illness, stress, depression or medication.

The media, in many respects, is both raising awareness and responding to increasing public interest. Television has shown many programmes aimed at different audiences, from soaps to serious dramas and documentaries.

Perhaps one of the most significant offerings was the account of Iris Murdoch's experience of Alzheimer's disease. Her husband, John Bayley, wrote two books (1998, 2000) about their experience, which were later made into the film *Iris*, starring Dame Judi Dench.

A steady stream of novels written by friends and relatives of people with dementia has continued to appear. Two of the most significant, in the sense that they are works of literary merit, are *Have the Men had*

*Enough?* by Margaret Forster (1989) and *Scar Tissue* by Michael Ignatieff (1993). The latter book was shortlisted for the Booker prize. As referred to earlier, we are now starting to see books written by people with dementia about their experience.

As staff in the field of dementia we too have a role in making sure that we share good information when we get the chance. The vast amount of readable and authoritative material produced by the Alzheimer's Societies is freely available in many languages. It is very easy to download information from the various websites. It is well worth having a good stock of it, not least to gently put right some of the misinformation so freely available. There are still far too many people who do not understand that dementia is a disease and not part of normal ageing. Memory does seem to deteriorate in old age to a degree, although this may be more about being unable to recall things rather than their not having been recorded in the first place. Dementia is a wholly different phenomenon and is a very great deal more frightening.

## Conclusion

Good communication is central to good social work with people with dementia. In this chapter we have covered the many different people with whom social workers need to communicate as well as different methods of communication. We began with some input on how to communicate with people with dementia with different degrees of impairment and we included seeing behaviour as communication. Of course this is not limited to people with dementia. We all communicate through our behaviour. Other sections of the chapter were more practical and are included because we see social workers as needing to be reflective about communication skills in all aspects of our work.

### Further reading
Killick, J. and Allan, K. (2001) *Communication and the Care of People with Dementia*, Buckingham: Open University Press.

# SIX

# Social work assessment in a changing world

## Introduction

This chapter considers the crucial skills of assessment, which apply equally to reassessment and review. We have assumed that readers will have a basic knowledge of them and that what is needed here is a discussion of the additional issues that relate to dementia care. We have struggled to provide generally applicable information and guidance because of the considerable differences between the countries of the UK and between individual local authorities within them. We mention diagnosis again since it is an essential first step in assessment. We are very committed to shared assessments but we also provide some views on when social workers should be the lead professional. We comment on the use of forms and protocols. Naturally there is input on protection, rights and risk. We comment briefly on care management and multiple providers and provide some thoughts on admission to long-term care. The chapter concludes with a section on income maximisation, which, although not always carried out by social workers, is very important.

## Diagnosis

The importance of a good diagnosis is a recurring theme of this book and is mentioned again here because it is an integral part of assessment, indeed some local authorities require it from the GP or consultant in order for people to access services. For social workers the issue is how to ensure that this is done. A GP skilled in dementia will be able to make a diagnosis for most people. She or he should take a good history from the patient and other informants, to obtain evidence of cognitive impairment and to rule out other diagnoses. A blood test should also be done. People in the early stage, when diagnosis is very tricky, and difficult complex cases, should be referred to a consultant psychiatrist and/or neurologist.

One of the problems is the uninterested GP who does not have the skills to make the diagnosis and needs to be encouraged to make the referral. This can be a very delicate business but one at which CPNs and community nurses are real experts. Working in an integrated team alongside CPNs clearly has advantages for social workers in the dementia field. As we saw in the previous chapter, nurses and social workers come from different 'tribes'. One of the particular advantages possessed by the nurses who belong to the medical tribe is their easy access to doctors and their considerable experience in persuading them to pursue investigations.

Getting an early diagnosis is a key issue for positive and negative reasons. The positive ones are that patients and families can make plans, obtain information and receive whatever help is available. The negative is that an early diagnosis is occasionally a wrong diagnosis. A wrong diagnosis is a problem because of the implications for the patient and the family and this makes GPs understandably anxious and leads them to prevaricate.

However, the development of the cholinesterase inhibitors, controversial though they may be, has forced GPs to consider the importance of obtaining a diagnosis that differentiates Alzheimer's disease from other dementias. These drugs were initially marketed by the pharmaceutical companies as being effective in the early stages of Alzheimer's disease. Like so much about these drugs, medical opinion is now divided about their effectiveness and also about their value in the symptomatic treatment of other types of dementia.

In spite of the uncertainty surrounding them they have had one very clear beneficial result. Because they exist, carers are asking GPs to prescribe them. This has led many more GPs to refer their patients on to secondary care (consultant/hospital) level to obtain a differential diagnosis. Cholinesterase inhibitors can usually only be prescribed initially at secondary level, although once the patient has been discharged back to the primary care team the drugs come from the GP's budget.

In England and Wales, decisions about prescribing pharmaceutical drugs in terms of the cost–benefit ratio are now made by the National Institute for Clinical Excellence (NICE), set up by the government in 1997, in an attempt to address inequalities in prescribing and the 'postcode lottery', which has always bedevilled the health and social care world in the UK. This issue is what is called 'technology effectiveness guidance', which in Scotland goes out to GPs through an organisation called NHS Quality Improvement Scotland, which adds additional comments for Scotland. There is a similar process in

Northern Ireland. Social workers need to understand that dementia drugs are under constant review and that there are controls on what can be prescribed, as well as to appreciate that they only help a small minority.

## Assessment

Because assessment is such a huge topic, we focus in this chapter on assessments in the community. We would like to see multidisciplinary assessments from the outset as they have in Australia with their Aged Care Assessment Teams. In the UK social work/services departments have very different practices regarding and attitudes about how the initial point of contact is managed. Call centres receive and redirect all initial calls in some large urban authorities. In other areas there are single appointment booking systems for different client groups or the more traditional duty desks. Whatever the initial contact we must remain committed to the fullest possible assessment of people with dementia and their carers, which includes assessment of their health needs. We are aware that this is not always possible.

Staff undertaking assessments may come from a range of professional backgrounds and are often not part of a multidisciplinary team. We feel strongly that social workers should be the lead professional in complex cases and unstable situations and that from the outset we should do a full assessment rather than simply completing the forms. This will save time in the long term and is much better for the person with dementia and their family. It is not yet clear whether the increasing numbers of Community Mental Health Teams and Memory Assessment Centres/Clinics for older people will undertake more initial assessments. Clearly it would be best if they did.

Our commitment to shared assessments is based on our view that different professions each bring their different strengths. In our experience, medical and nursing staff are good at using their eyes and their nose. They can read volumes into pallor and posture. Social workers are better at using their ears. They can hear between the lines when people describe their circumstances. In general terms, most occupational therapists are good at looking too and often notice the curled-up edge of the carpet and the inaccessible controls of the fire.

The pressure on budgets has resulted in a perverse incentive on social workers to stress the difficulties and lack of ability of the person. Experienced and effective social workers have learned which 'buttons to press', competing with their colleagues to make the best case for their client. The bottom line is that social workers will not readily obtain the funding they are seeking if they paint a picture that stresses all the positive factors in the situation.

## The use of forms, protocols and dementia-specific tools

As we have discussed in Chapter Three, every local authority in the UK is now required under the SAP to have an assessment tool shared with the health authority, which means that all staff use the same form. We want to consider carefully the use of forms, rather than a looser, less structured, professional assessment since forms and protocols are now universal as a result of single shared assessment policies. There is a complex underlying issue here about whether forms are meant to be a reflection of the professional assessment or of the service user agreement.

One aspect which is universally true is that forms tend to focus very much on the problems and difficulties experienced by the person rather than what they can do and what they can contribute. The idea that people with dementia can make a valid contribution to society (the citizenship approach) is a recent development in the field. Another weakness of the forms is that they often leave out the emotional and motivational aspects of the life of the service user as well as detailed information about biography and personality, which is so vitally important. It would be good if social workers could bear in mind the specialist dementia assessment tools, which tend to identify unmet emotional needs as well as the practical ones.

## The tendency to measure only what can easily be measured

Some forms may ask whether or not you can go upstairs and whether or not you can bathe yourself. Others focus on likely causes of stress, such as incontinence or behaviour problems. However, research suggests (for example Nolan et al, 1990) that it is the carer's subjective perception of events and circumstances that is more important in determining stress, and to some extent the outcome, than the events themselves. This is very difficult to pin down on a form.

Forms are also not so good at recording the key issues of relationships and motivation. This has been found to be critical in research by Levin et al (1994). Other research (Levin and Meredith, 1988) has underlined the importance of the relationship before the onset of the disease in people's capacity to continue caring. People who said they intended to go on caring, come what may, usually were able to care for longer than those who were less certain. This sounds obvious, but a lot of research has concentrated on factors that are more measurable, such as the combination of services that enable people to carry on, rather than the motivation of the key participants.

Before Mr Broom was diagnosed with early-stage vascular dementia, his wife had become increasingly unhappy in the marriage. His daughter and her husband were very supportive so the social worker set up a care package of day and respite residential care, which should have kept the situation stable for some time. However, Mrs Broom asked for more and more days at the day centre and more frequent respite short stays. Mr Broom became very agitated, telling a care worker that he felt like an unwanted parcel being passed from hand to hand.

Eventually there was a crisis. Mrs Broom refused to take her husband home from the short stay respite because of her own ill-health and he was admitted in crisis to another home. This affected him badly. Eventually Mrs Broom admitted to the social worker that the relationship between them had irretrievably broken down before the diagnosis. So a different discussion took place, involving Mr Broom, about their future. Once he understood the truth he settled well in the new home, rather to everyone's surprise.

## Dementia-specific tools

The assessment tool *Building on Strengths* (2003) was developed by the Alzheimer's Society in collaboration with Dementia Care Matters. It provides an assessment tool that builds upon the person's existing strengths and abilities, stressing that everybody has some. It provides us with an opportunity to use the citizenship model to which we have referred in Chapter Two. A version of this tool is widely used by Alzheimer's Society branches providing day and community support.

Occupational therapists have solid experience in assessing self-care skills. The work of Jackie Pool (1999) in developing an assessment tool (PAL – Pool Activity Level) based on observation of how the person performs a domestic activity is an invaluable contribution to the field of assessment. Careful observation of a person making a cup of tea or a sandwich can give the trained occupational therapist a general idea of the stage of dementia in which the person is living. Following this assessment the occupational therapist has learned how to adapt tasks to fit changing abilities. Although not precise, tools such as this are far less intrusive and potentially humiliating than the MMSE (www.mimimental.com), which is a widely used and respected tool for measuring cognitive impairment but which is often used as if it has wider applicability.

## In which situations is social work assessment needed?

There are many different routes into the health and social care system and we need to be clear about the situations in which social workers should be the lead professionals. It seems clear to us that social workers should be completing the assessments in situations of complexity, uncertainty and change. This view is supported by the definition of social work that we quoted in the Introduction: 'The social work profession promotes social change, problem solving in human relationships and the empowerment and liberation of people to enhance well-being' (www.iassw-aiets.org).

As partnership teams, in which different professionals work together, become increasingly common, social workers face new challenges. In order to practise effectively in teams we need to be much clearer about which situations and areas of practice require us as social workers to take the lead role over health colleagues. This, in turn, leads us back to remember the value base that is specific to social work and to identify our own particular strengths and skills as a profession.

### Changing Lives *(Scottish Executive, 2006)*

This report identifies the situations where social workers are particularly well equipped to be the lead professional. These are when:

- '• The individual or family's social situation is unusually complex with a number of interacting factors affecting assessment and decision-making
- The child or adult is at risk of serious harm from others or themselves and requires skilled risk assessment and protection
- The child or adult is likely to put others at risk of harm, distress or loss and a response needs to take account of the individual's interests and welfare and the well-being of others
- The child's or adult's circumstances, including their health, finances, living conditions or social situation, are likely to cause them or others serious harm, social exclusion, reduction of life-chances

- The situation requires assessment of, and intervention in, unpredictable emotional, psychological, intra-family or social factors and responses
- Relationships, rapport and trust need to be established and maintained with a child, adult or family who find trusting relationships difficult
- There is a high level of uncertainty about the best form of intervention and/or its likely outcome
- The circumstances are such that there are significant risks in both intervening and not intervening, and fine judgment is required
- The person is facing obstacles, challenges, choices and/ or life-changes which they do not have the resources to manage without skilled support
- Prescribed or standard service responses are inadequate, and sensitive, creative and skilled work is needed to find and monitor personalised solutions and
- The child's or adult's situation is getting worse, either chronically or unpredictably, and is likely to need additions or changes to interventions.' (Scottish Executive, 2006, p 29)

The report points out that this does not mean that professional responsibility in these circumstances rests exclusively with social workers but that social workers should be involved. It all applies to work with people with dementia and may help other professionals to understand the particular knowledge, skills and approach we bring.

## Protection, rights and risk

Use of the law in relation to the care of people with dementia is about trying to achieve a balance between human rights and proper protection. In Scotland, social workers have been working within the 2000 Adults with Incapacity (Scotland) Act for some years now (implementation was phased). The principles at the start of the Act have provided very useful guidance in situations where it is not clear how to proceed. These principles in summary are:

- There shall be no intervention in the affairs of an adult unless the person responsible for authorising or effecting the intervention is satisfied that the intervention will benefit the adult and that such benefit cannot be reasonably achieved without the intervention;

- Such intervention shall be the least restrictive option in relation to the freedom of the adult, consistent with the purpose of the intervention;
- Account shall be taken of:
  - the present and past wishes and feelings of the adult so far as they can be ascertained by any means of communication, whether human or by mechanical aid (whether of an interpretive nature or otherwise) appropriate to the adult;
  - the views of the nearest relative and the primary carer of the adult, in so far as it is reasonable and practicable to do so;
  - the views of any guardian, continuing attorney or welfare attorney of the adult who has powers relating to the proposed intervention. (Summary of 2000 Adults with Incapacity (Scotland) Act, Part 1, General Principles and Fundamental Definitions)

These are very helpful principles across a range of circumstances where we, as social workers, have to work out what to do for the best and they have had a real impact in Scotland. They are very similar to the new 2005 Mental Capacity Act in England and Wales and in Northern Ireland.

We also have to bear in mind that we have a duty of care, which any court will expect to see properly exercised if the situation goes that far. This is sometimes called 'beneficence' and it means that we should always work towards the best interests of the user of our service. Alongside beneficence is 'non-maleficence', which is not doing anything that harms the person; not an easy requirement when sometimes protection can be harmful in some ways. And into this complex set of moral imperatives there is also justice: that we should aim to be fair.

There are no easy answers but the principles of the legislation and these most-used moral imperatives are a good place to start. Simply clarifying the situation and the occasions where rights and risk conflict can be helpful.

Mr Sexton illustrates dilemmas very familiar to social workers in dementia care. For example, how do you decide when you are unreasonably restricting someone like Mr Sexton?

He was a big, energetic man who walked constantly, often getting lost and having to be brought home by the police. His wife, who was a good deal less fit than he was, walked with him until she was exhausted. She resorted to locking the front door and pretending she had lost the key. He became very aggressive and restless. The day centre could not manage him either. They felt unhappy at having to lock their doors, which restricted the other members. The day hospital was only able to keep Mr Sexton for assessment and diagnosis. Mrs Sexton became ill, probably through stress, and Mr Sexton has now been admitted to a nursing home where they have a digital lock and all the other doors have buzzers on them. He has made it very clear that he resents this restriction on his liberty, often becoming very angry. Seldom does he get very far, although he seems to get wings on his feet when he does manage to leave. Staff try to take him for walks and outings whenever they can. The nursing home is in another town, so he would never be able to find his way back to either his own home or the nursing home.

How are we to achieve a balance between Mr Sexton's civil liberties and the need to protect him from harm?

Contrast Mr Sexton with Mrs Lauder who has always lived at the same end of a small town as the care home where she is resident. She is always able to find her way back to the care home or be helped by locals who know her.

Another contrast is with Mr Deans who is the kind of example more often quoted because he represents the most feared outcome of the policy of leaving the doors of the care home open. He left his care home and was found dead the following day. Because staff have a duty of care, if the case ended up in court, they would have to show that they had completed a full risk assessment. This would be demonstrated by examination of records as well as interviews with the staff.

## Freedom of information

European legislation, which has a general application, has impacted on social care in unexpected ways. The passing of the Data Protection Act in 1998 and the 2000 Freedom of Information Act gave people the right to know the information that is held about them by public and private bodies. It tried to strike a balance between the rights of individuals and the sometimes competing interests of those with legitimate reasons for using personal information, which covers both facts and opinions about the individual. It has clear guiding principles. The data must be:

- fairly and lawfully processed
- processed for limited purposes
- adequate, relevant and not excessive
- accurate and be up to date
- not kept longer than necessary
- processed in accordance with the individual's rights
- secure
- not transferred to countries outside the European Union unless the country has adequate protection for the individual. (Summary of 1998 Data Protection Act, Schedule 1, Part 1)

The Information Commissioner's office is an independent regulator set up to deal with complaints under the Freedom of Information Act, the Environmental Information Regulations and the Data Protection Act. The Data Protection Act impacted on the work of social workers among others when it was passed, because it meant that we need the consent of the person to process information.

The fact that records are now expected to be read and agreed by the respondent can further inhibit the use of professional experience and expertise. In the case of dementia where the person may lack the capacity to read, understand or convey their consent, it is common practice for the carer to act on their behalf when assessment forms have to be completed. As we hear more of the voices of people with dementia themselves, this common practice is beginning to feel inadequate. Whose needs are we actually assessing? Are social workers really expressing the needs of the person with dementia or are we expressing the needs filtered through the experience of the carers?

Staff would also have to show that unreasonable restrictions were not in force, in line with the policy on the Protection of Vulnerable Adults.

## Mental Health Acts

Within the UK there are three laws concerning mental health: the 1983 Mental Health Act (England and Wales); the 1986 Mental Health (Northern Ireland) Order; and the 2003 Mental Health (Care and Treatment) (Scotland) Act. The last of these is the one that has been most recently revised. The 1983 Mental Health Act for England and Wales is under review.

The legislation exists to make the difficult judgements about civil liberties versus protection – the rights versus risks issue – with which many staff are still wrestling. We sincerely hope that the 21st-century legal reforms will result in the better protection of the human rights of people with dementia in all the countries of the UK and make the job of taking very difficult decisions easier for all professionals working in this field.

Assisting with difficult decisions on when to detain people is the daily bread and butter of approved social workers/mental health officers and a discussion with them is always useful. No law will ever be perfect. But it is not sensible to take the stand that says that people with dementia should never be subject to mental health legislation. There is a curious ageism about this. Some approved social workers, used to working with adults of working age with mental illness, are extremely reluctant to apply the force of the law to a little old lady with dementia, even though she is putting herself seriously at risk by her behaviour, because it seems to them to be too draconian. Conversely, many staff are unwilling to put the time and effort required into considering the mental health legislation for an older person, whereas they would not hesitate for a younger person at similar risk.

## Are we assessing needs, risk or available services?

There is an important question to be considered about what and why we are assessing. Are we assessing need or risk? Are we assessing it in order to meet it or to ration what is available? Manthorpe (2004), in an excellent chapter on risk-taking and dementia, asserts that, because of high thresholds before entitlement to social care services and the rationing of health care, 'managing risk has replaced meeting need as a key objective' (p 139). We need to be clear about this because if it is risk we are assessing rather than need, we need to be transparent about it.

## Risk assessment

Manthorpe (2004) points out that there are two ways of looking at risk: one is danger and the other is liberation. She reminds us that the 'acceptance of risk is becoming synonymous with adult status' (p 137). A focus on danger all the time can result in diminishing the personhood of people with dementia by treating them as less than fully adult. We always need to be able to ask whose needs are being met: the person with dementia, the relative or the staff?

This is where the issue of risk assessment is so important. A careful assessment of the identified risks, including the strengths as well as the weaknesses of the person and their situation, will go a long way to reducing the anxieties of staff and relatives and will make it possible to reach agreement on the way forward. It is this anxiety that has traditionally driven staff and relatives to err on the side of caution, supporting measures that deprive people of choice and liberty in an attempt to keep them safe. The careful recording and sharing of the risk assessment with all involved is vital.

Manthorpe (2004, p 141) reminds us that risk assessment is 'as much an art as a science in that it builds on shaky and incomplete evidence bases and incorporates values and images, emotions and contexts'. Some risks are given much more attention than others. People who cannot work their cookers and people who go out for walks in the middle of the night raise considerable anxiety whereas the risks of loneliness, isolation and boredom are of less concern. Similarly, the risks at home are generally of more concern than the risks of long-term care in spite of evidence of risk of depression, for example.

Although the assessment forms have a set of boxes to tick, giving the social worker a final risk score total, it is important not to focus too much on this. Rather we should be looking at ways of reducing the risk in order to help the person to maintain their independence. It may actually be helpful to write a risk reduction plan. It is often helpful to discuss a risk assessment with a colleague – two heads are better than one and someone else may well have a different perception of acceptable risk.

Having completed a full risk assessment in this way the social worker should find it much easier to put the case for preserving the choice and independence of the person with dementia to their carers. Many carers are so concerned for the person's safety that they can lose sight of well-being and quality of life altogether. There is no such thing as a risk-free environment, even for newborn babies, but many carers strive desperately to achieve one. If people with dementia are going to enjoy their best possible degree of well-being they must be allowed to take some risks. It is very important to have as much information as possible in order to complete a holistic assessment of risk in the context of well-being.

Most social workers are now very familiar with risk assessment. However, they may be less familiar with dementia-specific risk assessment. We have already referred to *Building on Strengths* (Alzheimer's Society and Dementia Care Matters, 2003), which has a good section on this subject including forms that can be adapted to the specific situation.

## Areas of particular concern in dementia assessment

*Translating difficulties into need for services*

> Miss Harris, who we met in Chapter Three, became more paranoid as her dementia progressed. She was unable to explain to herself why she constantly lost her keys, her purse and her groceries and blamed the woman upstairs. She began to believe that the woman upstairs had magical powers to penetrate her walls and sneak in to steal her belongings. She said she could manage on her pension, but was unable to go out of the house to do her shopping in case the neighbours slipped in and robbed her.
>
> What did Miss Harris need? She claimed she needed nothing except the removal of her neighbour upstairs. Another neighbour, who was constantly being disturbed by Miss Harris to help her find her keys or her purse, said that she thought Miss Harris needed to be assessed to see if her paranoia could be treated. This neighbour also wanted Miss Harris talked into a frame of mind where she would accept help with her shopping and meals.

> Mrs Dvorjak gives us another example. She is incontinent and clearly needs help, but does she need a better sign on her toilet, or a downstairs toilet, incontinence aids or treatment for a urinary tract infection? A form that lists difficulties does not tell you much about needs. Mrs Dvorjak might be depressed or demoralised, and therefore she is not motivated to go to the toilet. There might be several ways of helping her with her depression and low morale, which might ultimately improve her incontinence.

*People with dementia have constantly changing needs*

Many couples manage to cope by sharing a delicate blend of skills; sometimes the physically disabled but mentally alert person is the brain and the other, with dementia, is the arms and legs. If the physically disabled one becomes ill a previous assessment becomes redundant overnight. A few weeks later the status quo is restored but perhaps there is a loss of nerve in either or both. People with dementia function a lot less well when they are anxious, and sometimes a disturbance to a familiar routine may cause such anxiety that they never fully recover past competence.

## Many people with dementia refuse services

Much of this is related to fear. They know that their ability to cope is on a knife-edge and they have often developed their own elaborate ways of remembering. Often these are about having everything they need in plain sight, so there are piles of food and clothes on every available space inside the house. If these were tidied away they would be lost. They are also, probably rightly, afraid that if an outsider knew how poorly they were coping they would not be allowed to continue as they are.

> Miss Harris would probably have said that she needs nothing except the removal of her upstairs neighbour, although it might have been just possible to get her to admit her distress at her failing memory. She had everything she needed for her meals lined up on her sofa where she could see it. This looked chaotic to outsiders since it included empty packets to remind her that they were finished.

It can be too easy to accept the refusal of services by someone with dementia as something about which nothing can be done until there is a crisis. The key to working with someone who refuses services is, as usual, about building up a relationship of trust. Wiggins and Fahy (2005, p 149) describe their approach as phases and the first step of the initial phase is: 'Win a level of baseline trust, so that the client will comfortably allow us into their homes instead of being suspicious of us. Sometimes it takes weeks of visits, where we are just chatting at the front door, before we are allowed into the house. Our staff need a mixture of skill, charm, and perseverance as they try to find ways to engage the client at that stage'.

They are talking about home care staff and these may be the right people to break down the barriers of fear and mistrust in the first place. Community support workers attached to CMHTs are also excellent people to carry out this role. We need to be able to explain this to managers of social work who often have unreasonable expectations of how quickly an assessment can be done and can accept service refusal as a reason for doing nothing given the pressures they are under.

## The capacity of people with dementia to perform for a short period

Many people with dementia are able to rally all their resources to appear mentally competent for the duration of a meeting, which they understand to be important. This is intensely exasperating for the carer who then has to convince the person doing the assessment that the person with dementia is not usually so competent. This is awkward for carers who can feel very disloyal. A longer visit is often a way round this since few people with moderate-to-advanced dementia can sustain such an effort for more than an hour.

> The social worker met Mr Harrold for the first time when he was in the assessment ward of the psychiatric hospital. She observed that he was sweating profusely. He made a point of addressing each nurse by name as they came past. Aware that his memory was being tested and that decisions about his future depended on the outcome of the assessment, he had written down the names and learned them off by heart. He made a supreme effort and held it together for the 15 minutes of their conversation. Some time later, his daughter showed the social worker the list.

## Some carers do not even see themselves as carers

Often people are not consciously aware that they have needs of their own until the whole process of assessment leads them to stop and confront the reality of their situation. Some have not liked to face the fact that the person they are caring for might be ill rather than simply old; for them the possibility that their relative may have a very trying terminal illness may be too much to bear. Similarly, people with dementia may not have stopped to consider their own needs or those of their relative. They are likely to know that something is wrong with their brain but often they have not faced up to it, far less talked about it.

> Mrs Bianco had wholly unrealistic expectations of what her daughter would be able to do for her either at the present time or when her dementia had progressed. Her CPN had to get mother and daughter together for a discussion in which the daughter was encouraged and supported to set limits. The planning of the help Mrs Bianco needed

was then on a much more open and practical level. This stood them both in good stead as time passed.

The whole process of assessment can be therapeutic if the person doing it has the necessary skills. It can provide the opportunity to review what is going on and the carer and the cared-for to address their needs, either together or separately. The fact that carers have a legal right to an assessment of their own needs makes it easier for social workers to embark on this delicate work.

Working with people with dementia and their carers is highly skilled and potentially very harassing, although it has huge rewards. Assessment is one of those intervention points with great potential to be a positive or a negative experience. Workers who wander into assessment without having thought through what might happen are unwise, and may find themselves unable to take advantage of the therapeutic 'windows of opportunity'. At the very least we should think through, before the assessment visit, what we would do if the person with dementia asks about the diagnosis; the carer confesses that they are not coping; they both get into an argument about how much trouble the person with dementia is causing for the carer – and so on. Joint visits with an experienced worker are an excellent way to learn.

## Moving into long-term care

At the beginning of this chapter we looked at current attempts to identify the situations in which social workers will always be involved. One of these is when there is a question of a move out of home into long-term care. This is a very major life event for the person with dementia and their carers. For any of us, moving house is one of the most traumatic events but moving into a care home has all sorts of associated implications of failure and being the last move of life. Ideally, the role of the social worker is to assist the family to match the person with the place or to do it ourselves. From the point of view of someone with dementia, considerations such as a familiar locality, skillful staff, a compatible style of life and a 'legible design' are all important. Explaining it all to someone with dementia may be a really hard test of communication skills. Time for visits to allay anxieties is important and can be much easier if the person with dementia has already been in the place for day or respite care. Trial periods can be helpful and reduce anxiety. Ideally there is a brochure explaining at what stage (if at all) residents have to move on to another home, and the extent to which the person can go on doing what they have always done (like going to the pub or the shops).

The ideal move is a planned one, with time to choose what is taken into the home. It is important for most people with dementia to be surrounded by familiar furniture and objects. You may have to insist on this since most homes will only welcome pictures, ornaments and perhaps a chair. Many relatives are self-conscious about the shabby state of the furniture of the person with dementia.

> Mr Strang had been an itinerant labourer in the Australian outback. His room in the care home had a lino floor with a camp bed and a few shabby shelves for his meagre belongings. He felt very much at home in it.

The person with dementia may need some ritual of departure like saying goodbye to neighbours. Photographs are useful at this stage (see Chapter Seven) to reinforce the event and to provide a subsequent reminder. Our role as social workers is often to make sure that the care home knows enough about the person in terms of biography, preferences, key people and the reasons for some behaviour that may be misunderstood. We discuss this in more detail in Chapter Nine.

Sadly, many moves are very hasty. A relative turns up from overseas and decides her mother cannot remain at home any longer; or there is a crisis either for the person with dementia (such as getting lost on the way home from the shops) or for the carer. Many crises relate to health and going into a home from hospital can happen without any choice or due process at all. Social workers get much criticism for holding up hospital discharges while proper arrangements are made and often we have to cave in to pressures to release beds. English social services departments are charged by the day by NHS Trusts for anyone occupying an acute bed who is ready for discharge. This has led to some very unsatisfactory interim moves before a final placement. Practice has become less stringent over time. However, from 2007 the policy includes people with mental as well as physical health problems. Rehabilitation is still sadly less likely to be given to patients with dementia, so they are often more disabled than they need to be.

Sometimes social workers have to do the rituals of departure retrospectively. Some people with dementia constantly try to get out of homes until they have been taken back to their house and are able to come to terms with the fact that they can no longer manage to live there. Very occasionally they are sufficiently restored to health that they can return to their own home. Besides insisting that every effort is made to enable the person to stay at home, our role is often to make sure that there is an understandable process for the person with dementia so that they are not constantly bewildered and bereft.

## Care management: multiple providers

In Chapter Three we referred to the main trend of care management being towards packages of care assembled from multiple providers, the aim being the best value in both cost and effectiveness terms. This can be problematic for people with dementia.

Mrs Fortune received 'support' from a daily visit from a support worker who was not able to undertake personal care. This was provided by a private company funded by the local authority as part of free personal care to help her up in the morning and in to bed at night. A voluntary organisation provided a shopping service, for which she had been financially assessed, and another agency provided day opportunities once a week in the form of a befriender. Mrs Fortune was completely bamboozled by the plethora of well-meaning visitors; there were 10 different people coming and going each week.

Other negative outcomes include the fact that providers can be smaller agencies with few opportunities for training and poor conditions of service for staff, or even individuals with no protection against exploitation at all. The emphasis on cost and charging was not, we think, fully understood prior to the implementation of the NHS and Community Care Act in April 1993. Perhaps more positively, there has been an incredible change since then in the availability of flexible services – including services that cover the weekends and overnight, if you are lucky enough to live where services are well developed. A real postcode lottery of dementia services is emerging.

Mrs Williamson illustrates how people can remain in the community with a lot of services, if they operate in the evening and at weekends, although rarely without the help of neighbours and family. Mrs Williamson was an 84-year-old diabetic woman with dementia. Some days she was very alert, but most of the time she was very confused, often failing to use the toilet so her flat could be very unpleasant. She lived alone on the third floor of a small block of flats in an overspill estate with neighbours who had moved in at the same time some 25 years ago.

None of her four children remained local although one son visited most weekends.

Her care plan consisted of four days of day care (in two different day centres, since no local day centre in her area operated more than two days a week), a daily home carer on weekdays, a putting-to-bed service every day, mobile domiciliary help at weekends and regular visits from her district nurse for her diabetes. In spite of this range of help the neighbours were called upon at all times of the day and night. Luckily one was a nurse, but she sometimes resented the intrusion in spite of being very fond of Mrs Williamson.

It is also true that in the days before care management individual social workers were totally unaware of the cost (per day and per head) of the services that they were offering. The devolving of budgets to the most local level possible was part of a policy to make social work teams accountable for the public money that they were spending on behalf of the service users/clients. This, in itself, has brought with it a great feeling of pressure as very difficult choices are made between people who badly need services. There never seem to be enough services or enough money to go round. The myth that care in the community is a cheap alternative to residential care has been exposed in work with all groups of service users.

Dementia is a challenging field to work in because it raises a host of ethical issues as well as practical ones. How much self-determination is reasonable?

There is no easy answer to this. Like all ethical issues the answer is a balance; in this case between the right to self-determination and the right to care and protection. Ethical questions need to be asked constantly by teams of staff as well as by individuals.

Miss Harris, for example, who we met earlier, wanted to be left alone. There was clearly a danger of malnutrition and self-neglect. If she was allowed to choose to remain at home and was later found dead, the staff who were visiting her might have been in some difficulty with their managers if they had different views of the balance between the right to self-determination and the duty of care. Would Miss Harris accept the concept of a 'companion'?

# Income maximisation

This is another important area in the lives of people with dementia and their carers where assessment is a crucial part of the process. Social workers will make sure that an income check is carried out as part of the assessment process.

Being old in the UK means you have a good chance of being on a low income (Phillips et al, 2006). Many people on pensions are living on an income just above Pension Credit levels because they have a small occupational pension or some savings. Very few people on pensions have incomes anywhere near the average wage. This means that constant vigilance is required by workers to ensure that basic benefits are claimed as soon as people become eligible.

Many people with dementia have very great difficulty in understanding the constantly changing benefit system and may require the help of an appointee. Carers may find the whole business too humiliating. You may find someone who is unwilling to claim because they have claimed before and been turned down. This makes people feel as if they have been trying to fiddle the system and they require a lot of support to try again.

Although filling in forms for the Benefits Agency is no longer regarded as part of the core task of social workers, it is the social worker's responsibility to ensure that people are maximising their finances, which means they must be made aware of their entitlements. If necessary they should be signposted to a local agency that does provide this service.

## *Providing as much detailed information as possible*

There are benefits that are available because someone needs care in the household. 'As a minimum, Attendance Allowance or the Disability Living Allowance care component should usually be claimed by all people with dementia, and carers should check their entitlement to Carer's Allowance' (Alzheimer's Society Information Sheet, 2005, www.alzheimers.org.uk). It is important that these are claimed by all those entitled to them. People need to spell out on the form, in precise detail, the help that is required.

> For example, rather than saying that Mrs Murdoch needs help in toileting, it is better to say that Mrs Murdoch needs help going to the toilet 12 times during the day and four times at night.

People with dementia may need quite a lot of help to understand forms. Often it is necessary to find someone they trust to help them. People who are losing their memories can become very anxious and suspicious, presumably because they know they are not in full control of their lives anymore.

## Obtaining advice in individual cases

Benefits Agency offices or Jobcentre Plus offices stock explanatory leaflets and forms and can also provide information over the telephone and send the appropriate forms. They may also be able to arrange for a representative to visit the person at home if they cannot get out. The Department for Work and Pensions also has a useful website that includes information on benefits (www.dwp.gov.uk) where people can download claim forms. For advice on the state pension and related benefits go to www.thepensionservice.gov.uk. The Benefits Enquiry Line is a national telephone advice and information service for people with disabilities including dementia, their carers and representatives.

Benefits Enquiry Line advisors have no access to people's personal records but can give general advice and send you the relevant claim forms and they have a forms completion service for advice on filling in claim forms for some disability benefits. However, they may lack the specialist knowledge of the dementia organisations. The Welfare Rights sections of social services departments have been drastically scaled down or axed altogether in many areas. If you are fortunate enough to have such a resource locally, the staff will be extremely experienced and can provide great support. In other cases the Citizens Advice Bureau (CAB) and generic voluntary organisations for the support of older people such as Help the Aged or Age Concern can advise.

## Help for people for whom English is an additional language

It is often difficult for people who are not fluent in English to discover what benefits they can claim. It is vital that they get appropriate assistance. There may be someone within their own community/ language group who can assist them in getting information and advice. The local Race Equality Council or CAB is a good place to start. The Benefits Enquiry Line can offer help to people who are not fluent in English. Some Benefits Agency offices now have access to a telephone interpreting service run by an outside company offering a wide variety of languages. As we have said, as social workers we need to know the common minority languages spoken in our area. Some leaflets are now translated into Arabic, Bengali, Cantonese, Gujerati, Punjabi, Somali, Urdu, Vietnamese and Welsh. Audio versions may be available, as well as printed versions, from your local Benefits Agency office.

## Appeals

The benefits world is difficult. Carers have to take a deep breath and apply, and be ready to appeal. They may need help and support to stick with it especially if they have been refused in the past. As we have said, the more detail given when the person applies the more chance of success. People also need to be encouraged to appeal if they are turned down because eligibility hangs on the arbitrary interpretation of words like 'requires frequent attention' or 'for a significant part of the day'. For this reason, having someone to help with an appeal makes a real difference.

The Alzheimer's Societies produce excellent fact sheets, which are obtainable online as well as through local branches and national offices. It is worth checking online to make sure that the advice you have is up to date. The national offices of the major voluntary organisations are meticulous about making sure that these are updated whenever changes are made. However, local groups may be run by volunteers who may not always have the most recent changes. Benefits are often changed so that making sure your information is up to date is very important.

## Specific benefits

The following, more detailed, information is taken from the Alzheimer's Society Information Sheet on Benefits (2005), www.alzheimers.org.

### *Attendance Allowance and Disability Living Allowance*

Attendance Allowance is payable if the person is over 65 when their disability affects them and Disability Living Allowance if they are under 65 when that happens. Disability Living Allowance has two components: mobility and care. It is the latter which is applicable to people with dementia. The person is likely to qualify for the top rates of Attendance Allowance or Disability Living Allowance care component if they need frequent help or prompting with personal care or supervision for prolonged periods or several times during the night.

They are likely to qualify for the lower rate of Attendance Allowance or middle rate of Disability Living Allowance care component if they need frequent help with personal care or supervision either during the day *or* the night. They may qualify for the lower rate of Disability Living Allowance if they can show that they need help with personal care for some of the day or cannot prepare a main cooked meal for themselves without assistance.

Application forms now come in a pack. The form is completed by or on behalf of the person receiving care. It includes details of the person's GP and other professionals who can be contacted about the person's level of disability and contains a section to be completed by the person who knows them best – their carer if they have one. There are always delays with receipt of Attendance Allowance/Disability Living Allowance and you may need to warn the carers about this. The carer may also need to be warned that local authorities' social work/services departments will probably charge for their services. They also need to be aware of the following information about Attendance Allowance/Disability Living Allowance:

- Benefits are paid in the name of the person and not the carer.
- They are tax free and do not depend on National Insurance contributions.
- Payment is not affected by the person's savings nor usually by their income.
- A medical examination is not normally required.
- They are paid at different rates, depending on the person's needs.
- They can be claimed whether the person lives alone, with their family, or with other people.
- Unlike Disability Living Allowance, the Attendance Allowance does not have a mobility component.

### Pension Credit

This is an entitlement for people aged 60 and over, introduced in 2003. It has two parts: Guarantee Credit and Savings Credit. Some people are entitled to both parts while others are entitled to only one.

Guarantee Credit replaces Minimum Income Guarantee (formerly Income Support) and works in the same way, by topping up a person's income to a set level. Savings Credit is extra money for people aged over 65 who have income above the basic retirement pension level or who have savings or investments. It is based on the total amount of income that a person has, including income received from private or occupational pensions.

You may find you have to advise people to claim their Pension Credit. Pensioners are major under-claimers even of this very basic benefit.

### Council Tax Benefit

If a person with dementia is severely impaired he or she may be able to get Council Tax exemption. The local Council Tax office will advise.

### The Social Fund

This fund can help people with low incomes and limited savings to meet certain extra expenses. Loans and community care grants from the Fund are discretionary. There is no standard amount awarded and savings above a certain amount may affect the amount the person receives. Benefits that may be paid from the Social Fund include:

- cold weather payments;
- funeral expenses;
- community care grants;
- budgeting loans;
- crisis loans.

### Carer's Allowance

Formerly known as the Invalid Care Allowance, this benefit can be paid to carers who spend at least 35 hours a week looking after someone receiving Attendance Allowance or Disability Living Allowance care component at the high or middle rate. The carer does not have to be related to or living with the person they care for. It does not depend on past payment of National Insurance contributions but it is taxable.

If the carer is under the age of the State Pension it gives them a National Insurance credit each week to help protect their rights to the State Pension. Carers must be aged over 16 when they first claim. In some cases, the person being cared for could lose some of their benefits if the carer claims.

If carers earn more than a limited amount each week after the deduction of allowable expenses, if they are in full-time education or if they are receiving more than a specified amount from certain other pensions or benefits, they cannot claim the Carer's Allowance. However, they may receive an extra premium if they are receiving certain other benefits, such as Income Support or Pension Credit.

It is very important that they seek advice before applying. Carers aged over 60 do not get any extra money but they will get an underlying entitlement to a carer's discount with Council Tax.

It is one thing to know what benefits are available; it is quite another to persuade people to claim them. The principles and the rules of eligibility for benefits are formidably complex and deter many people from making a claim. One of the most useful ways of motivating them to try is to get the support of a body such as a carers' group. Discussion of benefits and the realisation that other people have gone through the hoops, sometimes successfully, can give carers confidence because it diminishes the stigma. Workers in the field can cajole at length but it really needs someone in a similar position to show the way.

## Conclusion

This chapter on diagnosis, assessment and income maximisation has proved difficult because of the wide range of policies and protocols. We have tried to emphasise the integral role of diagnosis and to identify the key circumstances where the lead professional in an assessment needs to be a social worker. We have looked at the strengths and weaknesses of shared documentation, however desirable and necessary it is. We have also explored the fact that there are particular difficulties in assessing people with dementia.

### Further reading

Scottish Executive (2006) *Changing Lives: The Report of the 21st Century Social Work Review*, Edinburgh: The Stationery Office.

# SEVEN

# The care environment

## Introduction

This chapter covers four issues: food and drink, design, photography and assistive technology, which we feel are particularly important in dementia care. None of them are fields where the social worker is usually the expert, but social workers need to be sufficiently aware of their significance to alert or seek advice from other professionals.

## Food and drink

Food and drink play a big part in any work with people with dementia and their carers. In fact they play a big part in all our lives but we are so accustomed to them that we give them little thought most of the time. You will recall that food and drink were shown in Figure 4.1 in Chapter Four to illustrate the social approach to dementia. Here we take the three approaches to dementia (medical, social and citizenship) and apply them to food and drink to try and bring some order to a complex issue. This same approach has been taken in *Food, Glorious Food* (Marshall, 2003c), which is not a book specifically for social workers, but it does provide lots of ideas for readers who are interested in this issue. The Alzheimer's Society has an excellent project called Food for Thought (2004c), which provides a set of leaflets which social workers can recommend to carers (www.alzheimers.org.uk). Other useful material includes VOICES (1998), Crawley (2000), Marshall (2003a, 2003b) and Berg (2006).

The medical approach to food and drink and dementia reminds us that there are physical and psychological consequences of both undernutrition and dehydration. Both exacerbate cognitive impairment. Lack of sufficient liquid is especially important (Archibald, 2005) because it so quickly leads to infections such as urinary tract infections, which can cause delirium on top of dementia. Both are implicated in constipation, which can hugely diminish the functioning and well-being of someone with dementia. Meals with enough roughage and at least eight cups of liquid a day are essential. Another problem can be that many people with dementia need their food to be tastier either with spices, salt or sugar. Indeed they may develop a really sweet tooth and cause great concern at their unwillingness to eat a full meal. Sweet food can be made nutritious by imaginative care staff or carers; battles about eating the savoury courses are rarely productive. Social workers sometimes neglect both undernutrition and dehydration when doing assessments, which is yet another reason for collaborative working.

The medical approach would remind us to bear in mind the hearing and sight impairments of older people. People with dementia may be overwhelmed by noise and be unable to concentrate on eating. They may be unable to see the food on the plate or the plate on the table. More light and more colour contrast between the food and the plate and the plate and the table are the ways to resolve this. Mouth ulcers and painful dentures are also often missed unless staff are alert to their significance.

The medical approach would understandably be concerned with issues such as swallowing and there is a very good video/DVD *Oh Good, Lunch is Coming* (Dementia Services Development Centre, 2003), which explains why this can be problematic and how to provide the appropriate food.

The social approach focuses more on mealtimes and actually getting people to eat. Quite often it is not the availability of food and drink that is the issue but getting the unwilling person with dementia to take them. Mealtimes are one aspect. We know that people with dementia manage best when they are using well-learned skills, so making meals and mealtimes as familiar as possible is important. Social workers may need to find out what the habits and preferences of the person were in the past. Did they have a sandwich lunch at work, did they always lay the table with a tablecloth and salt and pepper, did they always have an appetizer, did they always go to the toilet and wash their hands before lunch and so on?

People with dementia can be easily distracted in noisy dining rooms in day centres, hospitals and care homes (Calkins and Brush, 2003). Social workers may need to suggest to staff that the person or a small group may need a smaller, quieter place if they are to eat well. Some will eat better if a communal dining room looks more like a cafe, which makes communal eating familiar.

Mr Rienhoff refused to drink in his care home, which was causing a lot of concern. The staff had been working for some time with the help of a local school to make an unused lounge into a 1940s cafe. When it

opened Mr Rienhoff knew instantly how to behave. He ordered coffee
and cake and drank without hesitation.

Cafes and restaurants also know how to make food look good and to
make the whole experience a pleasure, which is a useful set of
considerations for people with dementia.

Some people with dementia can no longer manage to sit at a table
to eat. They may be self-conscious about their diminishing skills in
table manners, if these have always been very important to them, or
they may be too anxious and restless. Finger food is now usually
available in communal settings although occasionally social workers
may need to insist that it is. Enticing, moist and easy-to-eat sandwiches,
nourishing kinds of cakes such as banana and carrot, tray bakes and
nibbles provided frequently throughout the day can help people to
eat plenty even if they cannot sit down at a table with others. Newton
and Stewart (1997) provide some really useful guidance.

In communal settings there is a potential for food to be an activity
yet it is rarely realised. There is planning, shopping, preparation, cooking,
table laying, eating (perhaps themed around festivals or countries),
clearing, tidying up, washing up and putting away. There are masses of
social benefits too. If you ask any of your clients about their experience
of the help they receive, they are almost certain to say they are bored
and would like to help more. Food and drink provide good
opportunities for helping and you may need to make this point where
possible.

Helping people with dementia who live on their own at home to
eat and drink well is really hard. Delivered meals are often unsatisfactory.
They come in containers that make no sense to the person with
dementia. They often need to be eaten right away rather than put to
one side for later. Some people are accustomed to eating with others
and simply fail to eat on their own. Others need more cues, such as
the place laid, before they recall what to do. Some people forget to
shop, or do not remember whether they have eaten. Others can no
longer work the cooker and they live on biscuits and cake. Sometimes
the problem lies with home care staff who may not be allocated enough
time to sit and eat with someone or who may not know how to cook
nourishing meals. Many well-meaning home care staff, for example,
buy fat-free food as 'healthy options' without understanding that older
people need full-cream milk and butter to get as many nutrients as
possible.

Social workers need to be alert to the reasons why people do not eat well at home and to use imagination and determination in their care planning. Imagination because there may be clever ways of resolving problems such as involving the local pub. Rarely does a meals service or a shopping service alone fix it. Determination because there may be problems in how home care is organised or commissioned and arguments may have to be assembled to change practice. Eating with someone else is often the answer but it is very difficult to organise. There is a dearth of literature on how to help people with dementia who live at home to eat and drink well.

The citizenship approach, with its focus on communication, reminds us to consider that eating and drinking provide opportunities for communication. Earlier we met two people with dementia who used food to communicate.

Mrs Hughes communicated her grief through food, and Mr Allan used food refusal as a way of communicating his anger and frustration. When Mr Allan was a child, his grandmother, who ran the household, would serve the same meal again and again until it was eaten. Mealtimes were a battle of wills, which he always lost. They continued to have a high emotional component for the rest of his life.

Staff and carers too communicate how much they care in the attention they put into food and drink. A meal that is plonked down in front of someone and removed half an hour later communicates loudly a lack of individual care.

We may also need to be reminded about the potential of food and drink for enabling people with dementia to give to us rather than the other way around. Do we provide opportunities for them to give us a cup of tea or a piece of cake? In the psychiatric units for people with dementia and behaviour that challenges in New South Wales (CADE [Confused and Disturbed Elderly] units) the staff and residents make all the meals together.

When a visitor entered the unit a lady rushed to make the British guest a cup of tea even though she was far too impaired to join the conversation or even to sit still and join her with the tea.

Food and drink also provide opportunities for 'agency', that crucial process of being able to make things happen for yourself. People with dementia can choose what they want to eat and drink if choices are made in a way they understand. This often means showing them the actual meal. Social workers may be the only professionals who fully understand the importance of agency and may have to insist that choices are given in a real rather than a token way.

## Design

Most people working with people with dementia will have given little thought to the design of buildings such as day centres and care homes unless they are particularly terrible or unless the social worker is a commissioner or on the staff of the Care Commission. As social workers we are not trained to see and understand the built environment yet it can be crucial in the extent to which the person with dementia can manage independently. R. Powell Lawton (Scheidt and Windley, 2003), the father of environmental gerontology, came up with the concept of 'environmental press', which means that the more impaired you are, the greater the importance of your built environment. This is clearest in the case of someone with mobility problems. If the building has stairs and steps then the less mobile person is effectively more disabled than they need to be. The same applies to cognitive impairment. Unfamiliar and confusing buildings cause disability. If people can find their way easily around a building, especially finding the toilet, then they will be less disabled.

It is worth mentioning here sight and hearing impairment. There are some useful texts on this by Brawley (1997), Calkins (2001) and Koncelik (2003). Visual impairment is common in very old people. Diminishing vision, glaucoma, tunnel vision and so on result in people being unable to see their environment clearly. Plenty of light is an obvious way to help. Colour becomes less important for orientation as the ability to differentiate colour diminishes in most older people; colour contrast thereby becomes more important. Landmarks are probably more useful than either colour or colour contrast and, if you think about it, most of us orientate by landmarks. When we are in a strange hotel with identical carpets and corridors we often remember our room because it is near a window or a fire extinguisher. Hearing also becomes more impaired (Koncelik, 2003). Presbycusis is another unpleasant and common ailment, which is the diminished ability to differentiate sound frequencies so all sounds come at once. This can be very disabling indeed and we need to ensure that environments for people with dementia are quiet so they can hear only what they need or want to hear. People with dementia have the same hearing and sight impairments as any other older person; what they lack is an understanding of them and an ability to learn ways of compensating for them.

There is a general international consensus on dementia design and there is now quite a substantial literature (Calkins, 1988; Cohen and Weisman, 1991; Cohen and Day, 1993; Netten, 1993; Hiatt, 1995; Centre for Accessible Environments, 1998; Judd et al, 1998; Day et al, 2000; Cantley and Wilson, 2003) for those who are particularly interested in this area. There are two ways of approaching the issue: one is in terms of principles, which can then be applied to any building or feature, and the other is in terms of features, which may be more applicable but inevitably cannot cover everything.

Many authors have made lists of principles, which are more or less the same and a slightly amended example from Judd et al (1998) is as follows:

- Design should compensate for impairments.
- Design should maximise independence.
- Design should enhance self-esteem and confidence.
- Design should demonstrate care for staff.
- Design should be orientating and understandable.
- Design should reinforce personal identity.
- Design should welcome relatives and the local community.
- Design should allow the control of stimuli.

The same book gives a list of design features:

- small size;
- familiar, domestic, homely in style;
- plenty of scope for ordinary activities (unit kitchens, washing lines, garden sheds);
- unobtrusive concern for safety;
- different rooms for different functions;
- age-appropriate furniture and fittings;
- safe outside space;
- single rooms big enough for lots of personal belongings;
- good signage and multiple cues where possible (for example, sight, smell, sound);
- use of objects rather than colour for orientation;
- enhancement of visual access;
- controlled stimuli, especially noise.

It all seems quite straightforward but it is, in fact, really challenging. Domestic style, for example, means that it will look like a real home, not easy when you think it is the workplace for staff too. Age-appropriate means that it should look like a home in the 1940s; many staff may have no idea what this means in spite of television dramas set in the 1940s and 1950s. Ideally rooms should be let unfurnished so that the room can be full of familiar furniture and objects but again this is not easy. Upholstery may not be fireproofed. Relatives may be embarrassed by mother's shabby furniture. Social workers can really have an impact on this if they take the time to explain why it is important both to relatives and to staff who may want the room to look smart and be full of new furniture.

Orientating layout usually means that people can see and be seen. This means a simple open layout without corridors, which are usually very confusing. However, fire regulations and a determination to model care homes on hotels means that ensuring this can be a struggle. Being able to see a toilet or toilet door at all times can be a way to calmness for many people with dementia. Safe 'wandering paths' are often specified and a completely confusing design results where residents can go round and round but never arrive anywhere. Yes, they need places to walk and places to go, but they also need to arrive. Space to walk can be provided sensitively with enough basic space and a careful arrangement of furniture. Two doors into the garden can be helpful so people go somewhere by going out of one and into another.

Gardens are really important (see Pollock, 2001, for practical guidance). They are important for sun, which provides essential vitamin D. Many people in residential care are vitamin D deficient, which increases risk of falling. Gardens are important for exercise and there is increasing evidence that exercise improves cognitive function. They are important for a range of activities from peace and quiet for reflection to hanging out washing, planting, weeding and so on. They can provide opportunities for reminiscence too.

> The Crabbit Care Home was planning a garden and realised that their residents were from two different kinds of background: mining and agriculture. They were able to source traditional equipment from both settings for the continuing enjoyment of their residents.

Clearly most social workers will not be able to do much about the basic design of a building but they can be aware of simple changes that are needed such as increasing the lighting (see Pollock, 2006, for guidance on lighting), improving the signage with words and pictures and ensuring it is not too high (about four feet from the floor is right for most older people), personalising the doors of the person's room to increase the chance that they can find it and generally raising awareness of the needs of people with cognitive impairment to have a building that helps rather than disables them.

This understanding can be applied in people's own homes too. In the same way that a ramp would be provided to someone with mobility problems, we should be thinking about signage for people with dementia. We should also be thinking about fixtures such as taps and light switches that make sense to them. Lever taps can be totally incomprehensible. People can forget what is behind doors or in cupboards so taking doors off or using glass doors can be very helpful. Pollock (2003) has written a useful guide to interior design for people with dementia.

Finally we need to think about our own offices. Are they 'accessible' to people with dementia? Can they find their way around easily? Is the toilet obvious? Will they be able to work the flush, paper dispenser and light switch? Do the chairs in the waiting room look like chairs? Is the lighting good enough? Is it too noisy? Ideally the 1995 Disability Discrimination Act guidance will increasingly include the needs of people with cognitive impairments, which will make our public buildings 'friendly' for people with dementia.

## Photography

Photography should be part of every social worker's repertoire now that digital cameras make it so easy. It has huge potential for people with dementia because it provides both reminders of the past and a record of the present for people with impaired memory. It can provide just the information people need to cope. There are many ways it can be used, such as:

- records of the past in life-story books, which we have mentioned;
- prompts to assist communication and consultation. This could be a photograph of an object such as a bath or chair, or it could be a photograph of a person. Social workers can often elicit an opinion if we say 'what would you tell the woman in the photograph about…?';
- assisting the making of decisions and choices;
- reminders of events in the near past or the near future (for example a photograph of the day hospital can ease anxieties about where

the person is going, or a photograph of a recent outing can stimulate the memory);

- orientation in a building such as personalising a bedroom door (it need not be a photograph of the person; a photograph of a horse or cat may have much more resonance);
- reminders of family members and who they are;
- pictures of favourite places for pleasurable memories and to ease conversation for visitors;
- photograph telephones to help people who are no longer able to look up telephone numbers;
- communicating visual information by email or on records;
- recording significant events and rituals such as leaving home for the last time;
- as a shared activity with a person with dementia.

Digital photography is easy and cheap. We can make a huge difference if we are able to see its potential for use with people with memory problems. It is likely to be even easier in the future as mobile phone technology develops.

## Assistive technology

The recognition by social workers of the value of assistive technology (telecare) for people with dementia is very patchy in the UK, but will undoubtedly become less so as more and more people with dementia live at home and our home care services struggle to cope. Various government policies in all countries of the UK will further propel this issue into the forefront, for example in the White Paper on social care in England and Wales *Our Health, Our Care, Our Say* (Department of Health, 2006). Woolham (2005b, p 4) has edited a most useful collection of papers about assistive technology and dementia care because he believes 'there is now considerable awareness of the potential of assistive technologies to manage risks arising from the impairments caused by ageing and dementia'.

We want to take a wider view here about the potential of technology. Given that some social workers will still not know what we are referring to we will explain the potential of a range of technologies. We will then address some of the issues of implementation before going on to consider some ethical issues. It is worth saying right at the start that we do not see technology as replacing any existing services but rather supplementing and supporting them: technology must be part of a proper care plan rather than an instant fix. Technology has many functions for people with dementia and can be of several types.

The functions can be listed as:

- reminding
- stimulation
- relaxation and diversion
- compensation
- environmental controls
- safety
- surveillance
- control
- communication
- coordination of services.

The types of technology can be:

- one-off items;
- items that activate something else;
- items connected to the telephone system (sometimes called telecare).

## Functions of technology

### *Reminding*

Reminder devices can be really helpful, probably to all of us. One that is useful for people with dementia is a light box by the front door, which goes on when the door is opened. Messages might say, 'remember your keys' or 'check back door is locked'. There is currently research on the value of pagers linked to computers to remind people to take tablets or to get ready for the day centre bus. Other research is looking at the potential for using computers with a familiar face or a little pet on the screen to remind people with dementia. Readers may blanch at the idea of a fake pet but it may work for some people and underlines the importance of detailed person-centred assessment.

### *Stimulation*

Increasingly people with dementia are committed to the idea that they need to keep their brains active. One way of doing this is through games and puzzles on the computer. They need to be achievable or the person will feel undermined.

Mrs Mancroft, who has dementia, claims that she needs to do computer games as soon as she gets out of bed in the morning in order to kick-start her brain.

### *Relaxation and diversion*

Numerous technologies are appearing to relax people with dementia based, on the whole, on the Snoezelen approach pioneered for people with learning disabilities (Van Diepen et al, 2002; Chung et al, 2003). People respond differently to different sensory stimulation so, once again, assessment is crucial. However, sensory stimulation is really important for people whose cognition is failing because responding to stimulation of the senses does not fail in the same way. Equipment can include music centres, slide projectors with rotating coloured slides, gently moving optic fibres, chairs that provide a back massage, and light-operated lamps for scented oils. Some care homes have whole multi-sensory rooms but they tend to be underused. It is often better to have the equipment on hand to use in the lounge or bedroom so that it can be tailored to the individual or group.

As a social worker you may be asked for advice about someone who is very restless and unsettled and sensory stimulation may be the answer. You may need to emphasise the importance of assessment first because it certainly does not suit everyone. Such an assessment might include responses to touch, moving light, smell and music. Of course multi-sensory work does not necessarily require equipment. A bathroom provides lots of opportunities if there is time to put on music, use bath oil and use soft lighting. Fabrics too are underused. A suitcase full of different fabrics – fur, silk, velvet, cord and so on – can provide hours of pleasure. Hand and foot massage can also be very soothing.

As a way of keeping people with dementia happily diverted, some relatives and carers are making personal DVDs or videos, which can be much appreciated by the person with dementia for whom most material on television is meaningless. Television is, of course, a widely-used technology with people with dementia but it is used far too often without proper assessment about what people can actually appreciate.

Mr Griffid thought that everything on the television was real and he became very anxious indeed about some of the events he saw. His

family decided to take the television out of the sitting room and he
rarely watched it thereafter.

In a South Lanarkshire care home they have adapted a lounge into a
cinema, using a big screen mounted on the wall. Familiar DVDs of old
films, historic events and football matches are shown with proper
intervals for ice cream.

### Compensation

Compensatory devices are those which compensate for deficits such
as the plug that opens when the bathwater reaches a certain height
that is activated by weight and thus prevents an overflow. Induction
cookers have great and underused potential since they do not even
get hot if the pan is empty.

### Environmental controls

Environmental controls are another underused kind of equipment.
Many people with dementia are no longer able to make the connection
between being hot or cold and turning the heater on or off. They can
also not make the connection between it getting darker and the need
to turn on the light. They can thereby become anxious and restless
without knowing how to remedy the situation. Heat and light sensors
are easily available. Thermostats linked to community alarm systems
are a more sophisticated way of helping people who fail to turn the
heating on or even turn it off when it is cold.

### Safety

Safety devices are the one kind of technology that is currently
understood by social services departments. They include devices that
alert neighbours or the community alarm service when the front door
is opened during the night (a magnet is fixed to the door and door
frame and activates the alarm when the door opens), devices that turn
off the cooker when a pan is left and gets very hot or burns the
contents, or the cooker is not lit (a smoke detector, heat sensor or
carbon monoxide detector are linked to a cooker control). Stephen
Wey (2005) describes three different responses to three different women

all of whom had problems with their cookers. Technology may not be right for everyone but it is important that it is in the social worker's repertoire for times when it would be useful.

> Mrs Reilly lived in a small block of flats. She had twice burned pans and a neighbour shared her concern about a possible fire with the social worker. The social worker was quite unaware of turn-off devices and she organised the removal of the cooker, which left Mrs Reilly at a loss. She could not work the microwave. Meals on wheels were organised, which she did not understand. Her agitation exacerbated her tendency to go out of her flat at odd times, which further worried the neighbours, and a care home placement was becoming likely.

Global positioning systems (GPS) are being developed to locate people who get lost when they are out walking. Until now the only equipment available for people who wanted to walk outside but were putting themselves at risk were devices that were worn usually as wristwatches, which activated an alarm when they went through some sort of barrier, either a radio one round the premises, or one on the door. GPS systems work using satellites to locate things or people. Some mobile phones have them but the phone has to be on and they rarely work in buildings or bus shelters. However, this technology is developing fast, which will be a huge comfort to those caring for people who want to walk a lot but sometimes cannot find their way back.

### Surveillance

The movement detector or passive infrared device (PIR), now easily and cheaply available as part of burglar alarms, has huge potential for people with dementia because it can activate all kinds of equipment, it can raise the alarm and it can be used for surveillance. On a small scale it may be useful to put one in the bedroom attached to a light switch so that when someone sits up in bed the light goes on and they can find their way to the toilet. There are some sophisticated systems available where the person's normal movements are logged onto a computer and it is only when they do something outside their normal routine that the alarm is activated. This is linked to surveillance because the information about their movements can be stored on computer. This can be used to monitor behaviour so that problems can be identified when patterns change. This is not without ethical concerns in spite of the fact that these are rarely raised by the providers.

Surveillance has been common in some sheltered housing schemes for a long time using pressure mats, devices attached to toilet flush systems and to doors. These are no different from movement detectors in terms of what they achieve and indeed are often used alongside them. The same ethical concerns arise.

### Control

Control systems are rarely referred to, but they are widely used. On the whole, we mean locks on doors. Even when they have keypads, the intention is to restrict the movement of the person with dementia. There are really major issues around the locking of doors, which are rarely addressed (Archibald, 2003). The Mental Welfare Commission (2005) in Scotland has an excellent document on restraint, which includes locked doors.

### Communication

Computers would seem to have great potential to assist people with communication problems, but this is not yet realised to any extent. Most people with dementia seem to be able to work a touch screen, which seems to be intuitive. Researchers at Dundee and St Andrews Universities (Alm et al, 2004; Astell et al, 2004) have found a way to offer people with dementia choices of topic in holding a conversation with a relative or carer. The system they have developed consists of reminiscence-based material presented in a hypermedia format on a large panel touch screen. Hypermedia allows the users to move easily and flexibly between choices of photographs, music and video clips.

The system acts as a conversation prompt and support for the person with dementia, tapping into their still relatively well-preserved long-term memories, while not requiring working memory to operate the system. In trials the system has shown the ability to facilitate an equality of control over the conversation between the person with dementia and the carer or relative. The material is on the whole general rather than local and it covers a wide range. It seems to stimulate many personal recollections.

The ENABLE project has evaluated a Finnish concept to give people with dementia choices by using a touch screen, for example choices about the music they want to hear (Topo et al, 2004).

Written communication using computers may be increasingly useful as people with dementia have some experience with them. Two people who have written about their experience of dementia (Davis, 1993;

McGowin, 1993) both claim that they were able to use a computer after they were no longer able to write. People with dementia who give lectures find Power Point very helpful because they have reminders on the screen. Email is helpful for some people with dementia because, unlike the telephone, the message is written down for them and remains until they delete it.

### Coordination of services

This is not just an issue for dementia care but has special relevance because the condition and circumstances of people with dementia and their carers can change so rapidly and services really have to be constantly aware of what is going on and what services need to be tweaked. There are numerous projects and systems to facilitate the speedy sharing of information.

## Types of technology

Underneath the list of ways technology can be used, presented above, we suggested three types of technology, which may need a bit of explanation:

- *One-off items*. Cash (2005) provides a most useful description of how some of these 'low-tech' items can be useful in practice. These included locator devices and a 'magi plug' that prevents the bath filling beyond a certain level. These items can be bought in ordinary shops or online, although Cash points to difficulties as manufacturers stop producing them.
- *Items that activate something else*. As we pointed out above the PIR can be linked to any number of things. It can switch on a light or sound an alarm by the bed of the carer. Cash includes one of these in her low-tech devices. A PIR can be linked to a nurse call system in a care home so, for example, staff can be alerted when an individual at risk of falling, steps out of bed.
- *Items connected to the telephone system*. By this we mean the telephone links to community alarm services. A huge range of devices can be linked, increasingly by radio rather than wiring. They can include thermostats, smoke detectors, carbon monoxide detectors, PIRs, pressure mats, front-door magnets and so on.

It is tempting, but we think unhelpful, to see some sorts of technology as positive and others as negative. It is the way technology is used that is positive or negative, not the equipment itself. People get very anxious, for example, about 'tagging' devices but they can be liberating for people with dementia who want to walk about a lot and for others in the units who do not want to be restricted because one of the residents 'escapes'.

## Implementation issues

Woolham (2005b) has many concerns about the rapid development in the use of technology for people with dementia. He fears that the momentum will be 'technology driven' with insufficient attention given to person-centred approaches, consideration of ethical and legal issues and best practice. He points out that consent is not easy in our field and that we must ensure that the technology is used within a therapeutic context with robust ethical approaches and protocols. One answer to his concerns is to ensure that we are better informed about 'best practice' in aspects such as how we should introduce technology; how we can can share experience; whether more work needs to be done on ethical considerations and protocols; and, most crucially, how we can refine our assessments to ensure that we know exactly what is required to benefit the person with dementia. He counsels against 'recipe-based' approaches.

His book is a commendable attempt to share current expertise about what works and what does not and it includes an excellent chapter from Faife (2005) who provides an honest and thoughtful account of how technology was introduced into Norfolk. She draws attention to the need for a shared agency approach including the housing sector, which is often more experienced than we are about technology, and to the importance of involving the person who actually installs the technology: the electrician who deals with the people and the practicalities. In the same book, Calder (2005) suggests a panel system to avoid installation on the basis of inadequate assessment. Any organisation starting down the road of greater use of assistive technology will struggle with staff anxieties. Faife (2005) recommends a smart house to display the items, information about where to obtain the items, their best use and how to assess for them. There is an urgent imperative in this field to share knowledge and experience. The combination of increasing numbers of people with dementia living at home, a diminishing workforce and government policies will mean that assistive technology will become a routine part of many care plans very soon. A useful guide to using technology has been written by Bjørneby et al (1999).

## Ethical issues

The most common ethical issue raised is that technology will replace individual contact. This is unlikely, given that devices cannot listen, cannot hold hands and cannot wipe tears. But technology can free up busy staff so that they can undertake these more skilled activities without having to spend all their time on monitoring visits, for example. We are facing a workforce shortage, as we stressed in Chapter Three. We should welcome technology if it enables us to make best use of human contact. It can also fill the gaps between visitors, especially at night, when constant visits to check that people are safe and inside the house are really impracticable.

An ethical question that should be asked all the time is 'who benefits from this technology?' especially for people with dementia when consent may not be possible to obtain. The answer can really clarify what is going on. There are no 'yes' and 'no' answers to ethical questions, but they do shine a light on why decisions are being made and they make it easier to see when decisions are person-centred and when they are not. The Astrid Guide (Marshall, 2000) provides a useful introduction to thinking about ethical issues. It recommends a protocol based on one developed by nurses for the use of restraint for situations where consent is not possible. On file should be a form that describes the problem, describes what else has been tried to solve it, explains why technology will help and includes a review date and by whom it will be reviewed. It should be signed and dated. Some social workers refuse to use technology because people with dementia cannot give consent. This is an inadequate response to some situations and often results in admission to a care home, again often against the wishes of the person. As social workers we need to demonstrate ethical practice by asking searching questions, but it does not help if we are simply seen as obstructive.

## Conclusion

This chapter has looked at four important areas that are not exclusively in the domain of social work but can have a fundamental impact on the lives of people with dementia. There are other similar areas we might have chosen such as exercise, but these are touched on to some extent elsewhere. It seemed to us that food and drink, design, photography and assistive technology deserved a chapter.

## Further reading

Judd, S., Marshall, M. and Phippen, P. (1998) *Design for Dementia*, London: Hawker Publications Limited.

VOICES (1998) *Eating Well for Older People with Dementia: A Good Practice Guide for Residential and Nursing Homes and Others Involved in Caring for Older People with Dementia*, Potters Bar, Herts: VOICES.

Woolham, J. (ed) (2005b) *Developing the Role of Technology in the Care and Rehabilitation of People with Dementia: Current Trends and Perspectives*, London: Hawker Publications Limited.

# EIGHT

# Making it work

## Introduction

In this chapter we consider ways in which we as social workers can use our own field experience to influence service development in the sense of setting up new services, and ensuring that the service we offer is as good as it can be. A busy frontline social worker will have few opportunities for setting up new services although opportunities to contribute to the work of others may arise. However, some social workers who come from other fields into commissioning, planning and service development jobs should find this chapter useful. Social workers are often in voluntary organisations with a specific service development remit. To this end we address user and carer participation, service development, service evaluation, training and personal survival. We start with some reflections on the pace and nature of change in social work settings, which we have already mentioned in Chapter Three.

## Factors in the wider society

Every kind of discrimination can apply to people with dementia. We include ageism (see DH, 2001a; Bytheway, 2005), mental illness (see Chapter One), racism (see Chapter Three), sexism since the majority of older people are women and homophobia, which is emerging as an issue in dementia care (see Chapter Three).

As social workers we are trained to be aware of these issues of discrimination and can help care staff in homes and other professional colleagues to become aware of the conscious and unconscious prejudices we all have.

### The pace and nature of changes in social work organisations

We are working in a period of much change. The field of adult social care is under great scrutiny with guidance, initiatives, targets and performance indicators coming from government offices in a steady stream. At the same time there is constant structural reorganisation. These changes should be strongly influenced by the people who will have to implement them and there should be the necessary resources to implement them. Sadly, this is not usually the case or if there are resources, they are tied to very specific criteria. There is also a real danger that strategic decisions are made by managers who have not practised in the field for a very long time and who may be driven by the imperative to cut costs. An additional counterproductive pressure is the very short timeframes for change. It is easy, as a frontline social worker in this context, to become cynical and demotivated and we hope this chapter offers some positive encouragement.

We have already referred to *Everybody's Business* (CSIP, 2005). It usefully points out that 'commissioning is a cyclical process that involves:

- Understanding the market
- Aligning system partners
- Joint strategic planning
- Applying resources
- Reviewing and evaluating'. (CSIP, 2005, p 20)

We cover much the same ground here.

## Service user and carer participation

There is an increasing trend towards consulting service users and carers and this looks likely to continue as a strong policy imperative. We are seeing in health a development of 'expert patients' (DH, 2001b) and we may well see a parallel development in social care of 'expert users'. People with dementia and their carers must, however, be one of the least consulted groups, for several reasons. The first is attitudinal. Senior managers are not often up to speed on the enormous strides that have been taken in consulting people with dementia and their carers. Involving carers is more common than involving people with dementia and there are some groups of carers who have made a major contribution to planning and other meetings.

There are social barriers to meaningful consultation that need to be overcome. It can be very intimidating for a carer to walk into a boardroom with top NHS Trust and social services managers and say what is on their mind. In addition, the use of initials, acronyms and jargon can be absolutely bewildering, making the meeting incomprehensible and participation for the lay person almost impossible.

Are planners always aware that a carer who is looking after someone at home, who attends a consultation meeting that lasts two hours, may have to pay for someone to stay with their relative for four hours to allow for travelling? And that if the meeting overruns the carer will be further out of pocket?

There is increasing awareness that people with dementia have views and preferences they want to share but obtaining these views requires a considered approach by people who understand the communication needs of people with dementia (Allan, 2001; Alzheimer's Disease International, 2003). There are now some excellent examples of good practice from which we can all learn. The Southern Health and Social Services Board of Northern Ireland set about preparing their dementia services plan by organising a special day for a group of people with dementia and their carers at which it was able to determine the concerns and priorities of the participants and this formed the basis of the plan (McAndrew and Taylor, 2006). Many of the skills of consultation in such meetings involve techniques developed with people with learning disabilities, which include the use of artists who draw on large sheets of paper providing a visual cue and a memory jog for the participants with memory problems. The setting is important too. It needs to be quiet and comfortable so that the people with dementia remain relaxed and are able to concentrate.

The Dementia Action Group in Scotland is a group of people with dementia who support each other in speaking out about the needs of people with dementia and they have become skilled at coping in situations that would be intimidating to most people with dementia. One of the members made an invaluable contribution to the user group advising the 21st Century Social Work Review (Scottish Executive, 2006). The 'Collaborative' on dementia care in the north east of England developed a very strong group of people with dementia and carers to advise right through the process (Cantley et al, 2005).

Staff at the coalface should know individual service users and carers who could usefully be involved in the planning process and may well know what their support needs are if they are to work with planning and development colleagues. Staff in voluntary organisations will increasingly be expected to involve people with dementia as well as carers in advisory and planning groups.

## Service development

Service development is an area of work that some people do without thinking and other people never think of doing. It ought to be firmly part of the repertoire of skills of everyone in this field because there is such a severe shortfall of services. The ideal approach is when a member of staff identifies a gap in services based on analysis of good information, and gets the right group of people together who produce a plan that is then set in motion. This is very rare. More often a group of staff, such as a local team, collect information but omit the careful analysis and rush straight into a project. This is usually a project they have read about in *Community Care*, the *Nursing Times* or the *Journal of Dementia Care*. It may or may not be relevant to their local needs.

Another way things happen is that a group of activists identify resources and set up a service to qualify for the available finance. A frequent example of this is the church group with an underused church hall. The problem with this approach is that the services are often in the wrong place because places with extra, unused resources are not always in areas where there are people in greatest need. The most usual approach is when money suddenly becomes available and there is a mad planning phase and a project that meets the criteria and seems possible is submitted. The result is all around for us to see. If you are a person with dementia or a carer it is a complete lottery what services will be available to support you. It all depends – most unfairly – on where you live.

This sounds very critical, whereas it is, in our experience, how the world works. It is very hard to collect information, analyse it carefully, work out what is required and where the service should be, and then to wait for the opportunity and the money. It is equally hard to motivate a group of activists if there is little chance of success. People are usually so busy that they only make space for meetings and working parties when they can see a pay-off. Planning is, in a sense, everybody's job and nobody's job. It should happen at various levels with joint planning doing the broad-brush identification, and joint groups at a lower level setting about the local implementation phase. The various levels of planning and the different planning remits can be confusing, but knowing how it all works makes it possible to feed the right concerns, information and ideas into the process.

Team discussions about individuals can indicate where there are shared problems for which planning is required. The trouble with dementia is that there is often so little interest and so little awareness of both need and possibilities that very little happens unless real enthusiasts set about making it happen, with or without enough information collection and the right people on board. So what are the skills required for service development, assuming that you are a frontline worker or a first-level manager?

## Information collection

First is information collection. What is the population of your area? Are there lots of young older people or old older people? Ideally, you need to obtain a breakdown in five-year sections: 60-64, 65-69, 70-74, 75-79, 80-84, 85-89 and so on.

Jorm et al (1988) found that the prevalence of dementia doubles every five years. This means that prevalence studies come up with very different actual numbers because of different numbers of people in different age bands. What all studies have in common is an exponential curve in the proportion of each age group with dementia. If you assume a starting point of 0.7% people with dementia in the age group 60-64 you can take it from there. You can thus produce a rough and ready estimate of the numbers of people with dementia using this formula.

You might then want to know a few things about your population such as the number living on benefits, the number of older people living on their own and the number of people from black and minority ethnic groups and the most common languages that they speak. Rural areas have their own particular problems such as access to services and transport (Innes et al, 2005). The figures will be based on the latest Census returns. Figures such as the basic population of your area and their characteristics are almost always available from NHS and social services/work departments' planners.

You then need to find out what services there are. Mapping of services is increasingly being undertaken by planners but you may have local knowledge of existing services of which they are unaware. Most statistics are presented at electoral ward level because that is how the Census does it and this can make it easier for you. You may feel that all this information collection and presentation is a big chore if you have already decided on the service you want to provide, but it is very useful information for making the case to potential funders or supporters. Your case could be demolished if you did not know that there was already a similar day centre in existence down the road or that population figures do not support your case for a new service.

All this preliminary work is best done by the group who are going to do the planning for the service, but sometimes you have to assemble a new group after the initial phase. It is worth considering the membership carefully. Busy people are always the best, they know how to get things done and they have the contacts. Obviously an interdisciplinary group is needed, but you might like to think about co-opting potential opposition in order to avoid later sabotage. People with dementia who are able to communicate effectively, carers and representatives from specialist voluntary organisations are needed not only for their undoubted expertise, but because they will be the people to give your service credibility in the eyes of other people who will be using your service.

When you are thinking about the kind of service you consider would meet the needs you have identified, it is always good to have a look at other similar services and try to talk to some of their committees to see how they managed to get things going. The *Journal of Dementia Care* is an excellent reservoir of expertise on setting up services and you may have a Dementia Services Development Centre nearby (see Appendix for details) that can offer assistance.

## Standards, principles, problem anticipation and outcomes

First of all you need to be sure that the service you are planning will meet the standards required for registration and inspection. The Commission for Social Care Inspection (CSCI), which covers England and Wales, published its minimum standards *Care Homes for Older People* in 2003 (DH, 2003b) and now also has standards for services such as home care and day care. The Scottish Care Standards (Scottish Executive Health, 2005) are more aspirational and user based. You will need to be certain that you meet the ones that apply to your service. Northern Ireland uses the CSCI standards at present.

You will find it useful to make a list of principles for your service. Cox et al (1998) provide an inspiring set of principles. This can be a good team-building job for the planning group too. Many organisations have lists of principles such as the ones in the Northern Ireland Mental Health Review (which has a section on dementia) (Bamford Review, forthcoming). The Scottish *Needs Assessment Report* for services for people with dementia (NHS Health Scotland, 2003) lists the 13 principles shown in Table 8.1.

The service you are planning is unlikely to score 13 out of 13 but it is worth considering which ones are important and on which ones you would be prepared to compromise. Another useful planning exercise is 'the worst possible scenario' approach. What if: the roof falls in; a service user runs away; a volunteer gashes his/her hand; somebody falls when using the toilet and so on? You will need to spend time on outputs and outcomes for the users and a timeframe for achieving these. Almost all funders need a plan with clear milestones about what is going to be achieved by when. Your day centre may, for example,

**Table 8.1:** The principles of a good service

- Care should be based on a good knowledge of the individual
- People with dementia should be trained, informed and empowered
- Carers should be trained, informed and empowered
- Services should reflect ethical practice, balancing risk and protection
- Services should be based locally in the community
- Care staff should be trained in appropriate competencies and supported
- Day and residential services should be delivered in small, domestic, home-like settings
- Day and residential services should promote a domestic, home-like philosophy of care
- Attention should be paid to the design of the built environment
- All services should be accessible
- Services should respond effectively in a crisis
- Services should be flexible and adaptable
- Services, including home care, should be available 24 hours a day, 7 days a week

start small and grow over a period of time as staff and volunteers become more confident.

Other essential jobs in the planning phase are deciding exactly for whom your service is intended. You would be amazed at the services that are set up without looking at this issue. Staff end up being unable to explain to people who might make referrals, which people would be appropriate for the service. They also fail to ensure that staff and activities are focused on the people who will attend.

Let us say, for example, that you are planning a day centre using a church or village hall. You have done your survey and your analysis and you know that the need is for day care for people with dementia who are physically very active and have behaviour that challenges staff to such an extent that they are rejected by existing centres. To provide good care for this group of people you need a room where all those who attend can be seen, a high staff ratio, lots of staff training and support and a highly interactive programme. Those who come will need to be kept busy and engaged, often on a one-to-one basis and always doing things that they enjoy and at which they can succeed. This work can be hugely rewarding. By contrast, if you found the need was for day care for people with good social skills and minimal behaviour problems, you could consider smaller rooms, fewer staff and less intensive activities. In order to communicate effectively with health colleagues you may need to use a mutually agreed dependency scale to ensure that your target group is well understood.

An important area to which insufficient attention is often paid when planning a new service is to work out which people are *not* suitable for your service as well as those who are. If everyone is clear about this from the outset it makes it much easier for all concerned. Carers can be given a leaflet that clearly sets out the parameters of your service.

## Making applications

Writing up the service you intend to provide as a proposal, either for commissioners or for a grant application, is a good way to clarify exactly what it is you plan to do. You can demonstrate that you have thought it through. Costs are often the key section and need to be presented very carefully, including the 'hidden costs'. The fact that the church/village hall may be free should often be presented as the equivalent amount of money being given by the church or parish council. Travel expenses are often a major item in the budget and can be difficult to calculate. Having identified the service you want to set up and whom it is for, there is a marketing job to be done by key staff. Key staff are usually the commissioners but they may consult specialist providers for their views so you will need to have won the support of people like consultants in old age psychiatry.

Even if you get a contract for certain people or for a group of people you will inevitably have to find other money and letters of support can be invaluable. You will need to write a service plan and/ or a business plan that includes costings. Applying for money and mobilising resources always take much longer than you expect. Sometimes small efforts like jumble sales are important just to keep the team together. There is always a point where people feel like giving up and there are always people around who will be discouraging. You may, in fact, not manage to set up the service you dream of but you will be prepared when the next opportunity comes along. Faife (2005) provides a good account of the development of an integrated technology service.

## Evaluation

All services should be regularly evaluated and this is often a requirement by those who provide funding/grants. It can be useful to cost at least the first evaluation into any grant application, because evaluations always cost more than most people imagine. There are several approaches to evaluation:

• observation;
• against planned outcomes and outputs;
• against principles;
• asking the users and carers.

Dementia Care Mapping (DCM) is a technique that is now widely used to systematically observe the behaviour of people with dementia within a person-centred framework in formal care settings. 'DCM is a tool developed by the late Professor Tom Kitwood and Kathleen Bredin in the late 1980s and was designed to assess quality of care from the perspective of the person with dementia' (www.bradford.ac.uk/health/dementia/dcm).

In 1992 the Bradford Dementia Group began delivering training courses in the use of the method. Courses hosted by Bradford Dementia Group are now conducted in Australia, Denmark, Germany, Japan, Switzerland and the US as well as the UK. It is continuously being updated and the 8th edition of the DCM manual was launched in 2004. A full account of the method, its philosophy and applications can be found in Brooker et al (2004).

The depth of the evaluations is usually dependent on the amount of funding. Ideally an outside body should do the evaluation but this is the most expensive option. At the very least a review of the extent to which the original plan has been achieved is essential, with some investigation of why it has gone off course if it has. Evaluation against the original principles can be a good group exercise if only to reinforce them and to be sure that everybody remains committed to them. There is a real danger that they are simply rhetoric. We have all been in care homes and day centres where there is a statement of principles in a frame in the entrance hall that bears very little relation to what is going on in the place and is rarely read by the staff.

## Training

There is disappointingly little on most professional courses about dementia and social work is no exception (Pulsford et al, 2003; Cunningham et al, 2006). Social work courses usually have input on community care within which there is a lecture or two on older people but it is likely that most social workers in the field will have to go on a sharp learning curve when they start working with people with dementia and their carers. However, knowledge is only part of what is required.

We also need social workers who can respond person to person with warmth, imagination and respect and have an ability to empathise with other people. None of these are acquired on professional courses. Some have a gift with people with dementia, and others will never have it no matter how much training you give them. Most of us are somewhere in between and we can thrive if we are given training that inspires us to examine our own practice and learn new skills. Training should consist of knowledge, skills and attitudes. The last is, probably, the most important and the most difficult to improve. There is a lot of ageism about training, with some managers believing that older staff will not change their attitudes. The reality is that some people are more receptive than others – always have been and always will be.

The skill for managers is in identifying this potential for change and supporting it with training and back-up. One of the most effective tools for managers is modelling good attitudes and practice. It is rarely worth changing the attitudes of one person in a team and expecting them to work like yeast. There usually needs to be a group involved in order to achieve a critical mass if there is to be any change. Much training is about reinforcing positive attitudes and giving positive reinforcement for good practice (Chapman and Hosking, 2002).

Staff often say they have no time for training. There are two answers to this. The most important is that you should not practise if you are not being constantly trained in the sense of building up skills. Dementia care is a world where new skills are constantly emerging that can make a real difference to people with dementia and their carers. As an example, we do now know how to communicate with people who have impaired language skills. We do know how to find out from them what they feel about the services they are receiving. We do know how to involve the person in their own assessment. The support that social care gives is likely to be the only sort of 'treatment' given – and we have to make it as effective as possible.

Staff in a group home for people with learning disabilities were finding it very difficult to care for Mr Young. He, like many people with Down's syndrome, developed dementia in his fifties. The staff needed training about dementia care. Equally important was their need for training in sustaining their customary rehabilitation approach in the face of constant deterioration. They tended to see his need for basic physical care rather than his need for encouragement in maintaining skills. Given

> encouragement and having tasks broken down into small steps, Mr Young surprised the staff by what he was still able to achieve.

The second answer to the 'no time for training' approach is that training is in part a matter of management style and some training can be woven into team meetings. We all have skills to share, or have read something we think might be useful. Case discussions, demonstrating skills on the job, 'shadowing' and joint visits can be woven into the working week. In a sense, no manager can afford not to be constantly offering training if standards are to be sustained, motivation kept high and good staff retained.

There is now a wide variety of training materials available, many of which can be shared between teams. Courses designed to meet the special needs of social workers can be found. Self-study packs, video- and DVD-based training courses, online courses and group-based training packages are emerging as well as the more conventional opportunities for training courses and workshops. The local Dementia Services Development Centre is a good place to start (see Appendix). It can be useful when social workers share new skills and approaches that they have learned on courses with their colleagues. Increasingly social workers practise in teams alongside a mixture of different professionals. This means that the scope for sharing new ideas and experiences across professional boundaries is greatly increased. This should be of great benefit to everyone in the long run.

## Personal survival

Perhaps this should be the first chapter of the book since the well-being of the staff will have a huge impact on the quality of the service for people with dementia and their carers. Working in this field can be very stressful. Many staff are unwilling to mention that they feel stressed because they are only too aware that carers manage, or have managed in the past, often alone, for far more hours than any paid person. It is stressful work because people with dementia require us to take the initiative, to be always giving, warm and human and to be creative and imaginative. It is rarely a relationship of equal exchange although some people with dementia strive to give to a relationship, and there is a great deal of satisfaction in the work.

Social workers know that working with carers can be very exhausting too, since they often offload a lot of emotion as well as their own stress. We are very likely to be working with the most angry and least constructive relatives. Many situations are fraught with conflict, difficulties and worries. Dementia is also a terminal illness so dealing with death and dying are inescapable, as we have already discussed. Sutton and Cheston (1997, p 162) were talking about psychotherapists when they wrote the following but we think it is useful for social workers too:

> We need to listen to the poetical, to the metaphorical aspects of stories that people with dementia tell. But this is hard. The stories that are told, the emotional pain that can be generated is immense. When we hear these stories we need to remember that it is not just the pain of the person with dementia that we are listening to, it is not just their losses that we are speaking of; these are also our own potential losses, our own future pain. We are listening to people talking about a pain that may well one day be our own or that of our husbands, wives, fathers and mothers. We cannot make this future 'better' in the sense of taking this pain away; we can only try and listen and to help the person feel they have been heard. This is as hard to do as it is necessary.

It is very difficult for social workers who know the people concerned and are only too aware of the stress and pressures of their lives to realise that they do not meet the eligibility criteria of the department. It is social workers who have to make the judgements about the degree of need that will decide whether they receive help or not. We are also confronted with terrible situations where the person and their carer do not qualify for help because they have too much money. These 'self-funding' families have to be turned away by social workers and if there is nowhere else in the locality to refer them to, we can experience a high level of guilt and distress about them. We often feel frustrated, angry and disillusioned about the system of which we are a part.

So how do we survive? How do we keep our motivation to respond to the specialness of each individual? How do we stay creative? In our view the first step is to ensure that we have support mechanisms, which ideally should include colleagues. Regular supervision or debriefing is invaluable because it allows time to reflect on practice and our own performance. Teamwork with other staff can be a source of support and ideas. In both cases we get out what we put in and in both cases we have first to acknowledge that we are not superhuman. None of us cope well all the time. We make mistakes and we all have our strengths and weaknesses. It is, in part, about trust. Nothing is more supportive than a line manager and colleagues you can trust and, of course, this is not always the case. However, it is worth testing and putting some effort into it. If work colleagues are not helpful, there are often support mechanisms in the community: professional lunch clubs, meetings of special interest groups for older people with mental health problems, even mutual support groups that meet regularly for lunch or for an hour after work.

It is important to know how to recognise stress in ourselves and to know what to do about it. Headaches, mouth ulcers, irritability, feelings of powerlessness and panic are a few of the well-known signs. There are numerous techniques for reducing stress, including talking things through. Relaxation needs to be learned and what works will vary from person to person. We need to learn what works for us and ensure that we take it seriously. Being able to recognise our own stress is useful in that we also need to be able to recognise when we have nothing to give to the people we are supporting. This may be a sudden and short-term problem, or it may be that we are just burned out. In the short term, some managers are wise enough to move staff who own up to being unable to do the job for some reason. Sometimes colleagues will bear the weight temporarily as long as it is perceived as reciprocal.

In the longer term, there may be no alternative but to stop. Some provider units will only take part-time staff on the basis that they are fresher, have more to give and do not burn out. We have heard it asserted, and there is a good deal of sense in the principle, that it is not possible to provide frontline care, full time, to people with dementia for more than three years. The job of the social worker as care manager contains particular stress factors, some of which we have referred to earlier. The feeling of being caught between the conflicting pressures of the urgent need of your clients and the limited resources available to help them can be very stressful. The high level of strain, distress and emotional turmoil that is experienced by many people with dementia and their carers can be very draining to work with on a daily basis. The three-year rule may apply to social workers commissioning services as well as to staff providing care. If we are constantly learning, either individually or as a staff group, then we are much more likely to solve problems creatively and to remain actively involved ourselves (Senge, 1990). One of the most motivating things to do is to keep learning, which is why we included a section on training in this chapter.

## Conclusion

We started this chapter with a brief review of some of the contextual issues that we have to consider in setting up and improving services and our practice. We then looked at how we might achieve this, covering a range of planning tasks, evaluation, training and personal survival. Working with people with dementia and their carers can be personally very demanding.

### Further reading

Cox, S., Anderson, I., Dick, S. and Elgar, J. (1998) *The Person, the Community and Dementia: Developing a Value Framework*, Stirling: Dementia Services Development Centre.

CSIP (Care Service Improvement Partnership) (2005) *Everybody's Business: Integrated Services for Older Adults: A Service Development Guide*, London: Department of Health.

NHS Health Scotland (2003) *Dementia and Older People: Needs Assessment Report*, Edinburgh: NHS Scotland.

# NINE

# Therapy

## Introduction

Therapy may seem to be an odd word to use in a book about people with dementia and their carers, but its use is quite deliberate. We are in the midst of an intensely exciting phase in dementia care in relation to therapy. In this chapter we examine the different therapeutic approaches that have been developed in recent decades. We are very much addressing the social approach to dementia in this chapter, mentioning only briefly the medical intervention of drugs. Understanding behaviour that others find difficult, is discussed in this context. We consider various factors, both internal and external, which impact on the person with dementia.

We look briefly at a selection of therapeutic approaches, including activities, counselling, the creative arts and complementary therapies. Social workers need to be knowledgeable about interventions even though we may not often be able to implement them ourselves. We need to be able to advise and assist colleagues and carers, and we may need to specify certain interventions in care plans.

## Why use the word 'therapy'?

The word 'therapy' speaks of a potential growth and change in all of us, even if we have dementia, so it is used to underline the positive nature of working with people with dementia. It is also used because all sorts of new therapies are emerging. Some people are using the word to mean that everything we do can make people better. We can, for example, as we have seen in Chapter Seven, design buildings that are therapeutic: buildings that enable people rather than disable them. We are also learning that many of the therapies used with other groups of people can, with some modification, apply to people with dementia and their carers. This whole book is about therapy, if it means that we are all working to make people as well as they can be; to function at the highest possible level within the limits set by the neurological damage.

The medical approach would tend to use the word 'treatment'. The difference between treatment and therapy is too complicated to address here; however, clearly there is an overlap. It is, of course, as yet impossible to treat dementia in the sense of reversing the deterioration of the brain. Cholinesterase inhibitors slow down the progress of deterioration for some people with Alzheimer's disease or Lewy Body dementia for some time. However, they are not a cure. Kitwood (1997a) believed that person-centred care could not only halt the progress of the disease but also help regain lost cognitive and functional abilities for some individuals. There is some research that suggests that it does (Sixsmith et al, 2004). Kitwood coined the term 'rementia' to describe this phenomenon.

Fortunately we are increasingly able to refer to research evidence and we will need to become more assertive about interventions that work and which should therefore be available. Brodarty (2003) undertook a meta-analysis of research on psychosocial interventions for caregivers of people with dementia and concluded that some interventions can reduce psychological morbidity and help people with dementia to stay at home longer. The Royal College of Physicians (2005) found that multidisciplinary psychosocial interventions can be effective in reducing the incidence of delirium in older patients admitted to acute hospitals. Similar beneficial results were demonstrated in the case of dementia and depression. Even if it is not possible to cure, or even to slow, the process of dementia for most people, it is undoubtedly possible in many cases to reduce the anguish and pain surrounding dementia by therapeutic interventions.

We have both visited many facilities providing care for people with dementia. Many staff tell us that the people in their centre or unit are 'too seriously demented' or 'too far gone' to benefit from any kind of therapy. This seems, to us, to say much more about the staff than about the residents. The staff have clearly run out of ideas. They are probably feeling a lack of support, recognition and training. They may be burnt out or demoralised. There is always something that can be done to engage the feelings of someone with dementia even if it is only through touch or music; responding to both of these seems to occur despite considerable neurological damage. It is too easy to 'blame' people with dementia for not responding. In this chapter we want to concentrate on work that is traditionally put under the heading of therapy: understanding behaviour, activities, reminiscence and life-story work, counselling, group work, family therapy, the creative arts and complementary therapies.

# Understanding behaviour

Our first therapy is what used to be called 'behaviour management'. This is a term we tend to avoid since it depersonalises the person with dementia. We prefer to talk about 'understanding behaviour'. A word that is much in vogue at the moment is 'detective work' because the approach is one of looking for clues and working out what is happening for the person with dementia that is making them behave in a particular way.

## Stress

Most of this book has been implicitly, if not explicitly, about understanding the behaviour of people with dementia better, in order to make it less stressful for them as well as everyone else. We believe that a lot of people with dementia are highly stressed and this impairs their functioning as it does for all of us. People caring for those with dementia are often highly stressed as well, not least by proximity to very stressed individuals and a feeling of being powerless to help them. A first plank in any care plan must be the reduction of stress, and the plan itself should assist the person with dementia, carers and paid staff alike.

As social workers we may have a very important role in persuading our medical colleagues that drugs to subdue behaviour should be a last, not a first, step. The fact that behaviour can cause such stress and distress means that carers and staff often look for a quick fix with medication. There is a great deal of evidence of overuse of sedatives with people with dementia, as we said in Chapter Four. We have a role in pointing out that medication may be necessary in a crisis, but cannot be the answer for the medium or long term, if for no other reason than that it becomes less effective over time and that it often has side effects.

## Interaction with other factors

This section deals with how we might approach the care planning process – first by understanding what affects behaviour. Social workers are familiar with the idea that systems impact on each other and we can grasp easily the notion that behaviour is a result of the interaction of numerous factors: internal, surrounding and in the world at large. We have tried to express this in Figure 4.1 in Chapter Four to which we refer to again since we now consider further some of the factors around our gentleman with dementia. We will be referring briefly to factors that have been dealt with in much greater depth in earlier chapters but we mention them again to make the point that they all need to be considered in case they hold the key to understanding.

There is a similar figure in Stokes and Goudie's (2002) useful book, which makes the point that behaviour is speech and action, which is determined by thought, mood and motivation.

We start here in the middle of Figure 4.1, with a person who has a mind and a body, which are in part the ones he was born with, and in part the result of a lifetime's experience. This experience will be considerable since most people with dementia are older people. People will have had all manner of injuries and stresses, emotional and physical. They will have learnt all kinds of coping mechanisms, some more effective than others. Dementia is a stress of the first order and, in part, the way people cope with it will be a reflection of the way they have coped with other life events.

### Cerebral reserve

Current internal influences include the actual disease process – which part of the brain is affected and to what extent? Clearly, different abilities will be affected in different people where the disease has affected different parts of the brain. There is a view (Jacques and Jackson, 2000) that we all have a degree of cerebral reserve, which enables us to cope with some level of brain damage. The suggestion is that some people have a considerably reduced cerebral reserve so the signs of dementia are more apparent at an earlier stage. Cerebral reserve may be diminished by previous brain injury, life stress and so on. It is possible that people with learning disabilities have a diminished cerebral reserve because it is very stressful coping with a learning disability. This might again account for the substantial research (Gow and Gilhooley, 2003) that low educational levels are a risk factor for dementia. There is anecdotal evidence that black and minority ethnic older people get dementia earlier and once again the theory of cerebral reserve may account for this, since we know that being a member of such a minority in the UK since the 1950s has been a stressful business.

### Personality

It is clear that the sort of person you were, will, to an extent, affect the way you approach your dementia. It is, of course, impossible to determine accurately the cause of anyone's behaviour, and we are only suggesting a range of reasons that might be useful to consider in working out ways of understanding behaviour. The effect of previous personality then needs to be on the list.

> Mr Habib had always taken refuge in illness when life was too harassing. He enjoyed being looked after. He was quite comfortable being labelled ill and was quite calm and passive. Many others are very angry and frustrated by the whole experience.

### Past trauma

Defences can diminish in old age. It is possible that some of the behaviour we see now is the result of traumas in the past (Hunt et al, 1997), as we discussed in Chapter Four. Memories have been well suppressed throughout life but, without defences, they come to the fore. This seems to be true of the people who survived horrors of war, who are unable to block out the memories in old age and sometimes become profoundly mentally ill as a result.

Staff in care homes have reported occasions where it was clear that a resident had been sexually abused in the past, a fact unknown to relatives. The dementia led to the resident being unable to suppress the memory and her behaviour indicated that the memory was still vivid. Social workers may well be part of reviews of a person in a care home who resists intimate care with real aggression. It can be useful to suggest that past sexual abuse may be an explanation. Since sex is such a taboo topic in many settings, this may not have occurred to staff as a possibility. You will need to be alert to the fact that staff themselves may have been abused and find this whole issue very difficult indeed. A social worker should be in a good position to support and advise the staff about how they could best help her. See McCartney and Severson (1997) for further reading on this subject.

### Health-related factors

Current health and medication are crucial determinants of behaviour. Constipation affects everyone's behaviour whether or not they have dementia, but it is often overlooked as an explanation. In Chapter Two we mentioned the importance of distinguishing an acute confusional state from a dementia, since the former is often caused by illness and stress. This can, of course, occur on top of a dementia. The behaviour of a person with dementia will deteriorate very sharply if they have, for example, a urinary tract infection. As social workers we need to be very aware of the danger of making assessments that will be used to develop future care packages that are based on a temporary event, such as an acute confusional state.

> Mrs Crolla's behaviour was very hard to deal with since she became extremely aggressive whenever she had diarrhoea, which was increasingly often. Her dementia was thought to be deteriorating fast and long-term placement was being planned. An energetic doctor referred her for a full investigation and she was found to have Crohn's disease. After surgery she reverted to being a reasonable woman only mildly impaired by her dementia.

People with dementia may be unable to tell you what is wrong. Pain affects everyone's behaviour and we need to be alert to the possibility that someone's behaviour is telling us about their pain, psychological or physical. As discussed in Chapter Four, pain is a significant factor in the lives of some people with dementia. Medication is a major factor. Anyone who has worked in an assessment unit for older people with mental health problems will have stories of the dramatic improvement in people who are given a 'drug holiday' and taken off their drug cocktails.

## Mood

Mood is an important factor. People with dementia seem acutely sensitive to the mood of others and will often pick up that of relatives or staff instinctively. Sour and unhappy staff will often find themselves caring for sour and unhappy residents and vice versa. Earlier in this chapter we mentioned stress. Stressed staff equals stressed people with dementia. People with dementia are unable to rationalise or explain away the moods of other people and therefore they are especially vulnerable to these moods. Staff who are confident and working to a plan of care alongside colleagues and carers implementing the same plan will be less stressed. If, as the social worker, you develop and maintain good working relationships with the staff you can be an invaluable source of support to them, which may go a long way to reducing stress.

## Food and drink

We covered food and drink in Chapter Seven but in any attempt to understand behaviour they are important considerations. Both have a very profound effect on people.

## Noise

Dementia itself produces stress. A failing memory and a diminishing ability to work things out must be stressful whether or not the environment is stressful. We are learning to diminish stress by reducing stimulation overload such as noise, keeping the atmosphere calm and using techniques such as massage and aromatherapy.

> A recent visit to a 30-bed dementia unit showed how stressful such environments can be. Staff had made considerable efforts to divide the residents into small groups. Some were actively playing bingo, others were sitting in a conservatory, others were sleeping. The staff seemed quite unaware of the potentially stressful impact of old-time dance music, which played for a whole hour. Nobody seemed to be listening. We did not get the impression that the staff had checked that everyone in the unit really liked old-time music, let alone having it on all the time.

The connection between environmental stress and disturbed behaviour is often not understood by staff in care homes. It is ironic that some of the most disturbed people with dementia are cared for in the most stressful environments; big, noisy, confusing places with little personalised care. Many units still have hard floors and wall surfaces that amplify noise in addition to the usual racket of trolleys, voices, doors and so on. If a person in these units shouts all the time, the other residents and staff really suffer. The question of the built environment has already been covered in more detail in Chapter Seven.

## Weather and seasons

In the outer environment we have weather and seasons. The season may be particularly important. We are now well aware of the way that lack of sunlight can affect some people (Drake et al, 1997) and it may well be that certain people with dementia who spend a lot of winter time inside are also adversely affected. There is substantial research on the use of daylight light bulbs and behaviour.

## How do we decide what is affecting behaviour?

If all these are candidates for the key factors affecting behaviour, how on earth do we decide which to opt for? It is often when residents show behaviour that the relative or staff of a care home find difficult, that a social worker is called upon to give support and advice. You will be able to show the staff that the answer lies in careful monitoring of the difficult behaviour. What seems to happen just before and just after it? Asking the question 'why?' is the first step to understanding and working with behaviour that challenges other people (Jackson and McDonald, 1999; Jackson et al, 2002).

## A 'reasons and triggers' approach can often be very helpful

The *reasons* for the behaviour are usually the interaction of the person with the brain damage and one or more of the other factors including all the feelings they have about having dementia. The hard fact that carers and staff find particularly difficult is that it may be the interaction with them personally that is the problem. It is far easier to blame it all on the deterioration of the brain (which for some people of course may be entirely appropriate) but this explanation should be the last, not the first.

The *trigger* tells you why the behaviour occurred at that particular time, at that particular place, with that particular person, in that particular situation. Social workers can help care home staff to analyse situations and write down the triggers. Nurses will have learned this approach as the ABC approach (antecedents, behaviour, consequences). It can be helpful to suggest a unit meeting where all staff play detective and try to systematically work out what the explanations for the behaviour are. Sometimes an alert cleaner or cook can be as insightful as the care staff. As we have said again and again, you start this process by really knowing the person.

Is Mr Cieslik very aggressive at a particular time of day? When with a particular member of staff? Before or after food? When confronted with a particular activity? What are the staff doing to support him as he struggles to talk to them in a language that he learned as an adult and which he is now starting to forget?

Then the next step is to try changing the causative factors. Some people are very imaginative about this.

> Mrs Beale was the widow of a naturalist and she would not settle in her nursing home. She headed out through the door at every possible moment. One of the staff made the suggestion that she was used to watching animals and birds, so they bought a bird table and she was given food to stock it. She has not tried to leave the home since.

> Mr McDonald was urinating all over the residential home even though he had an en suite WC. A bucket solved the problem for him. It turned out that he had been a shepherd who was quite unaccustomed to internal sanitary facilities.

> Mr Dupont was always up and about and wanting to get out of the unit at 4.00 in the morning, when there were few staff on the unit, so they found this behaviour very stressful. It turned out that he had been a postman. Once they knew this, staff were more accepting of his behaviour and were sometimes able to take him for a walk around the block.

These examples emphasise the importance of the past because this is so often where the explanation lies. People tend to make sense of the present in terms of the more familiar past. However, the explanation can easily lie in the present.

> The Revd Peter Epworth would not join in the group activities that were organised in the home and would often disrupt them. Although he had been a Methodist Minister he refused to attend the church services. He had arrived with some books, including, of course, the Bible. However, it was only when his key worker brought in a diary for him that he settled down. He would write in it, consult it and could be calmed down when agitated by reminding him that it was in his pocket. It, rather than the Bible, was the prop he needed to recall his former life.

Sometimes the key lies in the daily routine.

Mrs Lorenzo, for example, would not eat meals at a table with the other patients in her assessment ward. She behaved in a way that was socially unacceptable at mealtimes, because the damage to her brain meant that she no longer recognised the plates and cutlery for what they were. A constant supply of finger food was the answer for her.

If the behaviour is the result of brain damage alone the answer may not be as obvious as in the case of Mrs Lorenzo, and there may be little that can be done. But in most cases there is something that can be done which will reduce, although not always eliminate, behaviour that other people find difficult, unless, of course, it is the person's usual personality. Planned intervention and a consistent approach by all the key people is essential.

If Mr Brown gets upset and abusive if he is rushed with his food, then it is important that his daughter and son-in-law know this before they look after him on the days they give Mrs Brown a rest.

Similarly, if Mrs Masih is very agitated whenever she is asked a direct question that she cannot answer, then it is important that everyone who relates to her knows this, especially all her extended family.

Social workers have a crucial role in contributing to the process of understanding behaviour with families and staff. We can also help them to work out ways to minimise stress for everyone concerned. We also have an important educational and supportive role with staff after the person with dementia has moved to a care home to live. This may be when we participate in reviews or it may be if there is a problem about the placement. We are also likely to be involved if the staff demand that the person should be moved, or in the case of a formal complaint being made. Helping staff in care homes depends crucially on trust which needs to be nurtured and maintained if the care staff are to make use of your different perspective, which can, on occasions, be very helpful to all concerned.

## Activities

Social workers need to understand the importance of activities because we are likely to have to be quite fierce about the need for them in many settings where boredom is prevalent. The phrase 'boredom is the equivalent of bedsores for people with dementia' may be useful to reinforce this point. Spector et al (2003) found that cognitive stimulation sessions had the same efficacy as the drugs currently available for dementia so we can insist that they are made available. We can also try to match the person to the type of activities available in a day or long-term setting when we are planning a placement. Activities are a central part of any therapeutic regime, even one happening in a person's home. There are a lot of purposes for activities, some of which we have alluded to in previous chapters but will explain much more fully in this chapter:

- meeting a fundamental emotional need;
- assessment;
- reducing behaviour that challenges;
- maintaining cognitive function and skills;
- enhancing self-esteem;
- sociability;
- recreation and relaxation;
- exercise.

Most people think of activities as a recreation in the sense of passing the time enjoyably, but this is a very limited view. Some people go further and think that activities are the responsibility of only one profession – occupational therapy – which is another very limited view. Kitwood (1997a) identified the need for occupation as one of the basic emotional needs that are seriously compromised by dementia. In our view almost anything you do with people with dementia is an activity that meets the need for occupation. It can be purposeful, planned and therapeutic.

For many people with dementia, especially those living in group settings, the day is profoundly boring. There is a lot of sitting and sleeping, interrupted by brief spurts of organised activity and meals. People with dementia are often described as apathetic, which is a rather negative way of describing the hesitant uncertainty and lack of confidence so often exhibited. Others are more active but often in a chaotic and sometimes disruptive fashion. It is almost always necessary for staff to take the lead in any activity, which is why this work is so exhausting. You have to give so much of yourself, all the time. Because what happens has to be planned and initiated by staff, it is referred to as 'activities'. What happens does not happen spontaneously; staff are responsible for each individual and for the group as a whole. Social workers can support staff if they understand both how important and how exhausting meeting the need for occupation through activities can be.

## What do we mean by activity?

So with a number of waking hours to fill as therapeutically as possible, where do we help staff to start? We start by knowing a great deal about the people with dementia from their life at home in the community – their backgrounds and preferences. We know how they would like to pass the day ideally, even if the whole day cannot be tailored for them. We use the term 'day' here while being very aware that, in some long-term care settings, the night is more important for some people as a time for activity.

> Miss Godber had been a nurse who became matron of the local cottage hospital. Now she was living in a nursing home. Every time the drug trolley appeared for the nurse to hand out medication, she became very agitated and verbally aggressive to others in the lounge. Her social worker came to see another patient and witnessed one of these episodes. She was able to suggest to the nursing home staff that Miss Godber might be feeling deskilled and frustrated because giving out medication should be her job. Together they worked out a safe way for her to be involved in the drug round. She was given the job of collecting the little plastic cups after people had taken their medication, in a special container, and then washing them up. Her difficult behaviour stopped.

As social workers our assessments should include preferences and the range can be daunting, for example, in relation to musical preferences.

> Mr Gilhooly liked to be on his own listening to classical music.

> Mrs Beattie preferred big-band music on all the time and she liked good, boisterous conversation.

> Mrs Mitchell liked the old ballads that her mother sang to her and also enjoyed singing bawdy cockney songs.

Mrs Macleod liked Gaelic psalm singing.

Mrs Corriere spoke only Italian and liked to sing along with opera.

Mr Campbell loved listening to his tapes of Gospel songs, which reminded him of his childhood in Jamaica.

How can such diverse needs be met? It is a great deal easier if people with dementia are in small, relatively homogeneous groups.

Mrs Macleod was actually in a Gaelic-speaking day centre where they sing psalms all day.

Mrs Corriere's day centre alternated English-speaking days with Italian-speaking days, since it was in the midst of an Italian speaking community.

Mr Campbell attended a centre for African Caribbean elders where his sometimes unusual behaviour was well tolerated, although not always understood, by the other people who attended.

Mr Gilhooly's relatives came and sang Bach choral music with him and even in his advanced dementia he could manage to join in.

Homogeneity is a tricky issue in dementia care. The experience of three nursing homes in Amsterdam, which organised their units on the basis of life experience and background, would suggest that there is less behaviour that challenges when the routines and activities are familiar. We need some really solid research to follow this through. It is also a great deal easier to meet individual preferences if there are enough staff or volunteers to allow for individual attention and one-to-one activities for some people some of the time. Relatives' involvement in long-term care can also provide this highly individual attention.

## Gender issues

Some preferences are gender based and since most care settings have a predominance of women, there is little offered to men. Some men are uncomfortable being with women at all, or to any extent, most of their lives having been conducted in the company of other men. In these communities, such as a fishing village in the west of Scotland or an old mining community in Derbyshire, a room where men can be together is really essential if they are to enjoy the time. As social workers we will, of course, be aware that in some traditional South Asian communities men and women socialise separately and will be sensitive to the great emotional pressure that may be experienced from someone from one of these communities who is expected to socialise in mixed company.

> Mr Patel became very agitated and angry when he was introduced to the day centre. It was impossible to persuade him to join in any activities and he absolutely refused to eat. It was not until the social worker, who understood about his culture, pointed out to the staff that it was not acceptable for him to mix socially with the women or the female staff at the centre that a solution was found. A small 'men only' group was set up, which met in a side room. There were only two other men and Mr Patel made the third. As he was physically more fit than the other two men he became the leader of the group and began really to enjoy his time away from home in male company.

> A day centre for younger people with dementia found that men came much more regularly than the women. The activities were therefore geared to their interests. The staff thought this happened because these were all men who were accustomed to going to work and being out of the house all day.

## Using the senses

Another set of considerations is related to the extent of impairment of the person with dementia. We have increasing understanding of how to reach people who are very impaired indeed. This is by using every possible sense: sight, warmth, touch, music and smell, since it is clear that senses remain when cognition is very impaired (Brookes, 2001). An example of this is the use of multi-sensory or Snoezelen rooms, referred to in Chapter Seven, originally developed for people with severe learning disabilities. Carers and staff who accompany the person with dementia have been seen to benefit too, perhaps because of the relaxing experience itself and perhaps because they feel they are doing something for the people with dementia. The sense of helplessness felt by many staff caring for people in the late stages of dementia can be very demoralising.

## Failure-free

Another characteristic of a therapeutic approach is that activities should be failure-free. This can be a real challenge. As well as maintaining cognitive and other skills, they have to be achievable. When we understand that there does not have to be an end product this becomes easier to develop. The process is everything – there may be an outcome but there does not have to be one.

> Mr Hansom had always been a workaholic and needed to feel he was doing something useful. He would sort postcards into countries. It did not matter how long it took him or indeed if he did it wrong.

> Mr Burns 'helped' his wife by sorting the grit and brown bits of lentils out of jars of lentils.

We have all seen people with dementia playing games in centres where, for example, they have thrown a beanbag on to a dartboard–type mat. In the group there are often people who have no idea what to do and no understanding. For them the game exacerbates their sense of failure especially when the other participants get irritated with them.

Elsewhere we have seen quizzes being conducted where the group is asked questions until the participants begin to get the answers wrong. When they then become irritated and angry, their response is put down to the dementia. Much more appropriate for many people are familiar games such as bingo with staff alongside the less able. Playing for money will add to the familiarity! For others it will be dominoes or knitting squares to make a blanket.

Social workers can help the staff at the care facility to make the day (or night) enjoyable as far as possible. Some people ask why this is important if the person with dementia forgets almost immediately.

This is to deny that the person with dementia has feelings. They may not remember why they feel relaxed and cheerful but they certainly have those feelings after a happy activity session where their emotional need for occupation has been met.

## An example of a group activity

Let us look at one activity to see how it can meet the objectives outlined above. Preparation of food in a day centre can be the main morning activity in which everybody participates. First there is a discussion over coffee about the meal, linking it to other meals. 'Today we are having Scotch broth followed by mince and potatoes' leads to all kinds of memories for some people. Then there are a whole set of chores that can be tailored to meet the skills of the members, after the hand washing, which is an activity in itself. Some people can wash the vegetables, standing up at the sink. Some can peel them. Peeling onions is more difficult than potatoes and some do not enjoy the tears. Some can check the barley for bits. Others can chop on a board at the table. Staff will know who can handle a sharp knife safely. Perhaps, like Mr di Rollo in Chapter Two, one of the men was a chef. Some people like to stir. Time is not an issue. This can take a good hour or two with lots of talk, lots of reassurance and lots of voiced appreciation for a job well done. Some appropriate music from time to time might add to the enjoyment, perhaps during stops for tea or coffee.

What else can be achieved through an activity like this? First, assessment; people are being assessed for improvements and deterioration in tasks with which they are familiar. They will have no sense that they are being tested and found wanting. There will be a potential for assessing memory, coordination, concentration and sociability. We discussed this in more detail in Chapter Six.

Second, 'behaviour management' or working with behaviour that challenges. Some people will have been given chores in such a way that they are distracted from their difficult behaviour, others to enhance their strengths. A very agitated person might be alongside a member of staff handing things out or stirring. A person who is very withdrawn can be given a job alongside others but not as part of the group. Remembering to give appreciation for the efforts of withdrawn people, however small, is especially important.

Third, maintaining cognitive function and skills; reading the recipe book, weighing the ingredients and so on. There are a range of mental skills for all levels within the total task of meal preparation. The enhancement of self-esteem is obvious because there will be something that almost anyone can do for which the staff and others can be grateful and appreciative. There is no end of failure-free tasks.

Enhanced sociability is one of the results of this kind of work. There is no competition. All work together and there can be lots of good talking at the same time. As the smells waft from the cooker, memories are stirred and appetites stimulated. Sometimes an old song will come to mind. Sometimes the meal itself may be one chosen to recall old memories. In Scotland there is much to talk about when making broth. As a social worker supporting staff in a day centre you could find out about similar meals that are traditional for the people who are attending the centre.

Recreation and relaxation may be the least likely outcomes of such an activity but we all know that concentration on an enjoyable task can be one of the best ways of relaxing.

## Chores as activities

This may all sound a bit too good to be true and life may often be much more chaotic and difficult. One of the points we are trying to make is that familiar, daily chores have huge potential for purposeful planned activity, which is good for individuals and good for the group. There are a hundred obstacles to this approach in most settings. There may be no kitchenette (Gresham, 1999), or none to which residents have access, there may be no budget for the food that is inevitably wasted as sugar goes into the potatoes rather than salt, or the cake mix falls on the floor. The finished product may well be inedible. There may be seen to be too many risks. It may only work with small groups and so on, but it is worth fighting for. The following experiences show what is possible.

Mr Channing was a big, restless, aggressive man in his long-stay ward but, when transferred to a unit where he could spend the day ironing and vacuum-cleaning, he became a person who made a huge contribution to the unit.

A very similar man, Mr Scott, was in a traditional 30-bed ward where he was very aggressive and doubly incontinent. He was transferred to an eight-bed specialist unit. He was able to take charge of the tea bar where he laid out the cups and did all the washing up. He became the heart and soul of the unit, and was no longer incontinent.

These two stories make two additional points. One is to take care about gender and activity preferences and ensure that we are not using stereotypes to decide on activities. The second is one we have made frequently, which is the need many people have to be useful and to be thanked for their contribution.

Seeing personal care as an activity rather than a task is one which some people working in the field are finding increasingly helpful. If staff view bath time as an enjoyable, relaxing activity instead of a care task to be accomplished within specified time limits, the whole experience can be transformed. Intimate personal care is often an extremely stressful experience for people with dementia in care homes. However, if staff can be helped to see that this is a good period of one-to-one time that can be used to encourage personal conversation and reminiscence, life can be transformed for both parties.

This section on activities as therapy could fill a whole book and is therefore only an introduction. There are many additional resources available. Perrin is an occupational therapist whose work (Perrin and May, 1999; Perrin, 2005) provides a useful resource for social workers. Archibald's books on activities (Archibald, 1990; Archibald and Murphy, 1999) provide more information on this subject, as does Knocker (2003).

## Reminiscence and life-story work

Reminiscence is an essential activity for people with dementia whose memories of the past can still be very vivid. It is best undertaken with a real knowledge of individual history, and care needs to be taken about painful memories. Reminiscence has many good outcomes such as reinforcing identity, building self-esteem, encouraging meaningful communication, and shared humour (Schweitzer, 1998). Age Exchange is a charity that produces a rich supply of resources on reminiscence, including reminiscence-based activities involving relatives (eg Bruce et al, 1999). Gibson (2006) has written a really authoritative book on the subject.

In this section we are going to concentrate on life-story books. They need not actually be books: they might be a collage, a videotape, a box of items. However, we will only talk about books here. A life-story book can be an immensely helpful tool, with many uses. It helps us to understand what activities are likely to be enjoyed by a particular person. It also gives us clues about the reasons people behave in the way they do and is also an important source of information about personal preferences, referred to in Chapter Five.

## Life-story books

As in the case of Mr O'Reilly in Chapter Five, there is often a need for a life-story book (Murphy, 2004; Gibson, 2005). This need not, of course, be a full life story, rather aspects of life and interests. Some people do not want to share the story of their lives, especially if they are ashamed of them or if they have been very traumatic. We shall see in the section on counselling, how important these past events and emotions can be in understanding present behaviour.

What is needed is a book showing what is important to a person. Often it is major life events: work, marriage, children. For others it may be their regiment or football club, their family being of much less consequence. These books give everyone the information they need to relate to that person: staff, relatives and visitors to the care home or day centre or to the person's own home. They are best if they are full of pictures.

> Staff have a good start if they know that Mrs Corriere sang in amateur opera or that Mrs Wang ran a takeaway restaurant with her husband.

A life-story book also provides a tool for one-to-one work. The family of a person with dementia often finds the point where they have to face the fact that they can no longer cope at home to be very stressful. As social workers we can suggest to them the possibility of creating a book of the person's life. It can ease the transition from one setting to another. Pictures of both places – the person's home in the community and of the place where they are now living – can go into the book. It is vitally important to include accurate names of the people in the photographs.

> When Mrs Robinson came to the home and kept calling for Tom, the staff had no idea if she meant her son, her brother, her lover, her husband or her pet dog. A well-labelled life-story book would have told them and they would have been able to talk to her about him.

Relatives are often at a loss to know what to do when they visit the person with dementia in a care home. Sitting side by side going through the life-story book and sharing memories can be very therapeutic. Sometimes aggressive or restless people can be calmed by the same process with a member of staff. Life-story books are best started while the person is still living at home and therefore as social workers we have a vital role in their creation. There is a real problem with the transfer of detailed information about the person's life between the community and the care home. Social workers are best placed to make sure that this vital information about the person's daily routines, personality, interests, value systems and life story does get transferred to the care home with the person.

> Mr Steele was very bewildered and upset when he arrived at the day centre and again when he arrived back home. Pictures of both places were put in his life-story book. His wife spent 10 minutes or so in the morning talking about home and then about the centre, using the book. Wherever Mr Steele went the life-story book went too. The staff of the day centre also went through the book at the end of the day. Mr Steele became much calmer about the transition.

## Counselling

Counselling people with dementia and their carers is part and parcel of any work in this field, if by counselling we mean listening intently to what is being said and offering what is called unconditional positive regard. To do this we have to be able to empathise with the strong feelings of others without being too dismayed or cast down ourselves.

### Counselling carers

Carers are always saying that what they need is someone to listen to them. They know there are often no answers and that little can be done but they want to use the chance of talking to someone else to work out their own plans and approaches. We all know the benefits of this but we sometimes forget that there are matters that cannot be shared within families and that talking to a sympathetic outsider can be enormously helpful.

In the early stages we may have to listen to the matrimonial difficulties, the grief as plans for the future perish, the intense ambivalence within relationships that become recognised as the difficulties mount. We may have to listen to anger, frustration and hurt as the person with dementia becomes more dependent. We may have to help people work through intense feelings of guilt when day care, respite care and then long-stay care are needed. One of the advantages of good counselling of carers is that it helps people to see situations more clearly and face up to the implications.

The Alzheimer's Association of Victoria found that they were getting a lot of carers coming in for counselling about two years after their relative had gone into long-stay care. The carers were often worried that they themselves had dementia. When they really talked it through it became clear that they had never worked through their feelings of guilt at giving up caring. Presumably, at the time, all the attention was on the person with dementia and it was nobody's job to listen to the carer working out his or her feelings. It has been our experience that the time when the person with dementia makes it clear that they now feel safer in the care home than their own home is a particularly stressful time for carers. This may well be more than a year after they have moved.

In a similar vein is the experience of chronically complaining relatives on a long-stay ward who were offered counselling. Talking through their guilt feelings, not only about relinquishing care but also about beginning to have a new life of their own, was felt to be very helpful and certainly diminished the complaints. As social workers we can help the staff in care homes by explaining the psychological processes involved. We have tended to see carers as saints who are willingly giving their all to care. What we often failed to see was the ambivalence and the anger that are inevitable but often well hidden because the carer is ashamed to mention them.

## Counselling people with dementia

The possibility that unfinished emotional business actually corrodes our coping capacities in time is one that underpins some approaches to counselling people with dementia. The work of Feil has already been mentioned in Chapter Four. Feil (2002, p 16) says that 'These very old people gradually taught me that they must pack for their final move. They sort out dirty linen stashed in the storehouse of the past. They are busy, irresistibly drawn to wrap up loose ends. This is not a conscious movement to the past. It is a deep human need: to die in peace'.

It is well accepted that children who cannot talk about their feelings will tell us about them through play. Communicating through allegory or non-verbally is perhaps similar with people with dementia. It is not easy. Making time to seize opportunities that arise for communication about feelings is often difficult and fluctuating lucidity means that people often want to talk when there is no time to listen. As social workers we can help staff in care homes to allow such conversations to take place instead of putting up the 'engaged' signal to prevent them. Staff often do this because they are uncomfortable talking with a person who is experiencing strong emotions although they will often use the excuse that they are too busy to do so. The time around the transfer to a care home and subsequent reviews are times when social workers can be legitimately involved in a counselling relationship with the person.

A few private psychotherapists are beginning to pioneer this type of approach. Some social workers are able to make referrals to specialist counselling for people with dementia in their area, including it in the care package if they can make a good enough case. This is one of those classic chicken and egg situations. People will not refer because there are no local resources and local resources will not be developed because there are no referrals. You will need to be proactive to break this vicious circle.

## Counselling staff

In this section on counselling we must not forget the needs of paid staff, who can have very strong and even more unmentionable feelings about their job, about certain people with dementia in their care, or certain carers. They may find some intolerable. They may find that difficulties at home are making them unable to give their best at work. They may be unable to cope with the sadness of a lot of the work. We are not proposing full-scale psychotherapeutic counselling, but rather opportunities for talking about their work with someone who has made time and space to listen carefully. This is called supervision or debriefing and it can be immensely helpful. Issues raised in supervision are often resolved by discussing them in a problem-solving manner.

Sometimes very difficult and painful issues arise as they did for Mrs Roberts. Mrs Roberts worked in a nursing home and seemed unable to cope with Mr Dryden who made suggestive remarks and tried to grab her breasts when she was helping him to wash. Mrs Roberts had been sexually abused as a child by her grandfather and Mr Dryden's behaviour was triggering the powerful childhood emotions associated with the abuse. She found talking about her feelings extremely difficult in the staff group. She was finally able to talk about her experiences to her supervisor in a one-to-one situation, which she found immensely helpful.

# Group work

## Group work with carers

Group work usually needs a very great deal more thought and planning than it gets (Haight and Gibson, 2005). Carers' groups are often seen as an obviously 'good thing' without the organisers properly matching up the aims and methods. Group work theory has some very useful principles, which are largely ignored. If, for example, you want to run a group where carers become very close and feel able to share personal worries, then it has to be a time-limited, closed group. This makes it more likely that it will be a group where the relationships are so strong that it becomes self-sufficient. The group then decides for itself what it wants to do.

The usual, more open, kind of carers' group is an odd hybrid, which is meant to do everything and does nothing well. It is meant to provide mutual support, which it does at a fairly superficial level unless people form friendships that go on outside the group. It is meant to be information sharing, which it does quite well except that people seldom feel able to ask about and share their own difficulties. It is often meant to both sustain existing members and welcome new ones, whereas, in fact, new members of any group, where there are already strong links, will have a hard time working their way into the group.

These open groups are often expected to voice opinions about the services received and their gaps and yet rarely are members given the confidence to do this. They are often meant to be groups that run themselves in time and yet only in groups where people know and trust each other well does this happen. Social work time is often allocated for a time-limited period to start the group off and then withdraw. The reasoning behind this is that a group will then run itself but in fact the group rarely becomes independent, having been accustomed to relying on a strong professional.

## Group work with people with dementia

As far as people with dementia are concerned, group-work skills are even less well developed except with people who have had an early diagnosis, as we mentioned in Chapter Four. There is an increasing amount of very useful literature from people who have run such groups (Yale, 1998; Bender, 2004). They are small, intimate and very intense groups with what seems to be a steady membership of the same people (that is relatively closed) who come to trust and rely on each other a great deal. Sharing both the feelings and experience about techniques that are helpful in coping with problems like a failing memory seems to be very helpful. They are also a good source of insight for staff into what the worries are of people who have been told they have dementia, at a stage when they are able to talk about it and make some decisions.

We have already discussed the contribution of people with dementia to our present understanding in Chapter Four. McGowin (1993), a woman with dementia, decided to help herself by helping others. She started a support group for other early-diagnosed people. She felt people needed help from others 'walking through the same maze'. Bryden (2005) gives us a particularly valuable insight into the experience of dementia. She belongs to an internet group called Dementia Advocacy and Support Network International (DASNI), which was founded in 2000. DASNI does exactly what it says it does. It is an online support network whose members come from a wide variety of countries. One third of them have dementia (Bryden, 2005).

Groups of more impaired people with dementia usually involve activities such as reminiscence (Gibson, 2006). Most group care settings are by their very nature group work yet the skills and insights from group work are seldom applied. We have in mind our knowledge about the phases of a group sometimes referred to as 'norming', 'storming' and 'reforming', which are, generally, a process of sounding each other out, a phase of turmoil as people feel safe enough to test the group, and then a phase of closeness. Knowing this can be very helpful for both staff groups and groups of residents or members. If the numbers are too big it is unlikely to feel like a group. There ought to be a great deal more work in small groups within settings where the same people gather each day or week to do something together with a strong emphasis on it being special and different from the normal routine.

John Killick ran a film group called 'Going to the Pictures' in a day hospital. A small group of service users with some communication difficulties meet once a week with the leader to look at video clips and short films. They then have a discussion session, which takes off in all directions and is often hilarious.

SONAS aPc groups, developed in the Republic of Ireland, provide a structured format for a group activity with people who are moderately or severely impaired with their dementia. 'Sonas' is the Irish Gaelic word for well-being and the format has been developed to stimulate all the five senses to create a feeling of well-being. Having completed a training course, staff in care homes are given a CD-ROM to use as a template for running the SONAS groups. This model can also be used on a one-to-one basis (Threadgold, 2002).

## Family therapy

Family therapy, which has grown out of systems theory, is traditionally practised in dysfunctional families usually in relation to distressed children. Clearly it is useful when families are under stress because one member has dementia but it is not to be undertaken without proper skills and support. There will be times when social workers see whole families. Sometimes, the diagnosis is given to a whole family including the person with dementia. Sometimes care planning meetings involve the family as a whole, as agreement is worked out about who will do what, at what time. Sometimes, when there is a crisis, the whole family is assembled to try and sort it out.

Thinking of dementia as a family problem rather than a problem for the person, or the person and the carer, can be very constructive. Sometimes you become aware that the problem is actually elsewhere. There might, for example, be a difficult adolescent, but everyone avoids dealing with that and scapegoats 'granny' who has dementia. There may be prolonged resentment that 'granny' has all the attention and the husband or teenage daughter may feel short-changed.

A common experience for social workers in the field is working with a family where the person with dementia has several adult children who cannot agree between themselves about the best way forward. One of them, often the one who is living on the spot and feeling under considerable pressure, will want the person to go into long-term care. Other siblings, living at a distance, may want their parent to remain at home. The fact that as social workers we are aware that the subtext for this story is often that some of the siblings do not want the family home to be sold to pay for long-term care, calls for particular confidence and skill. Sometimes a crisis like dementia can bring families closer together as they struggle to provide comfort and support for each other. Sadly, this often leaves out the person with dementia who may not even have been told the diagnosis.

The social worker's goal is to help the family to arrive at the decision that is best for the person. Understanding that the family operates as a closed system and that a change in one part of the system will affect all the other parts, is a useful way of looking at these situations. Decisions around dementia and particularly the decision to move the person into long-term care, often seems to produce considerable conflict within a family. When you analyse the situation, using the tools of systems theory, you will often discover that the conflict is not really about the parent with dementia but is much more to do with sibling rivalry and conflicts that have their roots way back in the past.

Families can be very complex in structure, particularly as more and more people have a succession of marriages or partnerships. There are two tools used by practitioners working in a systemic way that can help with the analysis of complex situations. A genogram is basically a family tree of all the family members concerned. An ecomap is a diagrammatic representation of a family system. There are conventions to these tools, such as using circles for women and triangles for men, single lines connecting people with weak emotional connections, double lines for strong connections and double lines with squiggles to indicate difficult relationships.

We have found that both these tools can be useful when a social worker is trying to get a clear picture of the family situation from a stressed carer talking either face to face or on the telephone. All you need to do is scribble down a genogram and/or ecomap on a scrap of paper to use for future reference. Ecomaps are particularly valuable as they will often show you where the closest bonds lie within the family. They may not be where you expect them to be at all.

There is very little easily available literature about this potentially useful way of working in the field of dementia care. Sherlock and Gardener (1993) have written a general introduction to the subject. Roper-Hall (1993) has applied the theory to work with older adults. Tibbs (2001) briefly explored its application by social workers. However, there is need for a great deal more work in this field. As we have said, the major therapeutic advances in dementia are likely to be transfers from other fields and this is a good example.

## The creative arts

In our explanation of the three approaches to dementia we mentioned the 'citizenship approach', which turns the other two on their head by looking at what the person with dementia can contribute as a citizen. There is increasing research (Miller et al, 2000) to underpin the experience of many in the field that many people with dementia go through a phase of remarkable creativity if they are given the opportunity and the materials. We should therefore seize opportunities for making this happen whenever possible; we will all be richer for it. One of the most famous artists to paint while he had dementia was Willem de Kooning. Others have come to the arts after the diagnosis.

James McKillop is an example. His 'befriender' realised that he had extraordinary talent in photography even though he had only taken family snaps before. Some of his photographs have been published (McKillop, 2003). John Killick, who has produced two books of poetry (Killick, 1997; Killick and Cordonnier, 2000) by people with dementia and has talked about the poems several times on the radio, maintains that people with dementia can be natural poets because they often communicate in pictures and metaphor. He works with very disabled people with dementia and the poems give a moving impression of what it must be like as well as being poems with their own intrinsic value as poetry.

Creative arts are also important as a way of helping with:

- self-expression;
- communication;
- social skills;
- self-esteem.

This should not be confused with art therapy, for which there is a whole profession and some solid research. There are similarly professions of music therapy and drama therapy where the research base is smaller but there is a lot of good practice. We are referring more to undertaking creative arts with the help of artists or occupational therapists. Useful references include Hill (2001), Craig (2003, 2004, 2005), Killick and Davis Basting (2003) and Kindell and Armans (2003), and there are some useful DVDs and videos (Mullen and Killick, 2001; Killick and Rose, 2003). Our intention here is to draw attention to their potential for providing an opportunity for people with dementia to give to society, as well as improving their quality of life. There is increasing interest in using creativity in other attempts to change the lives of people with other problems; in deprived communities for example or with alienated young people. We also want to say something here about music, which has particular importance for people with dementia.

## Music

Music has had a special place in dementia care for a very long time. The fact that the ability to communicate through music survives long after other forms of verbal communication have been lost is well known. The benefits of 'singalongs' in care homes and the joys for individuals of listening to familiar and much-loved music has become a given in dementia care. There are CDs of hymns and carols available, sung by church congregations, not by choirs, which give people with dementia from this tradition a great deal of pleasure (Morningside United Church, 2005a, 2005b).

However, the reasons for this have not been clearly understood until now. Archaeologists are beginning to study the role of music in human evolution and suggest that singing may be a very primitive function in the brain related to survival, which is why it endures through the ravages of dementia (Mithen, 2005).

A project called 'Singing for the brain' has started in the West Berkshire branch of the Alzheimer's Society. Groups include people with dementia and their carers and trained singers using the 'call and response songs' that occur in many different cultures, as well as singing rounds and canons. Warm-up exercises are being developed to re-establish the neurological connections between the voice and the brain before the actual singing session starts.

People are deriving enormous pleasure and a sense of well-being from these groups and the whole subject of the importance and value of song is now starting to be researched (Montgomery-Smith, 2006).

Gotell and Ekman (2001) found that staff singing while they worked improved behaviour in people with dementia even if they were not joining in the singing.

## Using dolls with people with dementia

The use of dolls in dementia care is now well established as a tool to assist communication. Dolls are also used to help to meet people's emotional needs (Scott, 2002; James and Mackenzie, 2005; James et al, 2005; Walker, 2005; Verity, 2006). There used to be strong resistance to the idea as it was perceived, often by families as well as professionals, that giving people dolls or soft toys meant that people were being treated as children. However, pioneering work undertaken, for example, at Merevale House (Moore, 2001), has shown that dolls and soft toys can be used as attachment objects, which help the person to feel secure. Looking after a baby gives us a role and a sense of purpose and dolls can make very good baby substitutes. The fact that the person with dementia can be only too well aware that they are 'playing' with a doll in no way diminishes their value. As with complementary therapies there has been considerable anecdotal evidence in support of the use of dolls for some years but empirical research has been missing.

The subject is now being seriously researched. The first study was published in 2005 by James et al. They examined the use of dolls in two homes for people who were classed as 'elderly mentally ill' in the north east of England. The views of 46 staff were collected about their use, 32 of whom felt that the lives of the people with dementia were much better as a result of using the dolls. Six areas were specifically monitored: resident interaction with staff, interaction with other residents, level of activity, happiness/contentment, amenability to care interventions, and agitation. Research such as this will help social workers to support care staff who may wish to use dolls with residents who meet resistance from families and vice versa. We are uniquely placed to be able to influence decisions like this as long as we have a relationship of trust with the care staff.

## Complementary therapies

There is now considerable interest in using a variety of these therapies, some of which have been in use for several years. Their main purpose is to reduce stress, particularly in people with dementia whose behaviour is seen as difficult and to encourage relaxation. We referred earlier to the use of Snoezelen. The main therapies in use, according to a study conducted by the Mental Health Foundation (Wiles and Brooker, 2003), are massage, aromatherapy, reflexology, reiki and herbal medicine, although there are many others. This research was the first attempt to provide empirical evidence in an area where there had been an abundance of anecdotal evidence for many years.

The study was conducted in the UK and Ireland in several centres. The sample was small ($n=85$) and self-selected, which means that it is likely that only those respondents who were particularly interested and enthusiastic replied to the questionnaire. However, within those limitations the study found that 'with due attention to issues of safety and the importance of informed consent, these therapies may have much to offer when seeking to improve the quality of life of clients and their carers' (Wiles and Brooker, 2003, p 36). You can find ideas on the many possibilities from Herzberg (2001), Brett (2002) and Thorgrimsen et al (2006).

Social workers who are familiar with the therapies that we have discussed in this chapter may well be able to influence the care that the people with dementia who they are supporting will receive. Staff in care homes will be receptive to suggestions from you as long as they are given within a relationship of trust. Even within the constraints of care management it is possible for social workers to remain involved with these families. At the very least the annual review provides you with opportunities.

## Conclusion

This chapter on therapies has covered a range of interventions on the basis that social workers need to have an idea of what might be in care plans even if we are unable actually to offer the interventions ourselves. New interventions are being explored all the time, which is why this is such an exciting field. The barriers and limited expectations are challenged by these interventions and they are responsible for much of the changing attitudes to dementia care.

### Further reading

Feil, N. (2002) *The Validation Breakthrough* (2nd edition), Baltimore, MD: Health Promotions Press.

Gibson, F. (2006) *Reminiscence and Recall: A Practical Guide to Reminiscence Work* (3rd edition), London: Age Concern Books.

Killick, J. and Davis Basting, A. (2003) *The Arts and Dementia Care: A Resource Guide* (1st edition), Brooklyn, NY: National Center for Creative Ageing.

Marshall, M. (2005) *Perspectives on Rehabilitation and Dementia*, London: Jessica Kingsley Publishers.

# TEN

# The future

## Introduction

In 2006, work with people with dementia is at a very exciting stage. The movement that began in the early 1990s has continued to flourish. There are now enough enthusiasts and experts, many of them social workers, to have reached a critical mass and the momentum for change has started. Formidable obstacles to change remain, some of which we have considered. However, new kinds of services, new skills, new theories and new approaches are emerging in all countries that already have a significant proportion of very old people. The growth in the use of the internet has led to much more collaboration between people in different countries. New ideas spread around the globe very fast now.

The issue will be to what extent all this enthusiasm can survive economic pressure. In this chapter we reflect on the past by considering how we might advise a hypothetical country setting up services for people with dementia from scratch. What have we learned about what works and what does not work? We conclude by reflecting on social work with people with dementia and what remains to be done if we are to contribute fully to improving the lives of people with dementia and their carers.

## Challenges facing the UK

In the UK, health and social care are under considerable pressure in spite of the additional funds allocated by governments since 2000. Advances in medical technology, increased expectations from the public, combined with our ageing population are placing severe strains on services. Work with people with dementia and their carers is never going to be the most important public priority; that will always be children.

Older people and mental health are priorities in all the countries of the UK, yet dementia constantly falls off the agenda. It is hard to know whether this is because of a deep personal fear of confronting this issue or because the challenge is too great and remains in the 'too difficult' basket. We need to be clever about attaching the issues of dementia to other priorities such as chronic and progressive conditions, depression and urban regeneration. A small impetus has come from the fact that there is a growing recognition that younger people get dementia too and service planners seem to find it easier to empathise with the predicament of this group.

## International challenges

Countries whose populations are not yet as old as those in industrialised countries will be facing the issue of dementia soon. The exceptions, of course, are the countries of sub-Saharan Africa, where the AIDS pandemic has decimated populations, and countries affected by the major disasters, natural and man-made, of the first decade of the 21st century. But generally speaking, countless people who have survived the diseases of childhood are going to be in the older age groups, and a proportion will get dementia. The numbers will dwarf those in the countries experiencing dementia now and the service shortfall is of quite a different order. This, combined with the rapid urbanisation of most of these countries, makes for a lack of the family networks that might just have sustained very dependent older people. We referred in Chapter Two to the fact that Alzheimer's Disease International estimates that 66% of the estimated 18 million people in the world who have dementia already are living in developing countries. What will we want to say to them about what we have learned so far in the UK?

## What have we learned so far?

### Putting the wishes of the person first

The first principle we will want to share is that of listening to people with dementia and their carers. It has taken a long time in this country for us to learn to listen to these 'experts from experience'. Listening to carers came first in the 1980s. It was a decade later when we learned to listen to the voice of people with dementia. In this country we have, on the whole, let professionals do the planning. A lot of dedicated professionals, with all the best intentions, have developed very interesting and valuable services but have frequently not incorporated the qualities that are valued by carers and people with dementia, such as flexibility and the ability to offer a 24 hours a day, seven days a week service. It is quite clear, when you look at a lot of our services, that they are, on the whole, run for the convenience of staff. Day care, for example, is usually only available during the working day, and provides a short day even then, yet a lot of carers struggle to get the person with dementia ready for picking up at 9.30am. They would find it a lot easier to take the morning slowly and then have the afternoon and evening to themselves. The fact that day care services shut down over the weekend and bank holidays means, as we know, that carers come to dread these times.

We have usually offered respite care in set blocks in some kind of institution, which is much easier to plan for and means that residential places are not remaining unoccupied. A judgement has been made that the people providing residential care services cannot afford to run them on much less than a near 100% occupancy rate, but flexibility is what people need. Alternate weekends off, or overnight stays for the person with dementia, once a week, or as needed, would allow carers to maintain their interests and generally keep their life going as normally as possible. This type of respite care might be much more valuable to people with dementia and their carers. It is safe to assume that it would also probably help to keep people out of long-term care for longer. Family placement, which works well with people with learning disabilities, is remarkably underdeveloped for people with dementia (Currie and Stopforth, 2006).

In the UK we seem to struggle all the time to make services person-centred. We seem to find it very difficult really to listen to, and respect, the judgement of carers and people with dementia, and to make our services adaptable to individual needs. There seems to be a tendency to slip backwards all the time to an easier option. Perhaps this is a fact of life. We are inclined to think it is also about professional arrogance – that we have to believe we know best to justify the fact that we earn a salary for what we do. Social workers who have listened carefully to people with dementia and their carers are often frustrated by the unresponsive nature of a lot of the services that are available. We have to recognise that much of this is discriminatory and would not happen with other user groups. As social workers, we take discrimination seriously in our values and we should probably be making a more explicit issue of it.

Yet, really listening and providing precisely what people need is a very complicated and difficult job; it requires enormous skill. Another reason why we find it so difficult to listen and respond to the needs of people with dementia and their carers may be the low self-esteem enjoyed by people working in this field. This results in people feeling that they are doing a mundane job because everyone around them, including, sadly, their managers in a lot of cases, think that working with older people with dementia is a mundane job. In the hierarchy of social work, working with older people with dementia often still comes far behind child protection and mental health in the perception of many colleagues. Society's ageism, discussed in Chapter Five, and sexism are behind this. Most younger people prefer not to think about ageing and dementia, seeing older people as a different and less worthy species.

So, as a first principle, we would want to say to people who are just starting on the road of caring for a significant number of people with dementia in their society: 'people with dementia and their carers are the experts first and foremost'. They know what they need and, to a degree, it will be different in each case, so services must be adaptable to individual needs.

The principle of putting the wishes of the customer first is related to the somewhat off-putting concepts of customer care, which are so omnipresent in all the successful service industries; from hotels to companies that replace car exhausts. It seems that, in service industries, if you are not constantly training staff and giving them incentives for customer care, they quickly slip back to serving their own interests. In a sense we are saying that staff are the equivalent of the machine in the manufacturing process and they all need the same degree of maintenance!

## Three approaches

Throughout this book we have emphasised that social workers need to be comfortable with three approaches to people with dementia: the medical, the social and the citizenship approaches. Our expertise is mainly in the social approach but we need to be appreciative of the other two and to integrate them when necessary. Social workers in most developing countries are likely to be aware of the medical approach to dementia; psychiatrists are the pioneers and have the status to develop clinical practice and services, albeit often on a small scale. Exciting work has, for example, been undertaken in prevalence studies (www.alz.org.uk) showing that many less developed countries have a lower proportion of people with dementia in their older populations. Use of a wider range of medical practice is also emerging with herbal medicine and ayurvedic medicine being practised as well as western medicine in India for example. Social workers in Soweto in South Africa are offering training in dementia care to traditional healers in order to reach people with dementia who practitioners of western style medicine never see (Tibbs, 1999).

However, western drug companies are supporting a lot of clinical services and they obviously embrace a medical model. As social workers talking to our peers in less developed countries, we would be wanting to share the social approach and perhaps even the citizenship approach. We would struggle to find a great deal of research to support our zeal but it is emerging, as we have hoped to show in this book. The importance of culture was shown in Figure 4.1 of the man with dementia; different countries and cultures have different attitudes to dementia and we need to be respectful of the impact of this. There is always a tendency for developed countries to want to export their models of services but, as McCabe (2003) found, this may be quite inappropriate.

## Status

We might also want to say something about the status of dementia care. Given how much we have learned in the last few years about the potential of skilled services, we need to be saying loud and clear that this is a field of care requiring the highest levels of skill. This is not just because we are working with older people and they deserve the best, but that we know that ours are the skills and expertise required.

What we mean is that we know people are acutely sensitive to their social and built environment. Their behaviour and well-being depend just as much on where they are and the way they are treated as they do on medication, possibly more. Therefore, to ensure that people function at the highest possible level within the parameters of neurological damage, all the skills and expertise we have acquired are essential. What look like normal housekeeping tasks, for example, are instead an individual plan of activities to achieve the maximum competence and confidence of the person. What looks like an informal gathering of carers is in fact a skilful use of group-work principles. What looks like a nice homely environment is in fact a very carefully designed building that helps people to find their own way wherever possible.

One of the mistakes we have made in the UK, in adopting the medical model so widely, is to assume that difficult behaviour is a symptom of dementia. This prevented us for a long time from exploring the reasons and triggers for the behaviour, some of which are to do with the way the person is treated. We have assumed for too long that a facility where people with dementia are calm, happy and content means that their dementia is not as advanced as people in a place where there is a lot of screaming and aggressive behaviour. There has been a frequent lack of recognition that the expertise and skill of the staff in the first facility is the key factor in keeping everyone calm and happy. This failure to recognise good practice has been very damaging. As well as reinforcing the old stereotypes about people with dementia and the way they behave, leading to further stigma, it has undermined the skills that staff had developed. Because their skills went unrecognised for so long, the status of work in this field has remained very low.

## The new culture of dementia care

We would want to share our optimism about dementia care. We would suggest that policy makers embrace the new culture of dementia care, one that is positive and rehabilitative. Because most of their expertise will be in clinical practice, it may be very pessimistic. They will be emphasising the issue of numbers and burden on carers. We will want to share our knowledge about the impact of raised expectations, person-centred care, therapeutic building design and all the other issues we have covered in this book that we believe make such a difference to the experience of dementia for both the person with the condition and their carers.

It is also important to encourage them to seize the initiative, to a sensible degree, from the medics. On the other hand they will have to ensure that an appropriate degree of medical expertise is available, both for diagnosis and input on the brain disease and also in treatment of concomitant physical conditions, the symptoms of which we know can be wrongly attributed to the neurological damage. The new culture of dementia care has to be based on a team approach, as does all rehabilitative care. We saw in Chapter One that once the great tree of the old culture of dementia care, based on segregation, incarceration and stigma, is well established, it is very hard to get rid of. It is much better not to let it take root in the first place.

## The way services are organised

We would want to say some clear things about the way services are organised. The split between health and social care is very damaging to people with dementia. Their needs are complex, rapidly changing and made up of health and social factors, which are often inseparable. Our system of care makes difficulties where none need to exist. A disproportionate amount of social work time in the UK is about untangling problems that arise between health and social care. It is in part about a power struggle between health and welfare organisations where each is trying to ensure maximum control over resources while at the same time playing 'pass the parcel' with people, like those with dementia, whose needs do not fit tidily into the remit of either organisation.

It is taking a long time to bridge the chasm between health and social care. Governments in the different countries of the UK are now making concerted attempts to make the two halves of the system work together through organisational change. But this, in itself, will not break down the social and cultural barriers to joint working. Just as we saw above, it is much easier not to create this division in the first place, than to change it when it has been well established, as it has in the UK for decades.

## Specialist services

The extent to which specialist services are needed will undoubtedly be something we will want to mention and it is hard to agree on what our experience in the UK has taught us. We have to acknowledge two things simultaneously; one is that most services will not be specialist and the other that specialist services can often be the best ones for many people with dementia. We have to balance reality with vision.

Most frontline services are not specialist. GPs, for example, probably only have 12–20 patients with moderate to severe dementia living at home, in an average-sized caseload in a community with a normal age spread in the population (University of Birmingham Department of Primary Care and General Practice, 2005). Yet they are a key service and are usually the first point of call. If they are not trained in dementia there is less chance of an early diagnosis, which can be helpful to people with dementia and families who want to be able to sort themselves out while they are able, and to make plans for the future. GPs are the gatekeepers to many other services. They need to know where to refer people and how to obtain the sustained support that carers need so badly over the months and years.

Similarly, the home care service is rarely specialist, yet if home carers are trained in dementia care they can encourage people with memory problems to seek a diagnosis and they can offer the necessary advice on where to go for help. They can also communicate with the person more effectively and deliver personal care in a way that will not frighten, frustrate or humiliate the person with dementia. These skills in communication may well be essential in helping people with dementia and their carers down the rocky path ahead. Non-specialist services are inevitably the way most people will be cared for. There are far too many people with dementia needing help for specialised care to be a reality for more than a tiny minority. Some specialist home care services do exist, for example in Nottingham. However, initially at any rate, people with dementia are most likely to be helped by non-specialist home care staff. Social workers should press for all staff who come in contact with people with dementia and their carers to be well trained and briefed, not just those in specialist services, and to insist that there is a role for specialist care.

In Bedford, there is a specialist community mental health team for older people with a team of community support workers, well trained in dementia care, attached. The CMHT completes the initial assessments and its community support workers remain involved with the family for a period of some weeks. The cases are then transferred to the area social work teams for older people. Training in dementia is given to the staff involved in both teams. Only the most complex dementia cases remain with the specialist CMHT, although any cases can be referred back to the CMHT after the transfer, according to an agreed protocol. In addition there is a strong working relationship with the local Alzheimer's Society, built up over many years, which is able to offer ongoing support to people with dementia and their carers through the various different projects that it runs.

It is often argued that the people who need specialist services are those with behaviour that others find difficult. If it is to be limited to them, there is an urgent need for all staff working with older people to have training about dementia up to a certain level. We could reflect on this in relation to social work. Is there a need for specialist social workers? If there is there will only ever be enough of us for the really very complex situations and all others will be dealt with along with other older people or community care users. These non-specialist staff will need to be able to understand most aspects of dementia care.

Having suggested that there is a need for some degree of specialism, if only for people with behaviour that challenges, there is a related issue about how this specialist service is provided. Social workers often have to decide whether a person needs a specialist care home, which inevitably means that the person with dementia has to move physically to the care they need. Ideally specialist help would be provided where the person lives.

Specialist care homes present another real dilemma, which is whether the person should move out once their behaviour has settled down. As social workers we have to be involved in the very tricky decisions about finding another placement. We have to weigh up the need for the person with dementia to stay somewhere they have got used to versus the needs of all the other people with dementia who need the specialist facility. We can find ourselves the champion of our person with dementia and can ignore the wider implications. However, this is a real dilemma given the shortage of such places and the additional costs. Ideally we would have enough services to offer what is best for that individual but this is easier to say than to deliver.

There are also issues about maintaining the quality of specialist services. They can become dumping grounds full of demoralised staff who feel neglected and taken for granted. Conversely, they can be wonderful resources of expertise, where training and placements are offered and much appreciated. Much of what we have learned since the 1990s was learned in specialist settings, which set out to show that a positive approach could really affect the experience of dementia for all concerned. In a sense, like everything else, the reasons for the specialism are the key. If they exist to take problems off the street or to hide them away, then they will be awful. If they exist to offer a rehabilitative service to certain individuals, who go there for good reasons, they are more likely to be therapeutic in style. Perhaps at least one specialist service is required in every locality to show what can be done and to be a local resource.

If this is to be a policy, then this specialist service needs to be multipurpose, offering a flexible range of services for people with dementia and their carers. So, the advice we should offer to our hypothetical colleagues in another country on this subject needs to be something like: 'concentrate first on raising the levels of expertise in all frontline staff, and set up specialist services for very clear reasons. If most of your services are not provided by statutory agencies, it may be very hard to persuade independent care providers to consider specialising in dementia care unless additional funding is available. Specialism requires extra training and quality control, which adds to the costs even though it can give more work satisfaction for staff'.

## The law

We might also want to say something about the law. Traditionally law in the different parts of the UK has been a very blunt instrument, with its all-or-nothing approach to the question of whether a person is mentally competent or not. In recent years we have seen a welcome change with the introduction of new laws to protect adults who lack mental capacity. This is very important if we are to protect the interests both of adults who lack capacity and those who care for them. One of the underlying assumptions behind new Acts is that a person with a condition like a learning disability, autism or dementia does not automatically lack all mental capacity. They may have capacity to make decisions about some aspect of their lives, but not others. The presumption is that they do have capacity and the onus is now on others to prove that they do not.

There have been other changes to the law in England, such as making the abuse of vulnerable adults a criminal offence, as it is with children. The various reforms of the Mental Health Acts will, it is hoped, produce better frameworks for the protection of people who are unable to consent to treatment. These changes can all be understood within the context of the European Convention on Human Rights, which became part of domestic law as the 2000 Human Rights Act. It has taken us a long time to get to the legal and theoretical acceptance of the fact that adults who lack mental capacity enjoy exactly the same human rights as everyone else. Working this out in practice may well take a lot longer.

## Public awareness

Finally, we would want to say something about public awareness. A well-informed public is a huge asset. The public probably understands that dementia is a devastating illness both for people with dementia and their families and that it is an illness and not part of normal ageing. People should understand that it needs to be talked about, that we have really suffered in the UK because people are still ashamed of this disease and tend to hide it.

If dementia was easier to talk about, then people would come forward for an earlier diagnosis and for help. There might be more public understanding, so that it was understood as a disease, like cancer or heart disease, and not something of which to be ashamed. There might even be more attention to the needs of those with dementia and their carers. Social workers are members of the public too and we often share these attitudes. We would want to say to our peers in developing countries, where social workers are often people of some influence, that they need to lead the way in talking about positive attitudes to people with dementia in whatever contexts arise. If we are not assertive about a social model with all its positive implications, we leave a vacuum which will be filled by the more pessimistic medical model.

It would be ideal if we could educate the public to see it as a form of disability and to understand that the attitudes that people with dementia and their carers encounter are as disabling as the disease itself. This is the case with most other disabilities. The public has to appreciate that there is plenty that can be done for people with dementia and their carers. We do not know how to stop the disease but we increasingly know how to make it less frightful for all the parties involved.

The hospice movement has managed to change attitudes to the care of the dying very successfully. Nobody thinks that hospices are a waste of money, yet people die in hospices. This is because the public respect the personhood of the dying; they see real people and they see themselves. We need to make sure that this is also true of people with dementia because it is just as true. One in 10 of us will get dementia if we live into our sixties and over.

This hypothetical exercise of talking to someone from a country whose population is not as old as ours is, in part, only making a point about the distance we in the UK have to travel before our services are as good as we know how to make them at the moment. The countries we have in mind are unlikely to have the infrastructure and resources to set up many services. What they can learn from us is what *not* to do and in what sort of direction they might wish to travel.

## Concluding reflections on social work with people with dementia and their carers

For a time, the change in the role of social work in the UK, following the introduction of care management, had a negative effect on our understanding of ourselves. It became hard to hold on to our core values and beliefs about our role as 'promoters of social change, problem solving in human relationships and the empowerment and liberation of people to enhance well-being' (IFSW, www.iassw-aiets.org). Social workers have always filled in forms, but the new electronic style of form, with tick boxes and limited space for qualitative judgements, led to many social workers feeling that their job had changed. The introduction of targets and measurable outcomes meant that electronic recording was inevitable but it did have considerable implications for practice.

There was and still is a danger that we only measure the things that can be easily tabulated on a computer. It is, for example, easy to measure how many calls have been received at the duty desk in one day. However, that information does not tell us how many people who called the duty desk were actually helped. Social workers have often felt that they had become nothing but glorified clerical officers.

Managers, if they need to pull a file from the cabinet for some reason, will say that they are unable to get a clear picture of the service user. The knowledge is in the social worker's head – it is not in the file.

At the same time the new awareness of the local budget, which imposes its inevitable constraints on social workers, has brought its own limitations. Too many forms to fill in, not enough time to spend with service users, fighting with colleagues for our share of the budget for the people with whom we are working, have led to a feeling of frustration, often described as feeling 'like the meat in the sandwich' – under pressure from all sides. Although there have been shining exceptions, we think that many social workers have found it difficult, in the face of these pressures, to keep their eye on the ball. The ball, in our context, is to improve the life and well-being of the person with dementia and those who care for them.

However, as we move into multidisciplinary teams and work alongside other professionals, we are beginning to remind ourselves of our core values and ask ourselves what is distinctive about the social work role. The *Changing Lives* report (Scottish Executive, 2006) is a useful reminder for us all. We really must become much more proactive in asserting the social and citizenship models for our service users. If we do not constantly remind ourselves of the value of these models, everything reverts to the default position, which is the medical model.

The reason why so much innovative and exciting practice has developed in the field of dementia care, as opposed to the generic care of older people, may well be because the situation in the old culture of dementia care was so dire that individual practitioners were driven to seek new answers. The old culture acted as a kind of greenhouse, the glass walls of which created a prison, which also became a hothouse for the abundant new growth of creative ideas. This greenhouse effect, thankfully, is entirely positive and shows no sign of diminishing.

It is not, of course, a bed of roses. The knowledge base for the social model, let alone the citizenship model, is still woefully inadequate with far too little 'evidence' of what works and what does not. We need to be candid about this without it being an excuse for inaction.

We think that first and foremost we must admit what we do not know. The potential for improvement in the world of social work with people with dementia and their carers has changed radically over the past years. However, in some ways it has only shown us what we do not yet know. We are only just beginning to learn, for example, about the importance of finding ways to meet the spiritual and the sexual needs of people with dementia. We are learning fast about the ways to involve people with dementia in their assessments and care but there is a long way to go. This also applies to the involvement of people with dementia in planning services.

We do not know nearly enough about the impact of dementia on people and families who were born outside the UK and have made their homes in the UK, especially those who are part of the post-colonial diaspora. We know that they want the same services as everybody else (Patel, 1999) but the subtleties of their understandings of dementia and the impact on families are insufficiently understood. We are not alone in this. The medics are having to consider culturally appropriate diagnostic techniques and the architects culturally appropriate design. This issue of cultural sensitivity is, in our view, going to be the area of greatest development in the next phase of changes in dementia care.

In some ways, social work is the ideal profession to spearhead many of the new approaches in dementia care because we have such a firm commitment to self-determination. We are also a profession that unashamedly pinches theory and practice from other professions and stirs them into the rich brew of social work. We are also increasingly working in multidisciplinary teams so we can enrich our knowledge and practice all the time. Working in a field of rapidly developing knowledge, skills and attitudes will not suit all social workers, nor will the imperative to work with other professions, but for those it does suit it provides a rewarding experience. It is also not a field for the timid. There is so much ignorance and discrimination that we need to be the sort of social workers who will stick by our guns and assert ourselves (in a carefully planned and strategic way, of course).

We hope this book has informed and enthused its readers. We think social work with people with dementia and their carers is a rewarding field to be in and neither of us would want to work with any other group. It is rewarding because it is so dynamic. From a purely selfish point of view it is a field that is both exciting and intellectually challenging. We do not have to look far for the challenges that face us. They have been discussed in various points throughout the book and they are formidable. However, we think social work in this field is exciting because we see new ways every day of widening expectations of what people with dementia can do and what we can offer them and their carers.

# Useful contacts

## Dementia Services Development Centres (DSDCs)

Details of all the centres and links are at www.dementia-voice.org.uk. All offer information, consultancy, training and research.

| | |
|---|---|
| South West DSDC | Dementia Voice<br>Blackberry Hill<br>Manor Road<br>Fishponds<br>Bristol BS16 2EW<br>Tel: 0117 975 4863<br>Fax: 0117 975 4819 |
| South East DSDC | Dementia Services Development Centre<br>South East<br>Canterbury Christ Church<br>University College<br>Canterbury<br>Kent CT1 1QU<br>Tel: 01227 782 702<br>Fax: 01227 784 408 |
| London DSDC | London Centre for Dementia Care<br>Department of Mental Health Science<br>University College London<br>Wolfson Building<br>48 Riding House Street<br>London WIW 7EY<br>Tel: 020 7679 9588/9<br>Fax: 020 7679 9426 |

Oxford DSDC        Oxford Dementia Centre
Institute of Public Care
Roosevelt Drive
Oxford OX3 7XR
Tel: 01865 761 815
Fax: 01865 762 015

West Midlands DSDC   Dementia Plus (West Midlands)
Warstones Resource Centre
Warstones Drive
Wolverhampton WV4 4PG
Tel: 01902 565 064
Fax: 01902 575 051

Trent DSDC        Trent DSDC
Division of Psychiatry for the Elderly
Leicester General Hospital
Leicester LE5 4PW
Tel: 0116 258 8161
Fax: 0116 273 1115

Northwest Dementia   Northwest Dementia Centre
Centre           Personal Social Services Research Unit
Dover Street Building
University of Manchester
Oxford Road
Manchester M13 9PL
Tel: 0161 275 5682
Fax: 0161 275 5790

Dementia North     Dementia North
Allendale House
University of Northumbria
Coach Lane
Benton
Newcastle upon Tyne NE7 7XA
Tel: 0191 215 6110
Fax: 0191 215 6193

| Scotland Dementia Services | Development Centre<br>Iris Murdoch Building<br>University of Stirling<br>Stirling FK9 4LA<br>Tel: 01786 467740<br>Fax: 01786 466846 |
|---|---|
| Wales (2 offices) | Dementia Services Development Centre<br>Wales<br>Practice Development Unit<br>Whitchurch Hospital<br>Cardiff CF14 7XG<br>Tel: 02920 336 073<br>Fax: 02920 336 385 |
|  | Dementia Services Development Centre<br>Wales<br>Neuadd Ardudwy<br>University of Wales<br>Bangor<br>Holyhead Road<br>Bangor LL57 2PX<br>Tel: 01248 383 719<br>Fax: 01248 382 229 |
| Centre without a geographical remit: | Bradford Dementia Group<br>School of Health Studies<br>University of Bradford<br>25 Trinity Road<br>Bradford BD5 0RB<br>Tel: 01274 236 367<br>Fax: 01274 236 302 |
| Ireland | Dementia Services Information and<br>Development Centre<br>Top Floor, Hospital 4<br>St James's Hospital<br>James's Street<br>Dublin 8 Ireland<br>Tel: 353 1 4162035<br>Fax: 353 1 4103482 |

| Australia | Dementia Services Development Centre<br>c/o Hammond Care<br>Level 2<br>447 Kent Street<br>Sydney 2000<br>Tel: 00 61 2 8280 8444<br>Richard Fleming, Director<br>rfleming@dementia.com.au |
|---|---|

## Alzheimer's Societies

| Alzheimer's Society (HQ for England, Wales, Northern Ireland and office for England) | Gordon House<br>10 Greencoat Place<br>London SW1 1PH<br>Tel: 0207 7306 0606<br>Fax: 0207 7306 0808 |
|---|---|
| Alzheimer's Society Wales | Heol Don Resource Centre<br>Heol Don<br>Whitchurch<br>Cardiff CF14 2XG<br>Tel: 029 2052 1872<br>Fax: 029 2061 5255 |
| Alzheimer's Society Northern Ireland | 76 Eglantine Avenue<br>Belfast<br>Northern Ireland BT9 6EU<br>Tel: 028 9066 4100<br>Fax: 028 9066 4440 |

## Elder abuse organisations

Action on
Elder Abuse

Astral House
1268 London Road
Norbury
London SW16 4ER
Tel: 020 8765 7000
Fax: 020 8679 4074
www.elderabuse.org.uk

WITNESS (against
abuse by health and
care workers,
previously PROPAN)

Delta House
175-177 Borough High Street
London SE1 1HR
Helpline: 08454 500 300

## Carers UK – the voice of carers

Head office

20-25 Glasshouse Yard
London EC1A 4JT
Tel: 0207 490 8818
Fax: 0207 490 8824

Carers Wales

River House, Ynysbridge Court
Gwaelod-y-Garth
Cardiff CF15 9SS
Tel: 029 2081 1370

Carers Scotland

91 Mitchell Street
Glasgow G1 3LN
Tel: 0141 221 9140

Carers Northern
Ireland

58 Howard Street
Belfast BT1 6PJ
Tel: 0289 043 9843

## Other useful organisations

| | |
|---|---|
| CRUSE Bereavement Care | Cruse House<br>126 Sheen Road<br>Richmond<br>Surrey TW9 1UR<br>Administration tel: 020 8939 9580<br>Fax: 020 8940 7638<br>www.crusebereavementcare.org.uk<br>Helpline: 0870 167 1677 |
| Counsel and Care (gives advice to older people and their relatives) | Twyman House<br>16 Bonny Street<br>London NW1 9PG<br>Tel: 020 7241 8555<br>Fax: 020 7267 6877<br>Advice line: 0845 300 7585 |
| *Journal of Dementia Care* (Editor Sue Benson) | Culvert House<br>Culvert Road<br>London SW11 5DH<br>Tel: 020 7720 2108<br>Fax: 020 7498 3023 |
| CANDID – Counselling and Diagnosis in Dementia | The Dementia Research Centre<br>National Hospital for Neurology and Neurosurgery<br>Queen Square<br>London WC1N 3BG<br>dementia.ion.ucl.ac.uk/CANDID |
| Age Exchange | Reminiscence Centre<br>11 Blackheath Village<br>London SE3 9LA<br>Tel: 020 8318 9105<br>Fax: 020 8318 0060 |

| | |
|---|---|
| PCaW – Public Concern at Work (advice and support for whistle-blowers) | Suite 30116 Baldwins Gardens London EC1N 7RJ Tel: 020 7404 6609 |
| Mental Health Foundation (publications on dementia) | London Office 9th Floor Sea Containers House 20 Upper Ground London SE1 9QB Tel: 020 7803 1100 Fax: 020 7803 1111 |
| Scottish Office | Merchants House 30 George Square Glasgow G2 1EG Tel: 0141 572 0125 |

# References

Abbey, J., Piller, N., DeBellis, A., Esterman, A., Parker, D., Giles, L. and Lowcay, B. (2004) 'The Abbey Pain Scale: A 1-Minute Numerical Indicator for People with Late-stage Dementia', *International Journal of Palliative Nursing*, vol 10, no 1, pp 6-13.

Ainsworth, M.D.S., Blehar, M.C., Walters, E. and Wall, S. (1978) *Patterns of Attachment: A Psychological Study of the Strange Situation*, Hillsdale, NJ: Erlbaum.

Airey, J., Hammond, G., Kent, P. and Moffitt, L. (2002) *Frequently Asked Questions on Spirituality and Religion*, Derbyshire: Christian Council on Ageing.

Allan, K. (2001) *Communication and Consultation: Exploring Ways for Staff to Involve People with Dementia in Developing Services*, Bristol: The Policy Press.

Allan, K. (2002) *Finding Your Way: Explorations in Communication*, Stirling: Dementia Services Development Centre.

Allan, K. (2005) *Dementia and Deafness: An Exploratory Study*, www.dementia.stir.ac.uk or www.deafaction.org

Allan, K., McLean, F. and Scott Gibson, L. (2005) *Dementia and Deafness*, Edinburgh: Deaf Action.

Alm, N., Ellis, M., Astell, A., Dye, R., Gowans, G. and Campbell, J. (2004) 'A Cognitive Prosthesis and Communication Support for People with Dementia', *Neuropsychological Rehabilitation*, vol 14, no 1/2, pp 117-34.

Alzheimer's Disease International (2003) *How to Include People with Dementia in the Activities of Alzheimer Associations*, www.alz.co.uk

Alzheimer's Society (2003a) *What is fronto-temporal dementia (including Picks disease)?*, Fact sheet no 404, www.alzheimers.org.uk

Alzheimer's Society (2003b) *CJD (What is it?)* Fact sheet no 427, www.alzheimers.org.uk

Alzheimer's Society (2004c) *Food for Thought: Promoting Quality: Food and Nutrition for people with Dementia. Practice Guides*, London: Alzheimer's Society.

Alzheimer's Society (2004a) *Policy Position Paper: Demography*, www.alzheimers.org.uk

Alzheimer's Society (2004b) *Policy Position Paper: Withdrawing or Withholding Treatment/Palliative Care*, www.alzheimers.org.uk

Alzheimer's Society (2005) *Lesbian and Gay Network Newsletter*, London: Alzheimer's Society.

Alzheimer's Society and Dementia Care Matters (2003) *Building on Strengths: Providing Support, Care Planning and Risk Assessment for People with Dementia*, London: Alzheimer's Society.

Archibald, C. (1990) *Activities*, Stirling: Dementia Services Development Centre.

Archibald, C. (1993) *Activities 2*, Stirling: Dementia Services Development Centre.

Archibald, C. (2003) 'Restraint', in R. Hudson (ed) *Dementia Nursing: A Guide to Practice*, Melbourne, Australia: Ausmed Publications, pp 107-17.

Archibald, C. (2005) *Rehydration and Dementia*, Stirling: Dementia Services Development Centre.

Archibald, C. (2006) *Sexuality and Dementia*, Stirling: Dementia Services Development Centre.

Archibald, C. and Murphy, C. (eds) (1999) *Activities and People with Dementia: Involving Family Carers*, Stirling: Dementia Services Development Centre.

Astell, A., Ellis, M., Alm, N., Gowans, G., Campbell, J. and Dye, R. (2004) *Comparing Personal and Generic Photographs as Reminiscence Aids*, Proceedings of 24th Annual Conference of PSIGE (psychology specialists working with older people), Durham 7-9 July, p 28.

Audit Commission (2000) *Forget Me Not: Older People with Mental Health Problems*, London: Audit Commission.

Audit Commission (2002) *Forget Me Not: Older People with Mental Health Problems*, London: Audit Commission.

Bamford Review of Mental Health and Learning Disability (Northern Ireland) (2006, forthcoming), *'Leading Fuller Lives': Report on Dementia and Mental Health Issues in Older People*.

Barnes, C. and Mercer, G. (2006) *Independent Futures: Creating User-led Disability Services in a Disabling Society*, Bristol: The Policy Press.

Barnett, E. (2000) *I Need to be Me*, London: Jessica Kingsley Publishers.

Bartlett, R. (2000) 'Dementia as a Disability: Can we Learn from Disability Studies and Theory?', *Journal of Dementia Care, Research Focus*, September/October, pp 33-6.

Basing, A. (2004) 'Timeslip Project: Freeing the Creative Voice from the Voices of Doubt', *Signpost Journal 3*, pp 15-17.

Bayley, J. (1998) *Iris: A Memoir of Iris Murdoch*, London: Duckworth & Company Ltd, also available as *Elegy for Iris* (1999) New York: Picador.

Bayley, J. (2000) *Iris and her Friends: A Memoir of Memory and Desire*, London: W.W. Norton and Company.

Bender, M. (2003) *Explorations in Dementia*, London: Jessica Kingsley Publishers.

Bender, M. (2004) *Therapeutic Groupwork for People with Cognitive Losses: Working with People with Dementia*, Bicester: Speechmark.

Berg, G. (2006) *The Importance of Food and Mealtimes in Dementia Care*, London: Jessica Kingsley Publishers.

Birrell, D. and Williamson, A. (1983) 'Northern Ireland's Integrated Health and Personal Social Service Structure', in A. Williamson and G. Room (eds) *Health and Welfare States of Britain: An Intercountry Comparison*, London: Heinemann Educational Books, pp 130–50.

Bjørneby, S., Topo, P. and Holthe, T. (1999) (eds) *Technology, Ethics and Dementia: A Guidebook on How to Apply Technology in Dementia Care*, Oslo: Norwegian Centre for Dementia Research.

Bond, J. (2001) 'Sociological Perspectives', in C. Cantley (ed) *A Handbook of Dementia Care*, Milton Keynes: Open University Press, pp 44–60.

Brawley, E.C. (1997) *Designing for Alzheimer's Disease*, New York: John Wiley & Sons.

Brett, J. (2002) *Complementary Therapies in the Care of Older People*, London: Whurr.

Brodarty, H., Green, A. and Koschera, A. (2003) 'Meta-analysis of Psychosocial Interventions for Caregivers of People with Dementia', *Journal of the American Geriatric Society*, vol 51, no 5, pp 657–64.

Brooker, D. (2001) 'Therapeutic Activity', in C. Cantley (ed) *A Handbook of Dementia Care*, Buckingham: Open University Press, pp 146–156.

Brooker, D., Edwards, P. and Benson, S. (eds) (2004) *Dementia Care Mapping: Experience and Insights into Practice*, London: Hawker Publications.

Bruce, E., Hodgson, S. and Schweitzer, P. (1999) *Reminiscing with People with Dementia: A Handbook for Carers*, London: Age Exchange.

Bruce, E., Surr, C. and Tibbs, M.-A. (2002) *A Special Kind of Care: Improving Well-being in People Living with Dementia*, Derby: MHA Care Group (and Bradford Dementia Group).

Bryden, C. (2005) *Dancing with Dementia*, London: Jessica Kingsley Publishers.

Burton, A. (1997) 'Dementia: A Case for Advocacy', in S. Hunter (ed) *Dementia: Challenges and New Directions*, London: Jessica Kingsley Publishers, pp 194–207.

Bytheway, B. (2005) 'Ageism', in M.L Johnson, P. Coleman and V. Bengtson (eds) *The Cambridge Handbook on Age and Ageing*, Cambridge: Cambridge University Press, pp 338–345.

Calder, C. (2005) 'Person-centred Approaches to using Technology in Practice Settings: The South Lanarkshire Dementia Technology Initiative', in J Woolham (ed) *Assistive Technology in Dementia Care*, London: Journal of Dementia Care, pp 28-33.

Calkins, M.P. (1988) *Design for Dementia: Planning Environments for the Elderly and the Confused*, Maryland, MD: National Health Publishing.

Calkins, M.P. (2001) *Creating Successful Dementia Care Settings Vol 1: Understanding the Environment through the Senses*, Baltimore, MD: Health Professions Press.

Calkins, M. and Brush, J. (2003) 'Designing for Dining: The Secret of Happier Mealtimes', in M. Marshall (ed) *Food, Glorious Food: Perspectives on Food and Dementia*, London: Hawker Publications Limited, pp 67-70.

Cantley, C. and Bowes, A. (2004) 'Dementia and Social Inclusion: The Way Forward', in A. Innes, C. Archibald and C. Murphy (eds) *Dementia and Social Inclusion: Marginalised Groups and Marginalised Areas of Dementia Research, Care and Practice*, London: Jessica Kingsley Publishers, pp 255-71.

Cantley, C. and Wilson, R.C. (2003) *Put Yourself in My Place: Designing and Managing Care Homes for People with Dementia*, Bristol: The Policy Press.

Cantley, C., Woodhouse, J. and Smith, M. (2005) *Listen to Us: Involving People with Dementia in Planning and Developing Services*, Newcastle: Dementia North, Northumbria University.

Carers UK (2005) *Older Carers in the UK*, London: Carers UK.

Cash, M. (2005) 'Exploring the Potential of Existing Low-technological Devices to Support People with Dementia to Live at Home', in J. Woolham (ed) *Assistive Technology in Dementia Care*, London: Journal of Dementia Care, pp 9-27.

Centre for Accessible Environments (1998) *The Design of Residential Care and Nursing Homes for Older People*, London: Centre for Accessible Environments.

Chapman, A. and Bree, P. (2006) *A CD Rom for Training Nurses about Dementia*, Stirling: Dementia Services Development Centre.

Chapman, A. and Hosking, R. (2002) *Bridging the Gap*, Stirling: Dementia Services Development Centre.

Cheston, R. and Bender, M. (1999) *Understanding Dementia: The Man with the Worried Eyes*, London: Jessica Kingsley Publishers.

Chung, J.C., Lai, C.K.Y., Chung, P.M.B. and French, H.P. (2003) 'Snoezelen for Dementia (Cochrane Review)', *The Cochrane Library*, Issue 1, Oxford: Update Software.

Clark, H., Gough, H. and Macfarlane, A. (2004) *'It Pays Dividends': Direct Payments and Older People*, Bristol: The Policy Press.

Clarke, R. (2003) 'A Sacred Space: Communicating with my Mother', in *Newsletter of the Leveson Centre for the Study of Ageing, Spirituality & Social Policy*, no 9, Septemberm pp 19-22.

Closs, J. (2005) 'Pain and Dementia', in M. Marshall (ed) *Perspectives on Rehabilitation and Dementia*, London: Jessica Kingsley Publishers, pp 211-20.

Cochrane, A. (2004) *Epilepsy and Dementia*, Stirling: Dementia Services Development Centre.

Cohen, U. and Day, K. (1993) *Contemporary Environments for People with Dementia*, Maryland, MD: Johns Hopkins University Press.

Cohen, U. and Weisman, G.D. (1991) *Holding on to Home: Designing Environments for People with Dementia*, Maryland, MD: Johns Hopkins University Press.

Colles, S., Kydd, A. and Chapman, A. (eds) (2001) *A Practice Guide for Community Nursing*, Stirling: Dementia Services Development Centre.

Commission for Social Care Inspection (2005) *The State of Social Care in England 2004-05*, www.csci.org.uk

Community Care Works (2005) *Alcohol Related Brain Damage*, Autumn, issue 50, Glasgow: University of Glasgow.

Cook, A., Downs, M.G. and Niven, C.A. (1999) 'Assessing the Pain of People with a Cognitive Impairment', *International Journal of Geriatric Psychiatry*, vol 14, no 6, pp 421-5.

Cox, S. (2000) *Housing Support for People with Dementia*, London: Housing Association Charitable Trust.

Cox, S. (2006) *Home Solutions 2: Housing with Care and Support for People with Dementia*, Stirling: Dementia Services Development Centre.

Cox, S. and Watchman, K. (2004) 'Death and Dying', in A. Innes, C. Archibald and C. Murphy (eds) *Dementia and Social Inclusion*, London: Jessica Kingsley Publishers, pp 84-95.

Cox, S., Anderson, I. and McCabe, L. (2004) *A Fuller Life: Report of the Expert Group on Alcohol Related Brain Damage*, Stirling: Dementia Services Development Centre.

Cox, S., Anderson, I., Dick, S. and Elgar, J. (1998) *The Person, the Community and Dementia: Developing a Value Framework*, Stirling: Dementia Services Development Centre.

Craig, C. (2002) *Creative Environments*, Stirling: Dementia Services Development Centre.

Craig, C. (2003) *Meaningful Making: A Practice Guide for Occupational Therapy Staff*, Stirling: Dementia Services Development Centre.

Craig, C. (2004) 'Reaching Out with the Arts: Meeting the Person with Dementia', in A. Innes, C. Archibald and C. Murphy (eds) (2004) *Dementia and Social Inclusion: Marginalised Groups and Marginalised Areas of Dementia Research, Care and Practice*, London: Jessica Kingsley Publishers, pp 184-201.

Craig, C. (2005) *Focusing on the Person*, CD, Stirling: Dementia Services Development Centre.

Crawley, H. (2000) *Food, Drink and Dementia*, Stirling: Dementia Services Development Centre.

CSIP (Care Service Improvement Partnership) (2005) *Everybody's Business: Integrated Services for Older Adults: A Service Development Guide*, London: Department of Health.

Cunningham, C. (2005) 'Clocks Must be Readable in the Dark', letter to *Journal of Dementia Care*, vol 13, no 5, September/October, p 8.

Cunningham, C. (2006) 'Determining whether to give Pain Relief to People with Dementia: The Impact of Verbal and Written Communication on the Decision to Administer 'As Required' Analgesia to People with Dementia in Care Homes', *Alzheimer's Care Quarterly*, vol 17, no 2, pp 95-103.

Cunningham, C., Archibald, C. and Rae, C. (2006) *The Need to Know: A Survey of Course Input at Pre-registration/Undergraduate Level*, Stirling: Dementia Services Development Centre.

Currie, R. and Stopforth, P. (2006) 'Adult Placements: Fostering a New Kind of Care', *Journal of Dementia Care*, vol 14, no 3, May/June, pp 20-2.

Daker-White, G., Beattie, A., Means, R. and Gilliard, J. (2002) *Serving the Needs of Marginalised Groups in Dementia Care*, Bristol: University of the West of England.

Davis, R. (1993) *My Journey into Alzheimer's Disease*, Amersham-on-the-Hill: Scripture Press.

Day, K., Carreon, D. and Stump, C. (2000) 'The Therapeutic Design of Environments for People with Dementia: A Review of the Empirical Research', *The Gerontologist*, vol 40, no 4, pp 397-416.

Dementia Services Development Centre (2003) *Oh Good, Lunch is Coming*, Video, Stirling: Dementia Services Development Centre.

DCA (Department for Constitutional Affairs) (1999) *Making Decisions*, London: DCA.

DH (Department of Health) (1998a) *Modernising Social Services*, London: DH.

DH (2000) *No Secrets: Guidance on Developing and Implementing Multi-agency Policies and Procedures to Protect Vulnerable Adults from Abuse*, London: DH.

DH (2001a) *The National Service Framework For Older People*, London: DH.

DH (2001b) *The Expert Patient: A New Approach to Chronic Disease Management*, London: DH.

DH (2003a) *Fair Access to Care Services: Guidance on Eligibility Criteria for Adult Social Care*, London: DH.

DH (2003b) *Care Homes for Older People: National Minimum Standards and the Care Homes Regulations* (3rd revised edition), London: The Stationery Office.

DH (2004) *Single Assessment Process Implementation (SAP) Guidance*, London: DH.

DH (2006) *Our Health, Our Care, Our Say*, Cm 6737, London: DH.

Drake, L., Drake, V. and Curwen, J. (1997) 'A New Account of Sundown Syndrome', *Nursing Standard*, vol 12, no 7, pp 37-40.

Drake, R.F. (1999) *Understanding Disability Politics*, Basingstoke and London: Macmillan Press.

Duffy, L. (1995) 'Sexual Behaviour and Marital Intimacy in Alzheimer's Couples: A Family Theory Perspective', *Sexuality and Disability*, vol 13, no 3, pp 239-53.

Erikson, E. (1963) *Childhood and Society*, New York: Norton.

Everett, D. (2000) 'Spiritual Care: Stretching the Soul', *Journal of Dementia Care*, vol 8, no 1, January/February.

Faife, D. (2005) 'Creating the Building Blocks for an Integrated Technology Service: Setting up the STIL project in Norfolk', in J. Woolham (ed) *Assistive Technology in Dementia Care*, London: Journal of Dementia Care, pp 34-44.

Feil, N. (2002) *The Validation Breakthrough* (2nd edition), Baltimore, MD: Health Promotions Press.

Folstein, M.F., Folstein, S.E. and McHugh, P.R. *Mini Mental State Inventory*, www.minimental.com

Forster, M. (1989) *Have the Men had Enough?*, London: Chatto.

Foucault, M. (1973) *Madness and Civilisation*, New York: Vintage Books.

Gibson, F. (1991) *The Lost Ones*, Stirling: Dementia Services Development Centre.

Gibson, F. (2005) 'Fit for Life: The Contribution of Life Story Work', in M. Marshall (ed) *Perspectives on Rehabilitation and Dementia*, London: Jessica Kingsley Publishers, pp 175-9.

Gibson, F. (2006) *Reminiscence and Recall: A practical Guide to Reminiscence Work* (3rd edition), London: Age Concern Books.

Goldsmith, M. (1996) *Hearing the Voice of People with Dementia: Opportunities and Obstacles*, London: Jessica Kingsley Publishers.

Goldsmith, M. (2004) *Ageing in a Strange Land: People with Dementia and the Local Church*, Edinburgh: 4M Publications.

Gotell, E. and Ekman, S.-L. (2001) 'Singing as an Intervention in Dementia Care', *Journal of Dementia Care*, vol 9, no 4, pp 33-7.

Gow, J. and Gilhooly, M. (2003) *Risk Factors for Dementia and Cognitive Decline*, Glasgow: NHS Health Scotland.

Grant, L. (1999) *Remind Me Who I Am Again*, London: Granta.

Gresham, M. (1999) 'The heart of the home – but how are kitchens used?', *Journal of Dementia Care*, vol 17, no 2, March/April, pp 20-3.

Haight, B. and Gibson, F. (eds) (2005) *Burnside's Working with Older Adults, Group Work Process and Techniques*, Sudbury, MA: Jones and Bartlett Publishers.

Herzberg, E.I. (2001) *Know Your Complementary Therapies*, London: Age Concern England.

Hiatt, L.G. (1995) 'Understanding the Physical Environment', *Pride Institute Journal of Long Term Home Health Care*, vol 4, no 2, pp 12-22.

Hill, H. (2001) *Invitation to the Dance*, Stirling: Dementia Services Development Centre.

Hodges, J. (ed) (2001) *Early Onset Dementia: A Multi-disciplinary Approach*, Oxford: Oxford University Press.

Howcroft, D. (2003) 'Sleep and the Person with Dementia', *Journal of Dementia Care*, vol 11, no 1, January/February, pp 33-8.

Hulko, W. (2004) 'Social Science Perspectives on Dementia Research: Intersectionality in Dementia', in A. Innes, C. Archibald and C. Murphy (eds) *Dementia and Social Inclusion: Marginalised Groups and Marginalised Areas of Dementia Research, Care and Practice*, London: Jessica Kingsley Publishers, pp 237-54.

Hunt, L., Marshall, M. and Rowlings, C. (eds) (1997) *Past Trauma in Late Life: European Perspectives on Therapeutic Work with Older People*, London: Jessica Kingsley Publishers.

Ignatieff, M. (1993) *Scar Tissue*, London: Chatto and Windus.

Innes, A., Archibald, C. and Murphy, C. (2004) *Dementia and Social Inclusion: Marginalised Groups and Marginalised Areas of Dementia Research, Care and Practice*, London: Jessica Kingsley Publishers.

Innes, A., Ashraf, F., Ismail, L. and Mackenzie, J. (2001) 'Supporting Family Carers of People with Dementia from Minority Ethnic Communities', *Journal of the British Society of Gerontology, Generations Review*, vol 11, no 2, pp 184-201.

Innes, A., Blackstock, K., Mason, A., Smith, A. and Cox, S. (2005) 'Dementia Care Provision in Rural Scotland: Service Users' and Carers' Experiences', *Health and Social Care in the Community*, vol 13, no 4, pp 345-65.

International Association of Schools of Social Work and International Federation of Social Workers (2001) 'Definition of Social Work Jointly Agreed 27 June 2001 Copenhagen', www.iassw-aiets.org

Jackson, G. and McDonald, C. (1999) *What Behaviour? Whose Problem?*, Stirling: Dementia Services Development Centre.

Jackson, G., Holloway, G. and Chapman, A. (2002) *People with Dementia and their Behaviour: 10 Questions to Consider*, Stirling: Dementia Services Development Centre.

Jacques, A. and Jackson, G. (2000) *Understanding Dementia*, Edinburgh: Churchill Livingstone.

James, I. and Mackenzie, L. (2005) 'Respecting Choices Made Here and Now', *Journal of Dementia Care*, vol 13, no 5, p 9.

James, I., Reichelt, K., Morse, R., Mackenzie, L. and Mukaetova-Ladinska, E. (2005) 'The Therapeutic Use of Dolls', *Journal of Dementia Care*, vol 13, no 3, pp 19-21.

James, I., Mackenzie, L., Stephenson, M. and Roe, T. (2006) 'Dealing with Challenging Behaviour through Analysis of Need: The Columbo Approach', in M. Marshall and K. Allan, *Walking not Wandering: Fresh Approaches to Understanding Dementia*, London: Hawker Publications, pp 21-27.

Jenkins, D. (1999) *Urinary and Faecal Incontinence*, Stirling: Dementia Services Development Centre.

Jokinen, N. (2005) 'The Content of Available Practice Literature in Dementia and Intellectual Disability', *Dementia*, vol 4, no 3, pp 327-39.

Jorm, A.F., Korten, A.E. and Henderson, A.S. (1988) 'The Prevalence of Dementia: A Quantitative Integration of the Literature', *Acta Psychiatrica Scandinavica*, no 76, pp 465-79.

Judd, S., Marshall, M. and Phippen, P. (1998) *Design for Dementia*, London: Hawker Publications Limited.

Kerr, D. and Wilson, C. (2002) *Learning Disability and Dementia: A Training Guide for Staff*, Stirling: Dementia Services Development Centre.

Killick, J. (1997) *You are Words*, London: Hawker Publications.

Killick, J. and Allan, K. (2001) *Communication and the Care of People with Dementia*, Buckingham: Open University Press.

Killick, J. and Allan, K. (2006) 'The Good Sunset Project: Making Contact with those Close to Death', *Journal of Dementia Care*, vol 14, no 1, pp 22-4.

Killick, J. and Cordonnier, C. (2000) *Openings: Dementia Poems and Photographs*, London: Hawker Publications.

Killick, J. and Davis Basting, A. (2003) *The Arts and Dementia Care: A Resource Guide* (1st edition), Brooklyn, NY: National Center for Creative Ageing.

Killick, J. and Rose, S. (2003) *Red Nose Coming* (video), Stirling: Dementia Services Development Centre.

Kimble, M. (2002) 'The Defiant Power of the Human Spirit: Mental Health in Later Life', in E. MacKinlay (ed) *Mental Health & Spirituality in Later Life*, Binghampton, NY: Haworth Pastoral Press, p 39.

Kindell, J. and Armans, D. (2003) 'Doing Things Differently: Dance in Dementia Care', *Journal of Dementia Care*, vol 11, no 2, pp 18-20.

Kitwood, T. (1997a) *Dementia Reconsidered: The Person Comes First*, Buckingham: Open University Press.

Kitwood, T. and Benson, S. (eds) (1995) *The New Culture of Dementia Care*, London: Hawker Publications.

Knocker, S. (2003) *The Alzheimer's Society Book of Activities*, London: Alzheimer's Society.

Koncelik, J.A. (2003) 'The Human Factors of Aging and the Micro-environment: Personal Surroundings, Technology and Product Development', in R.J. Scheidt and P.G. Windley (eds) *Physical Environments and Aging: Critical Contributions of M. Powell Lawton to Theory and Practice*, Binghampton, NY: Haworth Press, pp 117-34.

Levin, E., Moriarty, J. and Gorbach, P. (1994) *Better for the Break*, London: HMSO.

Levin, J. and Meredith, M. (1988) *Daughters who Care: Daughters Caring for Mothers at Home*, London: Routledge.

Lichtenberg, P. and Strzpek, D. (1990) 'Assessment of Institutionalised Dementia Patients' Competencies to Participate in Intimate Relationships', *The Gerontologist*, vol 30, no 1, pp 117-20.

Mackenzie, J. and Coates, D. in association with Ashraf, F., Gallagher, T. and Ismail, L. (2003) *Understanding and Supporting South Asian and Eastern European Family Carers of People with Dementia*, Bradford: Bradford Dementia Group, www.brad.ac.uk/acad/health/dementia/research/understandingcarersreport.doc.

Manning, W. (2003) *Delirium*, Stirling: Dementia Services Development Centre.

Manthorpe, J. (2004) 'Risk Taking', in A. Innes, C. Archibald and C. Murphy (eds) *Dementia and Social Inclusion*, London: Jessica Kingsley Publishers, pp 137–49.

Manthorpe, J. and Iliffe, S. (2005) *Depression in Later Life*, London: Jessica Kingsley Publishers.

Marriot, H. (2003) *The Selfish Pig's Guide to Caring*, Polperro: Polperro Heritage Press.

Marshall, M. (ed) (2000) *ASTRID, A Social and Technological Response to Meeting the Needs of Individuals with Dementia and Their Carers*, London: Hawker Publications Limited.

Marshall, M. (ed) (2003a) *Food, Glorious Food: Perspectives on Food and Dementia*, London: Hawker Publications Limited.

Marshall, M. (2003b) 'Nutrition', in R. Hudson (ed) *Dementia Nursing, A Guide to Practice,* Melbourne, Australia: Ausmed Publications, pp 60–9.

Marshall, M. (2005) *Perspectives on Rehabilitation and Dementia*, London: Jessica Kingsley Publishers.

Marshall, M. and Allan, K. (eds) (2006) *Dementia: Walking not Wandering. Fresh Approaches to Understanding and Practice*, London: Hawker Publications.

McAndrew, F. and Taylor, R. (2006) 'How all Voices are Heard for Strategic Planning', *Journal of Dementia Care*, vol 14, no 3, pp 22–4.

McCabe, L. (2003) 'Policy Transfer and Policy Translation: Day Care for People with Dementia in Kerala, India', PhD Thesis, University of Stirling.

McCartney, J. and Severson, K. (1997) 'Sexual Violence, Post Traumatic Stress Disorder and Dementia', *American Geriatrics Society*, vol 4, no 1, pp 76–8.

McGowin, D.F. (1993) *Living in the Labyrinth: A Personal Journey through the Maze of Alzheimer's*, San Francisco, CA: Elder Books.

McKillop, J. (2003) *Opening Shutters, Opening Minds*, Stirling: Dementia Services Development Centre.

McQuillan, S., Kalsy, S., Oyebode, J., Millichap, D., Oliver, C. and Hall, S. (2003) 'Adults with Down's Syndrome and Alzheimer's Disease', *The Learning Disability Review*, vol 8, no 4, pp 4–13.

Mental Welfare Commission (2005) *Safe to Wander*, Edinburgh: Mental Welfare Commission.

Metz, P. (1997) 'Staff Development for Working with Gay and Lesbian Elders', *Journal of Gay and Lesbian Social Services*, vol 6, no 35, pp 35–44.

Miesen, B. and Jones, G.M.M. (eds) (1997) *Care Giving in Dementia: Research and Applications*, London: Routledge.

Miller, B.M., Boone, K., Cummings, S.L., Read, S.L. and Mishkin, F. (2000) 'Functional Correlates of Musical and Visual Ability in Frontotemporal Dementia', *British Journal of Psychiatry*, vol 176, pp 458-63.

Mithen, S. (2005) *The Singing Neanderthals*, London: Wiedenfeld and Nicolson.

Moise, P., Schwarzinger, M., Um, M.-Y. and the Dementia Experts Group (2004) *Dementia Care in 9 OECD countries: A comparative analysis*, OECD Health Working Paper 13, Paris: OECD.

Montgomery-Smith, C. (2006) 'Musical Exercises for the Mind', *Journal of Dementia Care*, vol 14, no 3, pp 10-11.

Moore, D. (2001) 'It's like a Gold Medal and it's Mine: Dolls in Dementia Care', *Journal of Dementia Care*, vol 9, no 6, pp 20-2.

Morningside United Church (2005a) *Restoring the Soul: A selection of Favourite Hymns*, CD, Stirling: Dementia Services Development Centre.

Morningside United Church (2005b) *O Tidings of Comfort and Joy: A Selection of Favourite Carols*, CD, Stirling: Dementia Services Development Centre.

Mozley, C.G., Huxley, P., Sutcliffe, C., Bagley, H., Burns, A., Challis, D. and Cordingley, L. (1999) '"Not knowing where I am doesn't mean I don't know what I like": Cognitive Impairment and Quality of Life Responses in Elderly People', *International Journal of Geriatric Psychiatry*, vol 14, no 9, pp 776-83.

Mullen, M. and Killick, J. (2001) *Responding to Music*, Video, Belfast: Age Concern Northern Ireland and Stirling: Dementia Services Development Centre.

Muller-Hergl, C. (2004) 'Faecal Incontinence', in A. Innes, C. Archibald and C. Murphy (eds) (2004) *Dementia and Social Inclusion: Marginalised Groups and Marginalised Areas of Dementia Research, Care and Practice*, London: Jessica Kingsley Publishers, pp 113-22.

Murphy, C. (2004) 'The Critical Importance of Biographical Knowledge', in T. Perrin (ed) *The New Culture of Therapeutic Activity with Older People*, Oxon: Speechmark Publishing Ltd, pp 88-103.

Murray, A. (2004) 'Prisoners who Develop Dementia: What we need to Know', *Journal of Dementia Care*, vol 12, no 1, pp 29-31.

National Assembly for Wales (2000) *In Safe Hands: Implementing Adult Protection Procedures in Wales*, Cardiff: National Assembly for Wales.

Neno, R. (2004) 'Male Carers: Myth or Reality?', *Nursing Older People*, vol 16, no 8, pp 14-16.

Netten, A. (1993) *A Positive Environment*, Aldershot: Ashgate Publishing.

Newton, L. and Stewart, A. (1997) *Finger Foods for Independence for People with Alzheimer's Disease and others who Experience Eating Difficulties*, Adelaide: Creative State.

NHS Health Scotland (2003) *Dementia and Older People: Needs Assessment Report*, Edinburgh: NHS Scotland.

NHS Scotland (2006) *Alcohol and Healthy Ageing*, Edinburgh: NHS Scotland.

Nolan, M.R., Grant, G. and Ellis, N.C. (1990) 'Stress is in the Eye of the Beholder: Reconceptualising the Measurement of Care Burden', *Journal of Advanced Nursing*, vol 15, pp 554-5.

ONS (Office for National Statistics) (2005) 'Focus on Ethnicity and Identity' (www. statistics.gov.uk).

Oliver, M. (1990) *The Politics of Disablement*, Basingstoke: Macmillan.

Oliver, M. (1996) 'Theories of Disabilities in Health Practice and Research', *British Medical Journal*, vol 317, no 21, pp 1446-9.

Patel, N. (1999) 'Black and Ethnic Minority Elderly: Perspectives on Long-term care', in The Royal Commission, *With Respect to Old Age: Research Volume 1*, London: The Stationery Office.

Patel, N. (ed) (2004) *Minority Elderly Health and Social Care in Europe: PRIAE Research Briefing: Summary Findings of the Minority Elderly Care (MEC) Project*, Brussels: Policy Research Institute on Ageing and Ethnicity.

Perrin, T. (ed) (2005) *The Good Practice Guide to Therapeutic Activities with Older People in Care Settings*, Bicester: Speechmark.

Perrin, T. and May, H. (1999) *Wellbeing in Dementia: An Occupational Therapy Approach for Therapists and Carers*, Edinburgh: Churchill Livingstone.

Phillips, J., Ray, M. and Marshall, M. (2006) *Social Work with Older People*, Basingstoke: Palgrave Macmillan

Philp, I. and Appleby, L. (2005) *Securing Better Mental Health for Older Adults*, London: Department of Health.

Pollock, A. (2001) *Designing Gardens for People with Dementia*, Stirling: Dementia Services Development Centre.

Pollock, R. (2003) *Designing Interiors for People with Dementia*, Stirling: Dementia Services Development Centre.

Pollock, R. (2006) *Designing Lighting for People with Dementia*, Stirling: Dementia Services Development Centre.

Pool, J. (1999) *The Pool Activity Level (PAL) instrument: A Practical Resource for Carers of People with Dementia*, London: Jessica Kingsley Publishers.

Powell, J. (2000) *Care to Communicate: Helping the Person with Dementia*, London: Hawker Publications.

Pulsford, D., Hall, S., Keen, T., Stokes, F., Pusey, H. and Soliman, A. (2003) 'What can Higher Education Contribute to Dementia Care', *Journal of Dementia Care*, vol 11, no 4, July/August, pp 27-9.

Rankin, J. (2005) *A Mature Policy on Choice*, London: Institute for Public Policy Research.

Roper-Hall, A. (1993) 'Developing Family Therapy Services with Older Adults', in J. Carpenter and A. Treacher (eds) *Using Family Therapy in the 90s*, Oxford: Blackwell.

Royal College of Physicians (2005) *Who Cares Wins: Improving the Outcome for Older People Admitted to the General Hospital: Guidelines for the Development of Liaison Mental Health Services for Older People*, London: Royal College of Physicians.

Royal Commission on Long Term Care (1999) *With Respect to Old Age: Long Term Care – Rights and Responsibilities*, Cm 4192-1, London: The Stationery Office.

Sammut, A. (2003a) 'Developing an Appropriate Response to Emotional Pain', *Journal of Dementia Care*, vol 11, no 2, pp 23-5.

Sammut, A. (2003b) 'What about Me? Support for Dementia care Staff', *Journal of Dementia Care*, vol 11, no 6, pp 22-4.

Scheidt, R. J. and Windley, P. G. (2003) *Physical Environments and Aging: Critical Contributions of M. Powell Lawton to Theory and Practice*, Binghampton, NY: Haworth Press.

Schweitzer, P. (1998) (ed) *Reminiscence in Dementia Care*, London: Age Exchange.

Scott, B. (2002) 'Dolls in Dementia Care', Letter, *Journal of Dementia Care*, vol 10, no 2, p 13.

Scottish Executive (2006) *Changing Lives: The Report of the 21st Century Social Work Review*, Edinburgh: The Stationery Office.

Scottish Executive Health (2005) *Care Homes for Older People: National Care Standards (Revised March)*, Edinburgh: Scottish Executive Health.

Senge, P. (1990) *The Fifth Discipline: The Art and Practice of the Learning Organisation*, London: Century Business.

Shamy, E. (2003) *A Guide to the Spiritual Dimension of Care for People with Alzheimer's Disease and Related Dementia*, London: Jessica Kingsley Publishers.

Shenk, D. (2001) *The Forgetting*, London: Harper Collins.

Sherlock, J. and Gardener, L. (1993) 'Systematic Family Interventions in Dementia', in A. Chapman and M. Marshall (eds) *New Skills for Social Workers*, London: Jessica Kingsley Publishers, pp 63-80.

Sixsmith, A., Stilwell, J. and Copeland, J. (published online 2004) 'Rementia: Challenging the limits of dementia care', *International Journal of Geriatric Psychiatry*, vol 8, no 12, pp 993-1000.

Sloan, P. (1993) 'Section on Sexual Behaviour of Residents with Dementia: Guidelines to Explain how to Respond', *Contemporary Long term Care*, vol 16, no 10, pp 66-9.

Snowden, D. (2001) *Aging with Grace: What the Nun Study Teaches us about Leading Longer, Healthier and More Meaningful Lives*, New York: Bantam Books.

Spector, A., Thorgrimsen, L., Woods, B., Royan, L., Davies, S., Butterworth, M. and Orrell, M. (2003) 'Efficacy of an Evidence-based Cognitive Stimulation Therapy Programme for People with Dementia: Randomised Controlled Trial', *British Journal of Psychiatry*, no 183, pp 248-54.

Stokes, G. (2001) *Challenging Behaviour in Dementia: A Person-Centred Approach*, Bicester: Speechmark.

Stokes, G. and Goudie, F. (eds) (2002) *The Essential Dementia Care Handbook*, Bicester: Speechmark.

Sutton, L.J. and Cheston, R. (1997) 'Rewriting the Story of Dementia: A Narrative Approach to Psychotherapy with People with Dementia', in M. Marshall (ed) *State of the Art in Dementia Care*, London: Centre for Policy on Ageing, pp 159-63.

Swinton, D. (2001) *Spirituality and Mental Health Care*, London: Jessica Kingsley Publishers.

Teitalman, P. and Copolillo, A.L. (2002) 'Sexual Abuse amongst Persons with Alzheimer's Disease: Guidelines for Recognition and Intervention', *Alzhiemer's Quarterly*, vol 3, no 3, pp 252-7.

Threadgold, Sister M. (2002) 'SONAS aPc – A New Lease of Life for Some', *Signpost Journal*, vol 7, no 1, pp 35-7.

Throgrimsen, L., Spector, A. and Orrell, M. (2006) 'The Use of Aromatherapy in Dementia Care: A Review', *Journal of Dementia Care*, vol 14, no 2, pp 33-6.

Tibbs, M.A. (1999) 'Report of 15th annual ADI conference in Johannesburg', *Journal of Dementia Care*, vol 7, no 6, pp 8-9.

Tibbs, M.A. (2001) *Social Work and Dementia: Good Practice and Care Management*, London: Jessica Kingsley Publishers, pp 117-8.

Topo, P., Maki, O., Saarikalle, K., Clarke, N., Begley, E., Cahill, S., Arenlind, J., Hothe, T., Morbey, H., Hayes, K. and Gilliard, J. (2004) 'Assessment of a Music-based Multimedia Program for People with Dementia', *The International Journal of Social Research and Practice*, vol 3, no 3, pp 348-52.

Tsai, P.-F. and Chang, J. (2004) 'Assessment of Pain in Elders with Dementia', *Medsurg Nursing*, vol 13, no 6, pp 364-70.

Turton, J., De Maio, F. and Lane, P. (2003) *Interpretation and Translation Services in the Public Sector*, www.ind.homeoffice.gov.uk

Tutu, D. (2004) 'The Nelson Mandela Lecture "Look to the Rock from which You were Hewn"', tac.org.za/documents/speeches/TUTUMANDELALECTURE

University of Birmingham Department of Primary Care and General Practice (2005), *Quantity and Outcomes Framework Review Evidence to the Expert Panel*, www.popon.bham.ac.uk/primarycare/QOF/index.htm

Van Diepen, E., Baillon, S.F., Redman, J., Rooke, N., Spencer, D.A. and Prettyman, R. (2002) 'A Pilot Study of the Physiological and Behavioural Effects of Snoezelen in Dementia', *British Journal of Occupational Therapy*, vol 65, no 2, pp 61-6.

Verity, J. (2006) 'Dolls in Dementia Care: Bridging the Divide', *Journal of Dementia Care*, vol 14, no 1, pp 25-7.

VOICES (1998) *Eating Well for Older People with Dementia: A Good Practice Guide for Residential and Nursing Homes and Others Involved in Caring for Older People with Dementia*, Potters Bar, Herts: VOICES.

Wahidin, A. and Aday, R. (2005) 'The Needs of Older Men and Women in the Criminal Justice System: An International Perspective', *Prison Service Journal*, vol 160, pp 13-22.

Walker, B. (2005) 'Dolls: A Different Interpretation', *Journal of Dementia Care*, vol 13, no 4, pp 9-10.

Wanless, E. (2006) *Securing Good Care for Older People: Taking a Long-term View*, London: King's Fund.

Wey, S. (2005) 'One Size Does Not Fit All: Person-centred Approaches to the Use of Assistive Technology', in M. Marshall (ed) *Perspectives on Rehabilitation and Dementia*, London: Jessica Kingsley Publishers, pp 202-20.

Wiggins, B. and Fahy, J. (2005) 'An Australian Model of Community Dementia Care', in M. Marshall (ed) *Perspectives on Rehabilitation and Dementia*, London: Jessica Kingsley Publishers, pp 147-54.

Wiles, A. and Brooker, D. (2003) 'Complementary Therapies in Dementia Care', *Journal of Dementia Care*, vol 11, no 3, May/June, pp 31-6.

Wilkinson, H. (2002) *The Perspectives of People with Dementia: Research Methods and Motivations*, London: Jessica Kingsley Publishers.

Woolham, J. (2005a) *The Effectiveness of Assistive Technology in Supporting the Independence of People with Dementia: The Safe at Home Project*, London: Hawker Publications Limited.

Woolham, J. (ed) (2005b) *Developing the Role of Technology in the Care and Rehabilitation of People with Dementia: Current Trends and Perspectives*, London: Hawker Publications Limited.

Yale, R. (1998) *Developing Support Groups for Individuals with Early-stage Alzheimer's Disease*, San Francisco, CA: Health Professions Press.

# Index